James Hinton

**The Law-Breaker, and the Coming of the Law**

James Hinton

**The Law-Breaker, and the Coming of the Law**

ISBN/EAN: 9783337233198

Printed in Europe, USA, Canada, Australia, Japan

Cover: Foto ©Suzi / pixelio.de

More available books at **www.hansebooks.com**

# THE LAW-BREAKER

AND

THE COMING OF THE LAW.

# THE LAW-BREAKER

AND

THE COMING OF THE LAW

BY

JAMES HINTON

EDITED BY

MARGARET HINTON

LONDON
KEGAN PAUL, TRENCH, & CO., 1 PATERNOSTER SQUARE
1884

**Ballantyne Press**
BALLANTYNE, HANSON AND CO.
EDINBURGH AND LONDON

# PREFACE.

As the long years bear away the echo of that voice which was my very life, I feel, and all who loved him feel, that my husband was never more truly with us in spirit than he is now. The throbbings of his heart are repeated in ours who read his words, and his hope for the world—a hope whose credentials are the more perfect love of the whole human brotherhood—is ever finding a wider response.

It has seemed to me that the later manuscripts, of which this volume contains the first yet published, should no longer be withheld. The responsibility of keeping back thoughts which, surely, are now urgently needed, would be greater than that of presenting them in their present form, especially remembering, as I do, that I am carrying out his often-repeated wish that these manuscripts should be read, so that, if there were any truth in them, it might bear fruit. He used to say, "If my ideas are false, then the truth must be something better, and I am glad."

I need not apologise for the informal style and arrangement of these writings: they have the advantage of coming direct from the author himself, the passages having been written down each day as the thoughts came to him. I cannot tell how much he would have altered for publication, what strong words he might have withheld or even intensified, for he was ever open to fresh light and fresh impressions. It is certain that some obvious inaccuracies, such as that on p. 181, would have been corrected, but I have let them stand, feeling that these papers are a more valuable record of the writer's mind if left untouched.

The following letter, written to me in 1873, the year in which the chief portion of Part I. of "The Law-Breaker" was written, will perhaps throw some light upon his choice of the title : *—

"Here are two opposed sets of people: breakers of the law on one hand and keepers of the law—the good people—on the other. Now Christ stood between keepers and breakers of the 'law;' between Jew and Gentile; fearers and obeyers of God and outcasts disobeying Him. What was His method? It was not to bring, or try to bring, the breakers back to obey, to reunite them with the obeyers; it was to call breakers and obeyers alike to duties they both alike had disregarded. To bring them both alike to new, unthought-of duties, the fulfilling of which made the laws—which were so broken—not necessary. That was His remedy; to bring men to see and fulfil the duties the omission of which alone had made the laws to be imposed. He did not bring the refusers of the laws—the Jewish laws—to obey them; He supplied the omission—the want of love to God within the heart—

---

* An article in "The Modern Review" for April 1883, called "The Law-Breaker," by Miss Caroline Haddon, was written in ignorance of the existence of this series of MSS., but being founded on conversations with Mr. Hinton, it forms a useful commentary on the leading thoughts in this volume.

which had made the laws necessary. He put away the laws by putting away that which made the need for them. That was what He did when He stood in presence of disorder and division. And is it not He who has left us an example that we should walk in His steps? Are not disorder and division ever to be treated so? by seeking the things—the duty—the omission of which has made necessary the laws that are broken. How can we expect laws to be obeyed which are made necessary only by the omission of something? So what a fact it was that Christ took away the sin of the world. He took it away by bringing men—law-obeyer and law-breaker alike—to see a right, a call of God's, they had both alike overlooked."

I have no doubt that a feeling of surprise—almost of anger—will arise in the mind of the reader towards some portions of this book. It will seem as though many of our best and truest feelings were done violence to or ignored. It must be borne in mind, however, that in thinking, as in life, the process of development is carried on by temporary suppressions, in order that these left-out elements may be restored with fuller power when other hidden things have been duly recognised: remembering this, I think we shall find that any disregard is in appearance only.

In proportion as we have faith in the principle that in thought and in society life comes through death—that the good passes away only that the better may be—we shall be able to give up what seems highest to us, knowing that there must be a still higher aim set before the race. Such a yielding, however, Mr. Hinton always felt must only come at the unmistakable call of human needs. And if this principle should touch even what is most sacred and best in human life—there too we may summon all our faith and be ready for seeming loss, knowing that failure cannot be the end. It may be that our highest ideals can be realised without any change of form—only let us be sure that it is the true ideal we strive for, and not its appearance merely; that human needs do guide us, and not a right that is cruel. Because of the tremulous intensity with which we maintain our holy things, the mere thought of any change is like death to us. What if the needs of the perishing constrain it? Will not our treasure die to live?

If any social change is even hinted at, people are ready to think that a convulsion of society is meditated, an uprooting of our really useful regulations; but no one who reads carefully what Mr. Hinton says need be in fear of this. The change must come from within. Mr. Hinton believed that the desire for a truly human law of service must first be taught to children, and that it will take some generations to effect a general change. Meanwhile there may be much blundering and many lives sacrificed, but the *reductio ad absurdum* of our life is coming to be recognised, the system of competition and the avowed maintenance of the principle of "each for himself" bears fruits too evil to be endured, and we must begin anew on another basis. Perhaps we have missed the reading of the true basis taught us hundreds of years ago, and our mistakes, and the pain and distress of the world, may be guiding us back to its true rendering. It is this path that seemed the hope of humanity to one who suffered for the sorrow of the world more than is given to many. Of this hope he wrote to me in the last year of his life in these words :—

"All things come to me with one assurance of hope; because they always come as a better and completer vision of that great end which man's life is working out. All things come to me with one assurance; a better kind of goodness than men have been thinking of, of late, is destined for them, and the time is even now come for recognising it and beginning to seek it. All good and all evil, all successes and all failure, speak alike to me this one message: Seek a better goodness. Failure in the attempt at one thing is no evidence that the attempt at another will not succeed. So, love, I am always full of interests, and always have an inexhaustible source of joy. Always of *the thing* I desire I have a full assurance, one ever growing and becoming clearer and more convinced—only my 'quickly' and 'soon,' perhaps, are what seem to others very long and far off: by quick I mean two hundred years. That is the soonest for any great universal change that can be even imagined. And that seems quick to me; for besides that it is not long, one may think also of the many individual deliverances that will be achieved in the coming. And I hope more and more that there will be less of fighting and distress and pain in the process than it seemed as if there must be. The world is different from what it was; and its ears are more open, and its discontent and feeling that it does not know, and must be ready and prepared for the profoundest changes, greater than probably they ever were. The time is, above all, one of tolerance and recognition that there must be differences, and so the necessity of changes. We must not think too much that the course of things must repeat itself. We are the inheritors of the labours of the previous ages, and do reap the fruit of their toils and sufferings. And so much is achieved in the admission of Christ's thoughts, even in name."

I wish to record with gratitude my indebtedness to my friend Mr. Henry Havelock Ellis for his valuable co-operation in preparing this volume. It is at my request that he has written the following introductory remarks.

M. H.

# INTRODUCTION.

HINTON's intellectual activity falls naturally into the usual three periods. The first, the period of "anticipation," as he might himself have termed it, includes "Man and his Dwelling-Place," published in 1859, and ends with "Life in Nature," in 1862. The next period was one of suppression, of training in practical life, of preparation, mostly unconscious, for larger future activity. His temporary adoption of a literary career produced after 1862 nothing of permanent value, and on resuming the practice of his profession he ceased to write altogether. "The Mystery of Pain," which might be considered an exception to the general barrenness of this period, although published in 1866, belongs both in inception and largely in execution to the year 1862. The third period of Hinton's intellectual activity began at the commencement of 1870, or a little earlier, and was only ended by death in 1875. This latest and mature period was also that of greatest energy. Hinton wrote more during these five years than during all the previous years, although he published nothing except a few short articles. His new attitude towards moral questions was both the starting-point and the centre of his third stage, and it is curious to observe how this attitude had a reflected action on all that he wrote. It introduced a new vitality, a new freedom. It was not till 1870 that Hinton attained his own most characteristic note on many other subjects besides morals. He gained also a fresh power of expression, more simple and flexible than his earlier style; and the occasional force or felicity by which, rather than by its average excellence, his earlier style was distinguished gave place to a great extent—as, for instance, when discussing man's relation to Nature or the function of impulse in human action—to a lyrical passion which is of rarer and more individual strain. Perhaps this is best seen in some passages of the unpublished "Autobiography."

The first part of "The Law-Breaker" represents the transition from the second to the third period. Chronologically it extends from the end of 1871 to the end of 1874, although the last few pages only were written during 1874. In the development of Hinton's thought, however, it comes somewhat earlier; it shows in what way he considered his ethical conceptions to be related to the teaching of Jesus. This first part of "The Law-Breaker" is printed in exactly the same order as Hinton wrote it, with the omission of some passages that are either obscure or are mere repetitions, and also with, in a few places, slight verbal alterations, when such seemed necessary to bring out the writer's meaning. It has not been thought advisable to attempt any re-arrangement. Hinton himself considered that his thoughts had in the order of date a real organic relation. "A chief difficulty," he wrote, "is in the *order* of my thoughts; it is hard to get a good external order, an order for presentation. The right order for presentation is not the same as that for thought, and I have a difficulty here from the very fact of my thoughts being in good order in the latter respect. . . . I see why this should be. The order for thinking is a *vital* or organic order, an order of life or growth; the order for presentation is an *anatomical* order.

The various parts grow together; they are one and come contemporaneously, but for demonstration they must be separated, taken each one by itself, the very divisions being partly artificial."

A continuous argument runs through the whole of the first part of "The Law-Breaker." It is Jesus who is the breaker of laws, that is, of arbitrary laws, setting up instead the play of natural law, the response to human needs. But in His treatment of arbitrary laws Jesus was the type of all men of genius. Genius is the law-breaker. And Hinton is never weary of repeating that the man of genius is the man who first finds a new and easier path into which all may enter. He is simply the point of least resistance through which Nature passes into human life. So the method of Jesus, the method of all men of genius, has been the assertion of a law which is binding upon all, because it is the only law which all can fulfil. Even in asserting the authority of Christ, Hinton seems to say, the natural law of a true regard to facts is asserted, to the destruction of all rigid institutions. And if I had to choose a motto for "The Law-Breaker," it would be that which is so often repeated in various forms throughout Hinton's later MSS.: "Man's life is but genius writ large." This appears to be the main argument of the first part of "The Law-Breaker." It will be seen that it resolves itself largely into an attempt to give reality and vividness, a true natural meaning, to the words and actions of Jesus. Both those who accept and those who reject the authority of Jesus will not always be ready to receive Hinton's often careless and arbitrary method of interpretation. He himself seems to have been sensible of the weak character of his exegesis, and in the "Autobiography" he points out that he uses the New Testament writers in the same way as they used the Old. But when this is put aside it will still, I think, be found that Hinton's conception of the character and work of Jesus retains a considerable degree of force and fascination. He was a man with the yieldingness of genius, sensitive to the elemental touch of Nature, struggling, passionate, tempted, only attaining towards the end of his career the statement of that "new commandment," Love one another, which, as Hinton conceived it, superseded all other moral laws. Throughout this first part the reader will find many characteristics which will recall Hinton's earlier work. The conception of the *minus*, of a negative conceived as positive, is still used, though to a far less extent than in "Philosophy and Religion." Thus he generally prefers to speak of selfishness as "not-regard." There is the same over-emphasis in the frequent employment, for example, of italics, and in the use of capital letters for Nature, Man, Genius, &c., even when not distinctly personified, and for the personal pronoun referring to, for example, Jesus. This latter is so frequent that it has here been made invariable. Such pseudo-metaphysical expressions as "the self," in the sense of "selfishness," are constantly used, although the crude conception of altruism which marks some of the earlier writings, as well as the word itself (see, for instance, p. 287), gave place later on to a more exact and scientific conception.

The second part of "The Law-Breaker" is, unlike the first, made up of isolated passages from various series of MSS., especially that entitled "Genius." They are brought together because they throw various lights on the subjects touched on in the first part, and, although not arranged in chronological order, they cover the same years. Among them will be found passages of considerable importance for the right understanding of Hinton's later position in regard to genius, morals and religion. The passages bearing on theology have been introduced to show the last developments of many of the thoughts which occupy so large a position in the four volumes of printed MSS., and the volume of selections from them which has been published under the title of "Philosophy and Religion." It will be seen that Hinton still seems to retain implicitly the conception of God worked out in greater detail in the earlier MSS. as the reality rather than the cause of things —"whatever truly *is*"—or, as he wrote in the last year of his life: "God is the reason of things, the reason of our experience," and also in the sense (equally clear in the early MSS.) of humanity. In the later MSS., however, will be found a more distinct conception of the transitory nature of religions, of the permanent nature of religion. After 1873 there are few passages of either a theological or a metaphysical character. Metaphysics became for Hinton a kind of cosmic game. And in the "Autobiography," where chiefly, perhaps, this transformed metaphysics finds its place, God and Nature are beings of what might be called a mythopœic rather than a theological or scientific character.

I have been careful to point out the date of "The Law-Breaker." This is very necessary in the case of a writer who developed so continuously, so regularly, and, during his last period, so rapidly. In "The Coming of the Law," which was commenced in 1871 and written up till a few months before his death, it is possible to obtain a glimpse of the last developments of Hinton's ethical thoughts, and for this reason it forms the most important part of the present volume. The passages of which it consists have been selected from a series called "Subjects," and were doubtless intended for subsequent development. Although, unlike the first part of "The

Law-Breaker," "The Coming of the Law" consists of selected passages, these passages are in nearly every case given entire, as Hinton wrote them, and always in strict chronological order. A considerable portion of "Subjects" —that written during the greater part of 1874—is unfortunately missing in the MS. as it at present exists. It is possible that it formed part of a large quantity of MS. which Hinton himself destroyed during his last illness at St. Michael's. A word may be said as to the title here adopted. Hinton frequently used "The Coming of the Law" as a title during the last few years of his life, both in " Subjects " and as the heading of a distinct series of papers, which, with the exception of a few sheets, cannot now be found. It seems, indeed, to form a necessary antithesis to "The Law-Breaker." Another title which Hinton latterly sometimes adopted suggests itself: "The Mystery of Pleasure." But while this well indicates the relation which, as Hinton insisted, his later thoughts bear to "The Mystery of Pain," it seems almost too narrow to cover the new basis of life suggested by these passages, which contain, perhaps in a more clear and concise form than anywhere else, although for that very reason more liable to misinterpretation, Hinton's latest and most mature thoughts on morals. The short preface is that which he himself prefixed to them. Had there been no such preface, the following passage, written in 1871 as a preface to the second volume of the printed MSS., but which gave place to a simple glossary of words used with special meanings, might well have served as an introduction :—" These thoughts are rather communicated to than evolved from my own mind. Therefore I can without vanity assert that I believe them to be both unique and important. Yet I am in no haste to see them either arresting the attention or receiving the appreciation of the many. True faith can afford delay. At present I commend them to those souls who are as involuntarily attracted to them as mine has been and is involuntarily inspired by them. There is now a wide-spread, hard tension upon heart and life such as never was before. There will be as its results a spring; a level hardly glimpsed now will be seen and attained. 'I, if I be lifted up, will draw all men unto Me.'"

It is proposed that this volume should be followed, as soon as possible, by the publication of a selection of Hinton's writings on ethics, arranged in the best and most complete order of presentation. But I venture to hope that, in the meanwhile, these brief sketches may serve to exhibit in outline something of the mind of one of whom it may perhaps be said, that no modern man has shown a finer strain of ethical genius.

H. HAVELOCK ELLIS.

# THE LAW-BREAKER.

## PART I.

If I believe that Christ is divine, that is of no moment. We all wish to know what *man* He was; His mental constitution must express the laws of human nature, even as His physical life. His was the constitution of genius. And why should not even early superstitions have remained in His mind? Has not even the very best work been done under such conditions? Nay, is not some kind of enlightenment hindrance rather than help?

How should one "numbered with" transgressors not rule them? Has He not fulfilled the condition? This is to be said to them: "Here is the *pattern* of you. You are not what you truly are; you do not know yourselves, nor see yourselves aright. Here is the law-breaker, your model. Be what you are; at least *do* your own work; we do not ask you to do other."

It is seen that Christ introduced an enthusiasm of humanity; but we need to see how this very passion truly existed before (in the self-form) in superstitions. It is arbitrary still while thus thought of; it demands to be seen necessary. It was there, but against its own nature; that is, against service, bound against it by being in things; that is, dictated by regard to the self-goodness. But because in their beginning these forms were for service, in being swept away for service they are but fulfilling their own life.

That this law of life is what Christ's action expressed, is no argument that He was not God. Does not God ever work by means? Is not necessity the very stamp of His action? And had not the fulness of time to come, the preparation to be made complete? The work that is a function has exactly that character.

What Christ did was this: He asked, Is your right the true right? This is what is always wanted; to ask not only if we are doing right, but if our right is the true right. Is it not strange we go on so long not doing it? Here, in truth, is there not a use and meaning in political economy, formulating for man the proof that his rights are not the true rights, so that the answer is already given before the question is asked? Is it not striking that this is done now; so that there can no more be any question of the basis? It truly shows, though in a strangely inverted way, how much man has gained, how much more true life, or "force" ready to become our life, there is in humanity now; how ready it is for a new basis of its life, how full of passion for good not suffered to be true to its own nature. Man has been able now to recognise that there is another possible basis of life, so that he can draw the contrast, and say, "It is not that but this." This surely is most significant; it is as if he were conscious of a tendency within him to a different basis, so that he had need to define which it was, lest there should be a mistake. How full of meaning this is. And not only that he has not been able clearly to distinguish it, and say it, but that, in spite of his saying it, with its consequence of trying to accept it (and so with the utmost intensity binding the false rights on himself), in spite of his thus making himself invert his life and hold it against Nature, it has been able to exist and to show so much goodness.

Ever this is wanted: to ask not only if we are doing the right, but if our right is the true right. Christ has shown us the way; and as now there is a special preparation, as it were, for the asking of this question, a prepared demonstration that ours is the wrong right, so before He asked that question was there not a special prepared demonstration also then?

Is Christ seen in anything more than in this: "If the tree is bad let its fruits be bad?" His heart and thought were on the basis. See how we say now: we must act for self "in this world," but we can get some good fruits while we are waiting. We cannot, *so*: only deception. If it were true that we must have acting for self at the basis, our only wisdom would be to sweep away all goodness and all thought of it; and seek only pleasure—pleasure with prudence.

Does not the "temptation" become more intelligible? Thus "the kingdoms of the earth" is the temptation to use His powers for His own advantage. Conscious as He was becoming of the power within Him, here was the opportunity to use them and be a ruler. The Devil—the self—tempted Him. Then " Make the stones bread ; " again, use your power for yourself; a thing quite right to do, that you will do for others; do it to feed yourself. Is this the thought ? So does not the narrative mean the time when genius is tempted, when it comes first to be conscious that the old law is not the true law—the time when it is tempted to break the law for itself?

It appears then that we are not told of the first and second stages of Christ's life; that in which He obeyed the false law, and that in which He broke it not knowing it was right to break it, even unconsciously.

Christ broke the laws the Jews cared most about; He blasphemed God by making Himself equal to Him (at least they thought so); and did not keep the Sabbath. To keep the Sabbath was not a moral law, and for that very reason it is probable that the Jews cared about it most of all. For (is it not striking ?) the law which we care most about (that which is expressed in marriage) is ceremonial, strictly a ceremonial law; a matter of form and arrangement, not moral in any other sense than as the Sabbath is; not even so much so, probably; a matter in regard to which different usages have existed, different orders been advocated by men most worthy.

Is not this clearly the idea of "the Spirit" sent to us ? It is the removal from us of the necessity for restraint; for putting our powers, that is, to neutralise each other, and making them ineffective. That is giving us power indeed, but see what power it is; not any new one, but simply the use of the powers we have. And at least we may say that this is the best power *to give us*. (Before you give a sick man more powers than his own, first restore to him those that are naturally his.) It is the power above all for us; and is it not truly a power so great that we do not want more? That is giving us the true power of man; is it possible a man should want more? Is it conceivable a being should be advantaged by having more power than belongs to its nature? Give us the true human power, and that is the best and utmost gift that can be given us. And it comes simply by not having to restrain; that *is* it; and so this is what the gift of "the Spirit" must be. (Genius again shows this: its power is simply that it has not to restrain itself: which, again, is the same as saying that the self is cast out from it; for the self *brings* restraint.)

Could any thought be worse than ours of "virtue" in interfering with others' pleasures—being virtuous at other people's expense? For this is what it truly is. So do we not see Christ's words more truly, "Neither do I condemn thee;" silencing the crowd first, He also does not judge. And when He says: "Go, and sin no more," what is it He says? It is not: "Go, and see that man no more," but this, "Go and serve self no more; no more act for self; the one sin common to you and all the rest."

Can we not feel *how* Christ said those things the Jews counted blasphemy? Were they not forced from Him by the misunderstandings of His hearers, so that He was not even aware until He had said them? Would He ever have said them if they had not come thus unconsciously and unintended, though when said He felt them true? So will inconsistencies be found, especially in the early part of His life; even as in other men who have *made* the true laws? For instance, "My Father is greater than I;" and "I and My Father are one."

This is striking too, that Christ seems, if not always yet almost so, to have let the act of disobeying the law (whatever law He thus "fulfilled") precede the explaining and reason of what He did. The explaining seems to have come always as a reply to blame. This may not mean a distinct intention, an implied affirmation that that was the right way. May it not indicate rather the freedom from self-consciousness with which He acted, how perfectly He had fulfilled His own precept to become as a little child? Did He not say and do the things that incurred such blame wholly unthinking whether He were right or wrong, and only perceive as it were, when challenged, that there was a law that He had disobeyed, and which demanded disobeying? If this be so, the progress and history of His life in its outlines is clear; how the perception that the Jewish system was to be *fulfilled* and so pass away grew upon His mind, was forced on it by finding that He came, in following service, perpetually under its ban; that is, that the law assumed something in man which was not true of Him, and as He looked around perceived was not true (as it ought not to be true) of the men around Him (or if of any, only of the Pharisees in whom the false right had itself produced the deadness it supposed). Was that the secret of His pain about the Pharisees, that He perceived how they had been *forced* into inward evil, had used the very law to kill life within them? So He said: "Ye make him tenfold more the child of hell than before." And surely He not only felt that the condition within, which that "right" assumed, was not true of Him but that it was not true of those around, not true of the publicans and sinners to whom He turned for relief; seeing clearly that if only that false outside "right" were taken away their hearts were prepared for goodness, and that their evil outside did not mean that they were not. Do we not *see*, almost, His gradual, astonished, pained perception that that beautiful God-given system into which He had grown up within a loving home had become a whited sepulchre; that He was amid men who were under the grip of a law which forbade their doing service; so that when He unthinkingly did it He was to them a criminal? So did He not grow to feel that their law was the crime, and by degrees what the law required dawned on Him—*fulfilling*. He went about doing good, and perpetually men treated Him as a transgressor of the law, so that He perceived at last that their law was the "crime." How striking in Him is the twofold attitude to practical life, refusing some restrictions, and charging with guilt accustomed licenses.

Christ went about *doing*, this is why He saw; it was of himself He was speaking when He said: "If ye will do, ye shall know." This is the secret of knowing: the action following at once and *effortlessly* the seeing. When Christ said: "No man can come unto Me except the Father draw him," was He not really saying the universal truth of true work, that it cannot be done by trying, exactly because it is done by a not-doing? And this is a true thought for all His life and sayings; it was of the universal He was ever speaking—simply of the fact; and those around Him put on it its peculiar meaning, and so clothed Him with the theological character in which He stands before us. When we come to understand life, do not Christ's true relation and the true meaning of His words stand clear before us? Do we not see that He was simply saying the true things, the things that are true of all things, the things every man must say, if he truly sees? And then is that the key to the Gospels that this true seeing of His, the men around, even those who most entered into it, put into limited forms and made into theology, not seeing it as He saw it, as the simple truth of all things? That He saw it thus, is proved by the fact of His seeing it at all. How can it be seen but as it is presented to us by Nature? It may be said that Christ expressly asserted that what He saw He did not see in Nature, but that it was revealed to Him by God. But what is the meaning of this? Does not every one who truly sees Nature feel the same thing, that "God," some Being, is telling Him? Is that not a mark, inevitably and always present, of truly seeing Nature, that we have the feeling that some BEING is telling us, for is not that truly what it is? Is not Nature a Being, a conscious Being, and can we truly know her, and have perception of her, without this distinct consciousness that it is a Being telling us, revealing to us that which man's blindness has prevented him from seeing? So the men around Christ did not see how it was of the universal fact He spoke, and what He meant by saying His Father revealed things to Him.

Genius cannot doubt that every one will be good enough to do all it can do, knowing how far it is from being goodness in itself that does it; it is not goodness, only a passion. Is this indeed the plain and true meaning of Christ being tempted in all points as we? Was He not as bad as any of us, having in Him all that is mean, sensual, greedy, angry, just as we have; not good, only eaten up by a passion? So was not this what He meant, simply and plainly, when He said, "Why do you call Me good?" Did He not mean: "You would not if you knew?"*

Christ is to be seen by the history of genius. Is not the very same total change to be traced in Him? See how His soul must have been filled with reverence for the Law, the Temple, the whole service, with even its scruples and excesses—the whole life and hopes of Judea, in that home of His. What a sacred thing it must have seemed to Him! And when He came to Jerusalem, what He did was to refuse, with anger, to suffer a desecration which all the most reverend doctors accepted; He was scrupulous and jealous for the Temple beyond all. That is how He began, His soul demanding the most exact observance, refusing the most innocent and established licenses. He made all who saw Him recall the words: "The zeal of Thy house hath eaten me up." That is how *He* began who ended by saying with joy: "There shall not stand one stone upon another." The man who would not suffer money to be changed in the Temple said afterwards: "It does not matter where men worship, nor any Temple at all." Do we not see the whole universal life in Him? How He was driven to say that the whole system must fall, which lets even any of its right consist in opposing the service of men. That is enough; it is poisoned, and poisonous throughout; no fragment of it can be true or healthy if even any one point is contaminated so: its very life-blood is disease. If any part of it is forbidding service, we may know that *all the rest is license,* is serving self, sanctified and made to be accounted holy; wherever we find the one we may know the other also is. Yet that condition of the Jewish life simply meant that it had grown and become a higher and deeper thing, and

* So thoroughly did He recognise His oneness with mankind generally. —Ed.

that men were ready for a truer law, so that the very evil and hollowness were proofs of the readiness for good. And is not this natural and inevitable, the sign of a growing life? The chrysalis is a true illustration of it; the growing life *makes* the deadness which cramps and develops it. The motives are too powerful for the duties they are used to enforce; the right comes (as we see that by the necessity of the self-forbidding pleasure it must) to be in refusing service, and so in allowing ourselves license—for the one means and necessitates the other. And then such powerful motives come to enforce such insignificant practical aims; a stress too great is laid on things that are external; the very growth of the life causes a want of adjustment. Is it not visible in our own life—this great stress of motive on things that are so little? Enormous motives but no scope, even, for results. So here is the hope: the power of the motives *set free*, given liberty to produce its natural results, how rich it must be in fruits! And this comes with breaking the yoke that forbids serving; once break that down and the pent-up forces that choked and killed, how freely and potently they flow, for that very damming up and stagnating has given them new and intenser power, has raised and strengthened them to a fuller life. This is what we see in development. For this the self is made to forbid an end, answered by the union of pleasure and service, so that self must forbid it; and the service-producing powers, so dammed up for a time, are made higher, more perfect, more fully and deeply living. So the powers which have service for their natural fruit are rendered stagnant for a time, cannot have their effect, and it seems of course as if they were dead; but in truth they, too, do but lose their life to gain it. Set them free by putting away that restraint from service, and see what higher powers they have gained. That is what Christ did for man then, by setting free the powers restrained in Judaism; He called forth the same powers dissipated and lost among the Gentiles too, unknowing what they sought.

And see in our own life: we bring to bear on sacrificing nothing, or next to nothing, all the motives and spiritual powers which were in exercise in the extremest asceticism; there is an utter disproportion in the powers and the permitted results, a mere sham struggle, as it were, of opposing rights, and desires for good which is and can be nothing but a distortion of our life, our whole nature. For its permitted practical results our life (when it is religious) is overweighted with motive, and so it is made so miserable a distortion, with such stress on things of no true human moment, such tolerance of things intolerable, such wretchedness and unrest within, such paralysis without. Thank God for the unrest, at least; for one pledge of hope amid the gloom; that unrest means, it is, the struggle of the cramped-up, stifled powers which are to make life glorious; saying, "Free us, let us work, oh give us something to do that is according to our powers." The unrest at least there is, and it grows so strong, the bursting of the bonds must be near at hand. These powers of Christian motive that we compel to do *nothing*, how much they are adapted to do we see in the self-inflicted tortures of the darkest age: there we have the true measure of this force, that which is "natural," proportioned to them: how can our life stagger under their weight? No wonder that using them (not-using them) as we do, men say: "Let us put them aside altogether; they are mistakes inappropriate to our state." They are so, to *our* life. Either let them work or banish them. The extremest life of self-torture is the true measure of their force and nature; that, *or its equivalent*, they must do. What is the equivalent then? The banishing acting for self, the deliverance from the false law. The ascetic life was the "equivalent" of this; when that ceased it proved this was to come, and till it comes we are consumed and on fire with the disease (the dis-*ease* truly) of restrained, checked, cramped-up powers, that not being allowed to act according to their nature, rend and kill. These powers, Christ-begotten within us (but indeed also the common, inalienable inheritance of man), must bear fruit according to their kind, bring results fairly measuring their potency; the life of self-torture displayed them, and again the casting out of acting for self, the true rule of the desire for good, will do it. Either of these are worthy, proportionate, reasonable, but nothing else; above all nothing less. Can it be said that the forces which produced the one are incapable of producing the other?

Is there not a true parallel in the life of thought? The natural powers of the intellect were seen in the Greek speculation with its brilliancy, and they are seen again in science; but in the meantime they were suppressed, and bore no fruits. But science is the same thing as the Greek speculation; the power which produced the latter simply reappears in the former; it is the same thing, simply in a more perfect form, and that dark time, when it seemed to produce no fruits, was "unnatural" to man; impossible, that is, to continue, and it manifested its "unnaturalness" in the evils it produced, the tension, and restraint, and lack of proportioned action.

So Christ put away the restraints which kept these powers from producing their effect, and shut them up between license for self on the one hand, and restraints against service on the other. And we see that He assailed—as Nature does now—not the license, but the false, self-imposed, law-abusing restraints. It was the abuse of law against service, infinitely more than the breaking of it, that He sought to put aside. That banished, all was done.

Is it not evident how falsely the thought of goodness that is in a man's soul may be interpreted even through the very facts of his life; how because he takes pain, and even refrains from enjoyments accounted right by his fellows, and goes to the lowest place and shares with the wretched, it may come to be believed that he had a thought of goodness to which his true thought was utterly opposed; as if his thought was of goodness in restraint when indeed it was wholly the contrary, in perfect freedom to enjoy, to do all service wholly unrestrained from it by its being pleasure; when his true thought of good was in simple delight, unthinking of his own goodness; when his idea of the world was of a place in which pleasure should rule utterly unhindered by the self; and his thought of the means to it, also, the overthrow of all restraints which meant refusing service? Even although his thought of good might be this, nay, even *because* it was this—for taking the lowest part is its counterpart—men, under the dominion of self, might even be compelled to think that his thought of goodness was in restraining passion and refusing joy; because this very thought would make him refuse pleasures which his fellows followed, the pleasures against service; and take for his portion the lot of those who had least and were most miserable. This choice is *part* of that feeling, inseparable from it. But how it must deceive men under the rule of self; it must look as if it meant that he thought good was in refusing pleasure; and how should either his actions or his words prevent men thinking so?

Christ broke the Sabbath (as was then thought) to heal: now suppose breaking the Sabbath had been a thing that could not have been done without distinct and even great bodily pleasure in the doing, ought the man to have gone unhealed, and Christ to have said, "I must not break the Sabbath to heal him?"

In Christ's time was it not the case that all men who regarded worshipping God with any earnestness *were* ready to worship Him in spirit and in truth? What was wanted was simply the sweeping away the laws and restrictions that implied they were not so. It needed only that a clear space should be left, as it were, those weeds uprooted, those rocks and barren stones which choked the ground—and life sprang up. The ground was rich with seeds: that was what had been done all that time; the seeds of that life were being sown, and Christ was as the spring that called them into life. He was the Sun of Righteousness, and man's nature blossomed beneath His beams. The wilderness and desolate place was glad for Him, the barren soil burst into tumult, and became as a field that the Lord had blessed. And even so is it not now; yet again is He not to arise, with healing in His wings; healing of our death, the power again to call into glad uplifting of the buried seeds? For now are not all who truly care about goodness quite ready to put self wholly away as the basis of their life, to make it wholly a life of desire for good —quite ready and needing only the law and restrictions which imply the contrary to be swept away? Then when the path is made clear will not the buried life spring up?

Will not Christ's work renew and fulfil itself? These very laws, our very rights, are lies, untrue to the fact; implying what is false. How can our life flourish?

How strong *every* argument would have been against Christ's healing on the Sabbath: was the case so urgent? Why should He have set such an example to those ignorant people, so ready to take every advantage, so incapable of understanding—"this people which *knoweth* not the law"—why should He curse them more? What was the urgency? why could He not wait just twelve hours, at the very most twenty-four? the man who had been ill a long while, was in no danger; was it necessary to take things into our own hands as if we knew so much better than God, and break His laws merely for an impatience that could not wait a day? Did not God know when He ordained the Sabbath that sick people would have to wait to be cured? Did He not design discipline? is not the seeing of others' sufferings a lesson to us, as well as certainly a blessing to them, if we let God judge of the conditions under which we should try to relieve them? And had He not infinite means of making all amends? Nay, did not Christ before or after, as much as say so in one of His sneering parables? Ought we not to recognise what He ordained, and leave to another world what He had forbidden in this?

What Christ did above all was to affirm that *all* were ready, able, to worship God in spirit and in truth, and that what was needed was that the laws (the outside laws) which implied that they were not must be thrown down. And do we not see the special relation of His work to the *service of God* (as compared with now when it is rather in respect to the service of Man; thanks to His power). The service of God was what man then was regarding most, was the thing to which his regard was paid, in respect to which he imposed on himself the false laws which said: "You must act as if you were not serving God in your heart; as if your hands doing a service on the Sabbath would mean that you were glad not to do God's bidding because it inconvenienced you." (For that is what those laws of the outside mean, and must mean; they cannot but *keep* that evil on man by the very fact of their implying it; they treat him as an enemy to God, and prevent his even knowing when he is not. Is there any surer way to make any one bad than to treat him as being so; especially when he is not? That is what those laws on the outside do: is it any wonder that the time for sweeping them away is the very worst time of all?) Christ's work must have been especially with the laws which related to the service of God, for they were what were binding and ruining men then; and His so introducing *benevolence*, active good-will to man, was the expression of this, *was* the bringing out the serving God from the heart and in spirit; because that is God's true service. And so how plainly Christ did reveal God's will; He came to men and said: "You want to serve God? He does not want your outside deeds in reverence to *Him*: but in all ways to serve each other." Assuredly He did reveal God: that needs no proof besides.

Christ introduced a living law; but again, upon it man has erected a dead one, and so His work wants recognising again. But He has done it; and all. We need but to *see* that which He truly did. Is there not an image of it in mathematics? Newton introduced a living process, but still the ignorance erected on it a dead one again; so that again it is necessary to see what he truly did. Is the meaning this: that even *three* ordinates are necessary? May it be that Paul was to Christ as Leibnitz was to Newton; would Christ have felt that Paul was letting go of the *Life* he taught?

No invective ever was like Christ's: "Ye make him tenfold more the child of hell." Such anger and scorn never flashed through human lips as through His. And (is it not a striking thing?) the very utmost and bitterest indignation ever known to be roused in a human breast has been roused, not by vice or wickedness, but by cruelty in the form of piety and virtue,—by piety that was cruel.

This is to be observed of Him: it was upon the *goodness* of His time He worked; *against that* He set himself. In this He was a typical man. Christ overthrew a great system of rights or laws, and put an unity for them— the *one* from absence of which they all came: it seemed less, but how much more it was. And so it was with Copernicus. And now, for all these "rights" of ours an unity is wanted. Judaism supposed the not-serving God in spirit and heart, and so that multitude of external things was necessary or there would have been no serving God at all; they were means by which, not being within, it was made to be externally or physically. So at the mere putting clearly forth this true relation of serving God, it fell, dissolved away. We must think of this. How unjust it might have seemed to say that Judaism was a system of outside service and meant not-serving in the heart. Yet we see this would also have been true to say; it was true of the system, though not true of so many individuals who lived in it and were supported and nourished and guided by it. We see it was true of the

B

system, for at the touch of the thought of the true serving God it dissolved; in its fall was the blessing. And the same things are true of our external "rights;" though so much true devoted love has been nourished and guided by it, yet as a system it means and expresses absence of love, acting for self as the basis of the life; the right not being within has to be without. It is no libel on *it* also to say this; and in its fall the very blessing and power is to be. Do we think the dying of the body—which seems merely death—is a rising into fuller life, and cannot we believe it of the dying of the body of a law? (Is there not a real parallel here?) Are not these individual cases of true life rather the promise that a whole system of life is to come in the place of the dead one?

At the touch of seeing that the true service of God is in the spirit, all that system of Judaism dissolved like frostwork in the summer sun. And so our system of right things will dissolve at the sight that the true right is acting wholly not for self. It is just as the Epicycles dissolved, and every system of the "observation-true," at the perception of the fact; all are but a frostwork.

That is why the new thought is presented: it repudiates not only the badness but the *goodness* it finds itself in contact with. And saying that, how the secret of its power is revealed; repudiate the *goodness* too, and the badness shall be put away; but not without. For in truth the goodness is that by which the badness supports itself.

May not Christ's relation to our life be seen more clearly through the history of mathematics? The fluxion truly includes *all*, and though not applied fully, yet all that is needed is simply to apply it. Did not Newton mean *all*, when he spoke of the $x$ and $y$? And so when

Christ said: "The Sabbath was made for man," did He not sum up *the whole* of morals, say all that was to be said, mean all?  Saying, as we have to say, "Marriage was made for man and not man for marriage," is not adding anything; it is only saying again what He said, and what we have been as yet unable to see: Christ did it *all*.

As compared with the Gentiles, the Jews saw that Nature was not capricious: so Christianity,—which is truly the saying to man: "Your right must be as Nature's is; apart from *things*,"—must have come through it.  It could not have come from the Gentiles—at least till science had come; which more perfectly still banishes caprice from Nature.  But now through science have we not as it were a better Judaism?  Is not science truly as Judaism?  So that now more perfectly and fully still we can say: Man's right is to be one with Nature's, wholly in the action, and apart from things.

Man's having a "right" different from Nature's, is simply his being untrue to Nature.  And so Christ said: "Be as a little child."  He might have said: "Be converted and become as Nature."  "Truth is truth to Nature" applies to the moral life also.

It is an easier right; one which sums up in one little thing *all* they have been trying to do, and so opens the path of a larger and more perfect rightness to all, brings in a goodness that is more inclusive because deeper; setting free the wasted power that has been shut up in doing a needless, hard thing—in putting away what were good if rightly done, and which can be put away only at sacrifice of some good, and in restraining passion, which, if it had not been perverted, would have wanted no restraint. Do we want as much goodness as possible in men? Then why mix it up with these hard things? Why not have it (as it *may* be) without them? Is it possible that, without them, the same amount could be as hard? Anything as hard must be—by the equivalent of all their hardness—so much *more* good.

The impression Christ produced on those who did not understand Him, was that of a man who let his selfish passions sway him, "a gluttonous man." See the opposites in Him: this was His aspect, yet He was the man of sorrows. And that does not mean external sorrows; it was the pain of His work; the sorrow, the groaning within; and yet the free play of His passion, His passions as a man. There was the grief inside, the grief of doing what He had to do. Can it ever not be grief, that work of seeing the better good, the truer right? Ever not be agony, that giving up, ceaselessly renewed? It must be a thing loved, delighted in, held with every muscle of the soul, and wound around by every fibre of the heart, or it could not be rightly given up. Will it alter it to know, even ever so surely, that giving up is receiving? What! even self-restraint, abstinence, the things counted good and that good has brought, *forbidden*, and no pain—the very world travailing in birth and no agony! Shall it ever be?

And then again: that one passion for service, which is all passions, and lives by the life of them all, has this effect, that then it does not matter what *other* passions there are; all may be; all those that would come even to most evil; there is no reason any passion should not be, *within that*, as it were; it must be harmless; all the passions that make every form of evil and of crime can be, and to the full, within that bosom; all the *power* that is in evil also can be thus taken up and made a servant. Is this indeed the thing that constitutes genius? It not only may have, it must have, the passions which are the workers of ill. And so here is the guide to what we should seek in human life; not the absence, not even the control, of those evil-working passions, but their *using* a passion that will make it better for them to be than to be absent. Is it not native to genius not to think of, or care for, or inquire about right? That is what is in the bad, only completer and more absolute in genius when the conditions are fulfilled. And so is it not to this that it comes at last, to not thinking, asking, caring about right? This is its time of power; it fulfils the conditions of this, that is, it becomes as a little child. (When Christ bade that He spoke from His own experience.) It fulfils the conditions of this. Genius wants in it those passions that—not serving the one passion, or with self in them—make the evils; it *is* by their presence. Now in this is it one with the relation of organic life to the causes of its disease? The truer right comes by taking in the "passions" that have made "wrong" come; is this one with a higher grade of organic life coming by embodying, using, the sources of disease? Does not that too mean a change in the starting-point?

In the one passion of genius, also, is shown us what the union of two self-passions means; of two passions each with a negative in them, becoming the one true passion with the negative banished from each. Are these two passions, the passion which makes vice and the passion which makes self-goodness—that is, the passion for pleasure and the passion for right—each with the self in it? Unite them, and is it not the passion for service, which is right and pleasure one? In it we have the passion for pleasure and the passion for right, each with the self banished. But is this to be seen in the individual passions also?

Christ spoke from His own experience when He told His disciples they must be made *free* and become as a little child (which two things are indeed one). And was it not the same when He said to Peter that in his age another should gird him and carry him whither he would not? Had not He been carried indeed whither He would not? Was it His thought or design, His youthful ambition or hope, to overthrow the Jewish polity? Did He not recognise in Peter a nature like His own—one destined to be ruled and guided absolutely by another volition? And so was it He gave to him the keys, and said that on him as on a rock He would found His Church? (It is surely not unnatural that even His dearest disciples should have misunderstood Him in more instances than those of which the correction is recorded.) Look at what sort of man Peter was; among all the disciples there, was there one that seemed less like a rock? How weak he was; yet by that very weakness he was destined to be as adamant, through whom worked a power to resist which would move the universe.

Did not Christ see that in building upon him He was building on Nature herself, a rock that cannot be moved, because even in moving—and it moves to every breath—it remains unmoved?

"Greater works than mine shall ye do." Is not this thought the very same as that of the "angels" of those who have become as little children always beholding the face of the Father? That is, He having gone to the Father would stand in that relation; a thing He also expressly said: so the works He would do through others in the future (as He saw with joy) would be greater than those even which He did, or were possible to Him, in that life of His. In more than one way probably greater, not only because (how likely) the action through others *is* a greater and deeper action, but also because of the growing life of man which renders the very same action necessarily greater in its fruits and effects. So was this Christ's thought: "More, much more, shall I do through, and in these, my friends, and other men who will love me even as they, than I could do now."

But now is it not true that, though Christ said this, yet for any one of us to feel it true of himself or of any friend of his, would be a thing terrible to himself, and abhorred by every Christian? Are we bound by reverence for Christ to disbelieve His words? What does it mean? (I do not dwell on the meaning supposed—of the apostles doing greater "miracles.")

Now that we see Nature also bringing her call to a higher standard—no more to obey "laws," but to be free from that on which they rest—now that we see this which is her "gospel," may we not understand the other Gospel better which was so simple a parallel to it? For instance, may we see what the special wickedness of refusing it consists in? Is it not in regarding self in place of human need—the very same as that of thinking still of our pleasure when need calls? And then do not many parallels arise also? Christ called men to a higher goodness than the Jewish—a living goodness instead of one in an outward order; bidding them let that go; now is it not easy to understand "the sin of unbelief" and how unbelief was His great hindrance? What would it be but not believing that the truer goodness could be? That was *the* hindrance to His work; the thing men then (of course, as now, as ever) were tempted not to believe; the feeling in which the dominion of self over them would express itself. And then there must have been other feelings opposing the change, which we can perfectly perceive: the feeling: "No; I must be virtuous" (self-righteousness); the feeling: "If I did it, it would be for pleasure I should do it, and I will not; and I will not believe that it can be otherwise." May we not trace these feelings plainly wheresoever the call comes to man for a truer goodness, in a life that shall put away the carnal ordinances? Must they not ever be the same? So in respect to every "gospel," or call to a truer goodness, the "sin" is sure to be *unbelief*. For it is the very nature of a "gospel" that it is a call to a truer goodness. That is the good news; a deliverance is come; a new starting-point; freedom from that which has made our right false.

Man's worst evil is the false laws he puts on himself; and what makes them is regarding himself. What Christ did for him was to show him how to escape; the one chief and great blessing for which He never can be forgotten. So He came at an appointed and necessary time; when things were ripe for this change, for a true law taking the place of a false one. What sort of time? a bad one, but one of unrest; when goodness had sunk very low, especially that of those counted good, nay truly seeking good; when the vicious with all their license and greed (never worse or baser or less restrained) were yet nearer the kingdom of heaven than those in whom the "goodness" was. This is the sort of time.

Self-denial cannot be in refusing service, for what but self-regard can make us? So Christ—the law-breaker for service—said "deny himself and take up his cross, and follow me." What cross? Of course his going against the *goodness* of his age, incurring reproach, giving pain, breaking laws which were not true; that is the cross that comes, not in restraining, but in denying self, "bearing His reproach," how plain in the early Christians it was. Is it likely that when Christ spoke of His cross He meant His bodily privations? Was that the baptism He was baptized with?

How striking the parallel is between Christ's relation to the spiritual life and that of the fluxion in mathematics. Men going to right *things* again after Christ had shown all right to be in the action, was it not as the infinitesimal supplanted the motion? And Newton said that the very least things are not to be disregarded; yet he took all things as equal. So Christ said: "Whosoever shall break one of the least of these commandments;" yet which did He show Himself afraid of breaking? And alike of Christ and Newton do not men speak one thing by their tongues and another by their deeds? Christ said: "Be perfect as God is perfect;" we say that men must fall short and sin in this world; we break commandments and "teach men so." But why should not men be "perfect" with a true law? Why not let others' wants guide them wholly?

And farther: if Christ or Newton had lived, would not a different course of the world have been? If Newton, for example, would not he have urged the necessity of regarding the motion, and shown how it meant equilibrium, but by that very thing would not results essential to the perfectness of mathematics have been prevented from coming? So do we see another thing Nature does by causing men to die. She prevents their life from interfering with the suppression of their work, that is, with the very condition of its perfecting.

Thus also there were *inconsistencies* in Newton; points in which his thought was imperfect. Was it so also in Christ, so that it was needful for that cause also that there should be the suppression? Did His thought also leave the law of "things" not wholly put aside even though its foundation was? But if Christ had lived would He not have prevented the false right from superseding again His true one; and by that very means have kept back the needful perfecting through dying?

Christ said: "Be free from laws outside, and have them on the heart." And it is clear these go together; not being in the heart they must come on the outside; and further we see, in evils brought by the law on the outside, the call and the power to put them within the heart. This is the order, nor can there ever be other; it must come into the heart through being put away, *for others*, from the outside. The laws on the outside having to be put away because preventing good, are brought on the heart by that very process. It is not so much that they are, in that, brought to *be* on the heart, but by that man is made to recognise that they ought to be there, there fully and wholly, and must be, and that there can be no substitute for it, no evasion of it; and still more is made to recognise how far they already are there. He is prevented from putting away the true laws, the true heart-goodness, to another state. This it is, surely, above all; so long as man can put off the goodness within to another state, so long he will. The value of the evils of the laws on the outside calling man to remove them is above all this, that it stops his putting off the attempt to have them on the heart to "another state."

Is it not suggestive? That putting off to "another state" is like putting off till "another day;" it is the very same, and the very preachers who warn against the latter, themselves teach what they condemn. This is the very problem indeed: how to prevent man from putting off the very thought of having the laws truly, or on his heart, away from this world; and the answer lies, of course, in the evils brought by having them on the outside; make these intense enough, and it is done. The laws on the outside are but the sign of the absence of them on the heart; they arise from that; and so must bear the fruits of it.

By having, for others, to put away the laws on the outside, man is made to recognise that they are to be on his heart, and that the outside freedom is the sign of it; that his call is to fulfil the conditions of that freedom, the conditions of goodness to him not meaning less pleasure. It is a new thought of duty, the beginning of a new life; a new aim comes to him, and the freedom from law outside becomes a new thing. It had meant wrong and license; now it has become a new thing, the very power to make good be within. We see the total change; and especially how that " liberty " outside must be insisted on, and maintained. So the apostles insisted on it. "Stand fast in the liberty with which Christ has made you free." How natural and good it must have seemed to the early Christians to try and bring back the Jewish law.

They would naturally say: Why not have the laws in

the heart, and yet obey them externally too? But it could not be; that freedom outside is the very sign, and more than the sign, it is the *power* of the laws being on the heart. It makes us insist on the conditions for it being fulfilled. So the apostles said: "Stand fast." Your coming again under the outside law, will mean the power ceasing in the heart. Putting the law outside again will mean again being content with its absence from the heart; and, indeed, must mean that, for it will mean putting aside others' good. And the *effort* put there will mean its being withdrawn from within; the power will be in one form or the other; it cannot be in both; the laws not meaning others' good must waste the power. The outside law apart from service (and if it is service that *is* the law on the heart) *is* simply the phenomenon or exhibition of the absence of the law on the heart, and apart from that absence cannot continue; even as no phenomenon can without its cause. And again, the outside law could not come back because the life is not to stop, but to go on; it is but a beginning, and to stop were to decay; the liberty must be kept for power to advance.

Now, are the moral laws also, by being put away from the outside, made to be in the heart? We can see: do they or any of them sacrifice man's good? If they do their meaning is visible at once; they call for the conditions (of our goodness no more meaning our less pleasure) to be fulfilled. This freedom outside is in truth the phenomenon of the law on the heart, the mode in which it expresses itself; even as the law outside is of the absence of the law on the heart. The freedom is the "phenomenon" of the perfect law. Thus, this is the relation: that thought and feeling of freedom is of the phenomenal; the actual, the fact, is law. And is this universal? Is that whole conception of freedom the phenomenon, when it is true, of the perfect law?

Then also seeing what it means—that the conditions of needing no restraint, of having no reason for goodness to mean less pleasure, are fulfilled—we see also why it has had (rightly had, even when falsely dreamed of) a dazzling charm for men; how liberty stands now, in spite of all, as their great ideal. It is *because* it is the phenomenon of perfect law.

Then does it not seem as if one single law, thus compelled to be broken for service, was enough to make the complete change? Thus was not all done by Christ through that one law of the Sabbath? And now is not the one law that forbids service in the relation to woman enough? And in the life of thought is it not the same? One case is enough to bring the complete change: the moon alone was enough to establish the planetary motions. And this is natural, when we see what it is that is needed to be done; it is simply the bringing the new thoughts, the new aim, or rather the truer consciousness; for this is what it is, the true consciousness of what he desires and seeks, and of what he has attained and what he needs. It is a revealing of man to his own eyes; this above all. And so come Christ's words again in a new truth: "(the son of) *Man* is revealed in Him." In Him man recognised what he was, desired, could do; he looked afresh into his own heart and saw it more truly. He says his very thoughts of right were false, not only to God's will (the fact of Nature), but to his own being. And this now we need to see again. We do see it, thanks to one false law, so fruitful in ills that we cannot be blind to them longer. One law is enough to teach us all; let this law—it *means* all law—be upon the heart.

If there be the thought of a true life for man, there is one thing it cannot tolerate; and that is unbelief. We must believe, or how can the passion be given us? It is the despair that banishes it. We must believe man can be human; can be delivered from need to exact the laws which must mean torturing the weak. Here is what we do: we consent to make right mean what it does not mean, and then when poor wretches, with no chance of keeping it, do not keep it, we torture them with tortures we know we could not bear, and we know that it must go on, and there is no hope of its ending. And we will not even look on them as children and mercifully slay them: no, we are too virtuous; we will keep them alive and torture them—yet torturing ourselves most in our flaming hells of luxury, that burn the very fingers that grasp them into such cinders that they cannot even quit their grasp. Like hands clenched in torture upon electric balls, we are compelled by the very pain to clasp the tighter, unable to let go through the very pain. Who will stay the pain for us and set us free?

This is man's great deliverance: a law put off the outside by the demands of service. And by a law thus put off the outside, there is given a new consciousness, a new perception within. So Christ gave that to man: He endowed him with a sensibility in his soul which was not in him before. He calls man's moral feeling into a new being; so that that which was before felt all right, or at least inevitable, and succumbed to, became to him abhorrent and impossible. And so is not a new sensibility again to come to us from Him, making acting for self, through one seeing what it brings by means of the law it imposes—the law of not helping—as abhorrent and impossible to us as any other crime or cruelty?

This new feeling, too, must come by the same means: by having to give up the outside things that implied that acting for self was right; and together with which alone it could even seem right. For so long as man can have his life so that any evil state whatever within can *seem* right, so long it will be succumbed to; even the perception of its evil will not awake. Men had to be such that neither circumcision nor uncircumcision mattered at all to them, but only the condition fulfilled—a new life; and how was it done, how sought? By saying: Keep circumcision scrupulously, put away all neglects and breaches of it perfectly, first, and then, &c.? Or rather: Think wholly of the new life you are called to; seek that, and let circumcision be forgotten?

There only the law is truly broken when keeping it externally would be breaking it in the soul, and so to keep it it must be broken. And when it is once thus broken all is done; for it is shown to all that that is truly keeping it. For they want to keep it—all want, indeed, and some more than all things beside. They need but to be shown how; to be shown that keeping the law does not mean injuring their fellows, and cannot; that it is kept perfectly in serving them. Once that seen and all is done: who wants to injure others? (Or above all man want to injure woman!)

Is it the fact that there is no true serving or regarding God which is not distinctly regarding the service of man; and that any other is truly, at the bottom, acting for self (perhaps either for happiness hereafter; or for our goodness' sake)? Not one with serving man, God's service is a negation merely, a superstition. Is God's service indeed but one of the forms in which the absence of regarding man expresses itself? And then here is a key to false "theologies," and all superstition, to all the false invention of "God," our fathers' and ours alike. Why must man's not regarding have this false regarding "God" as one of its phenomena? A true insight lies here. Is it thus? The two opposites from not regarding (man) are: regarding self-pleasure and self-virtue. Now, has self-virtue the two forms of serving "virtue" merely and serving "God" against service to man? And if so, has self-pleasure two corresponding forms?

This is Christ's revelation: whatever seems to be God's law, but makes us an instrument, even passively, of ill to our fellows, is misread; it does not mean that. Were there the same things binding the Pharisees against that feeling for others that bind us? Have not fresh powers, fresh elements of feeling, come in now, for the very end that a farther work may be achieved? That is, now there are feelings, reasons, rightful emotions making us deaf to others' needs that were not then, nor could have come until long after all the questions that existed then had been laid to rest. And these farther feelings, have they not existed in order that, by bringing in anew the question of whether man's needs shall rule or not, man's life shall be still more deepened and enlarged? To give man's needs the rule over all other right involves much more now than it did then. And so we may see one reason why these very relations that make the new problem and the new difficulty have been introduced. They give to that simple demand to let human needs rule this increased power. For how interesting it is again; what comes to us is simply that simple thing that came to them: Work no ill; let what man needs be. The same power, but in new conditions. So has not God ordered human life that

that simple demand coming again and again—one demand, the very simplest that can be, to let that which is wanted be, and not ask about ourselves—shall have power again and again, to renew it? Nay, as often as ever again it shall arise, having been refused, will it not again and again make it new? (Only may we not learn once for all that it must always be; and so be ready for more teaching?)

Man's life had become such, in Christ's time, that a law of external order had set itself against human wants (under thoughts of holiness, Divine authority, reverence for God, regard to virtue, or consideration of "what all could do," or these and other reasons), and by that condition there was power in the simple saying: "All laws are for man's service," with the condition that that implies insisted on, to bring in a whole new life for man, a whole transformation of the world. Of course it made man's life new; how could it fail? The conditions involved it; all had been prepared. And whenever they exist—a law made to be against man's service, and under such thoughts—there again are prepared the conditions for a new transforming of man's life, a new coming of a law of life into the heart. Then again we may hear Christ's voice, and drink in the power of His life. In every such condition He comes to us anew and bids us receive Him; says to us: "Here I have shown you the path; walk in it; be followers of me. I have wrought out the task for you; eat of my flesh, and let my blood work in your veins. Here I have overcome: enter into my victory. This false law of things, that bids you be instrument of ill to your neighbours (because some one has told you God commands it, or another that human virtue depends upon it, or because you have never known it done otherwise except for evil, or doubt if all could do it), this false law letting evil be to another that you may be good, need never bind you more: I have delivered you from it once and for ever. Look to me, and you are lightened." And so by the virtue of that act how much He did for us; for every new case He gave us the key; unloosed for us every new bond; and though so long ago His fingers work along all the ages. And when that same problem comes again, weighted with immense, innumerable powers and pregnant with the enormous good that life thrown into them would bring us, still His power works for us; our weakness is made strong with His strength. It is as if His very voice spoke to us, as indeed it does: every sorrow that we suffer to be unaided is as the very sorrow that nerved His hand.

Baffled, cast down, visibly defeated by evil, despairing now, not hoping even, nay, making a sort of virtue of consent to ill and converting it into a dogma to which we prostitute the name of piety and call part of the "faith" —now in our despair, when we doubt and tremble and know not what to do; sure only of one thing (or rather two, which are one) that we must act for ourselves, and that there is a law of God (one law at least) which for no good to man or woman must be set aside one jot; despairing now, sure but of this one two-faced fact in all our moral life, like the very breath of God which they are (for His words as He knew and said were spirit and life), like the very breath of God His words steal across the desert of our souls: "Was man made for the law, or the law for man?" And the chain is broken. He has made duty clear again, the duty to be such that *no thing* shall forbid our serving.

Does it not seem wonderful how exactly Christ's deeds and words were those which we want *now?* They fit our very problem, answer our very doubts; things that might seem so past burn with a fresh light, and are as if now first new, the very thing our life demands. We turn in our perplexity "to see if before there was not known some better way," and behold, Christ has taught us.

One law alone was wanted to be the occasion of the revealing of the truth of all: one was enough, and so there is visible a reason that the Sabbath was placed as it was before the Jews. It was in order for Christ thus to reveal what the true obeying God meant; to furnish Him the means to show how fulfilling God's law was done in the heart, and must, called by human good, pass *away from* the outside deed that it might be there.

And so appears the meaning of His words that the man's sickness was for the revealing of the glory of God; that it might be shown the obedience He desired was an obedience in the heart, proved to be there by being perfectly fluent to human good (the only proof that can be given of an obedience in the heart); that it might be seen how much God wanted *His* honour against man's good. Was it not for "this glory of God" the man's sickness had been appointed? We might be willing to let God's will be done in others' loss that we could help; but that loss is expressly to teach us that God's will is that we should not. That is what it is for; to make us know *what* God means by obeying Him.

So now, have not these relations of man and woman, and the sickness unto death that has come in them, been made as one of their reasons for this very purpose, to reveal to us yet again "God's glory," to show to us the true "obedience" He requires? For 'this very purpose made, so that on the one hand is placed what we think a command of God (expressed in some dignity of good and right on man's part) and on the other—simply a poor sufferer, a poor suffering body, let us say. Here is the very meaning of God's glory again: how is man to obey Him? Well prayed he who said: "Show me Thy glory." Was not woman's need made that it might reveal God's glory in man's purity?

We say often we want Christ to come again; but in that act of His He *is* here.

How much of the sacrificing others "till I can be good" is practically due to the teaching that is called Christian. When one thinks of what has been done in Christ's name, is it not plain that the true pathos of His life is in that? Not in His death nor any of the things He did. A deeper pathos lies in the history of His thoughts than anything recorded in the Gospel. How striking the parallel is between Christ and Newton in many things, and in this perhaps even most. Newton said: "The least things must not be disregarded in mathematics; I warn you against that above all:" and the mathematicians swear by his name, and mathematics is one great disregarding of least things. So Christ: above all He warned us against putting our being good and obeying God above others' needs; and what is our piety?

Self-righteousness is inevitably one with making right consist in things, and purity a matter of the flesh. And it is proved that Christ's action was to put service above "being good," was to put away self-righteousness, because it made things nothing. Paul's words, even about circumcision, prove it; from that one little saying we can see all; it means others first: the question of right regarded from their needs, not from self. It is proved by that one expression that this was what Christ did. And now, if it be supposed that God has given us a law of things, of certain things to be done, and those alone, even against all visible service, does not this prove that that thought of God is but an expression of the regard to self; that it is but a hidden form of self-righteousness?

The regard for others makes indulgence and restraint alike not-self, and so the flesh nothing. That is the true *self-denial*. What mischief there is in the false use of that word; making it mean against indulgence instead of against self-indulgence and self-righteousness alike. Turning it against indulgence we turn it away from self, and leave that unassailed.

So the "believing in Christ" is putting away both self-indulgence and self-righteousness, and the latter first. Now, is not this to be for the race? Made a fact and placed in woman's hands, it rises to be a true life of man, a life in *all*.

Was Christ amiable or loving in the sense in which He is often spoken of as being so? The feeling that it is of no use to speak to some persons of any truer thoughts was never expressed with such contempt as: "Cast not your pearls before swine." And to His friend Peter, merely shrinking from the thought of His being killed, He said: "Get thee behind me, Satan." In truth we see a reason for Christ's being held Divine in this: that while genius was so unknown it was necessary to insist that He should not be judged by the same standard as other men. So plainly being the moral teacher of the world, yet His actions and words so hard to reconcile with what a man "ought" to do, was not that a reason for His being claimed as Divine, that so a different standard might be taken for Him? And then does He not fulfil it?

"Teaching for doctrines the commandments of men," exactly expresses our attitude. It is not teaching the commandments of men that misleads us, but teaching them for doctrines, for absolute commands of God; as if they were sacred things. And it does not mean an evil commandment of course, only one of man's, expressing his feeling of the best. And the reason of the wrong in it is that, being man's, it must be unfit to be made a fixed thing of. It will be a "thing," a rigid course of doing: God's command is to *love*—an act. Christ says: Put no rigid deed up as the right. And the consequence too is so clear: in vain do they worship God. Necessarily their very goodness is turned to evil. "Worshipping God" is the seeking of good, and with a commandment of man put as a doctrine this must be vain. It is a false right; our very desires of good are made to work against it, the falsity being in the premiss. Our *light* is darkness.

The commandment of men will always be that which is passion, restraining, a thing that is beautiful and right on the basis of acting for self; it may be known by this. And another character will be that it will be always the putting aside of something; of something pleasurable, naturally tended to and desired. (It will not else come to be commanded; there would be no occasion for its coming.) A commandment of men will express a good thing made evil.

It is evident how Christ, in place of the service of God merely, or even of the service of man *through* serving God, bid men serve God in serving man. His way of treating the Sabbath and the Temple shows this. And even more the saying: "He that hath seen *me* hath seen the Father." And above all His new commandment is: "Love one another." Now what is the newness here? He had Himself summed up the old: Love God first and most; then man. That was the Law and the Prophets. Now when He said: I give you a *new* commandment, must not the old one have been in the thoughts of all? What then is the newness He introduced? That it is no more: Love God, but: Love *one another*.

Putting God in that false way first—the service of God in the self-form—is essentially ascetic: that is, it bears the mark of regard to self, and it is indeed regard to self in the form of regard to God. For how can we, not for ourself, serve a Being who has no needs, who wants nothing from us? He has no needs to unite goodness with pleasure. That is the defect in Him as an object of service; He has no needs. And so the true thought of others' needs is that they are God's needs. It is right to put God first, only it must be in the true way. We rightly are to love others, and serve them because that is serving Him, and for His sake. He comes to us so to be loved. As Christ is an incarnation of God, so all men are His incarnation too; He takes in them more weakness, because so He serves us most; serves us in making it possible to us to serve Him.

Thus Christ, then, as it were, put God aside; came in His name, saying: Do not regard Me; love *one another*. He made God less; and behold from thenceforth God has been to man not less but infinitely more than ever He had been; dearer, closer, more omnipotent to command. (Is there not also a great interest in seeing how in this Christ was akin to Buddha?) And if Christianity disappoints (and who does not feel that even if it do not fail, yet we are disappointed ?) may it not be because it has let go of that great thought; and while Christ put man first, and recognised no serving God but in serving him, those who have claimed to be Christians have gone back and again put God as to be served apart from man? This struck me in speaking to Father Newman: he said that "*all* Christian bodies agreed with the Church of Rome in this, that God was to be loved and served first, and men in serving Him, and because He loved them and for His sake." Is it not likely that this is true, and that it has robbed Christianity of its power? Men have not grasped the thought of Christ's, not even those who have loved Him most; but have gone back to the heathen thought of a God to be served for Himself.

How wonderful is that saying of Paul's (and how it accounts also for the power he has had over men), that the very thing that most absorbed his soul, that he found best, truest, the sublimest power of good, should also pass away—Christ's relation to man. But we may understand how he should have been ready to feel even that; he had had an experience which taught it to him; he had had to give up his best, and had found it gain. So he knew what giving up the best and holiest and mightiest for good meant. Is not this how genius ever learns it? And its being able to do it is its power.

We should follow Christ in our efforts for the amelioration of the world, even as that was His great work and is our great work too: however far we may be from Him in any other respect, there at least we are one with Him. And He has shown us the type of all such labours, has revealed the only principle on which they can be successful (and so long ago He did it, and now science confirms it; the only true action must be that): it is putting away restraints from things, and putting away at the same time that which imposes them; putting away a restraint that lay on things, and bringing it upon the emotions. And this is manifest, if once we see *what* it is that brings restraints on things, and makes goodness to be in not-pleasure; what it is that makes some things "sensuous" or low, even although they serve. What can it be but disregarding service? That makes not only some things, but all things mean and low and degrading. But also, any putting away restraint that does not claim as part of it the new restraint within, fails too, and is not following Him. Here is the test: is it *both* these?

"A new and better righteousness,"—one possible for all. A better righteousness with giving up of restraints, with less of abstinence. That is the difficulty, the restraints to be abandoned; what we would avoid, what our friends urge us to avoid. What it means is that we want the force but cannot give up the form in which it is; we cannot *use* the instrument we have made. We want the power, but find it so hard to pay the price. So a man is wanted not valuing these things.

A right which means not-pleasure will and must mean having pleasure the ruler of our life. As the latter inevitably brings the former, so as inevitably the former brings the latter; they cannot be separated, any more than the two electricities.

And thus we may gain a key to how Europe now has come to be so utterly under the dominion of acting for self. It seems the effect of the banishing of pleasure which it carried to such an extreme. Did not that inevitably bring this result, absolutely implied within it, of giving over the life to self? As having the life centred round pleasure makes right centre round it too, and be in putting it away, so also does not a right centred round pleasure and made to be in putting it away *bring* a life bound under pleasure?

There is this good in our life, that it is the clear insistance, in practice and theory alike, that pleasure is not wrong, nor goodness in its refusal. There is this element of good, the breaking of the false bonds between right and absence of pleasure. Europe is doing that—the parallel of the intellectual work in the dark ages.

Again, in respect to Christ's turning men's regard from God to their fellows, see the "judgment." Those who were thinking about Him He "never knew;" those served Him who served their fellows without thinking of Him at all.

What is wanted, when the better right is to come, is not to bid men "Do," but to ask: "Why should I do this troublesome right?" So here was Christ's power. Not what He bid men do (had not others bidden that, or nearly all, before?) but: Do not have to do, learn: here is something you have not thought of. And this is visible in His "new law." Love, it says; but that is not the whole; had not that been said before, many times before? But the command is: Love *one another*. Is there not a not-doing here also? Love one another: is not the leaving off the chief power in it?

And see again His answer: What good thing shall we *do?* It is so natural a question. "Give us some practical directions; *what* things shall we do? How shall we carry out these principles? What should we do each of us?" (And John, too, had given a direct answer to that question.) But Christ's answer was as if He had said: "Do not *do* at all; have a *feeling*."

In the new law, certainly, the new thing was not the "love," it was "one another," and *instead* of God. And this is so striking in it, men are put strictly instead of God; God is left wholly aside. In this the new law contrasts with the old, which was: "Love God," but also added: "Love your neighbour," though in less degree. And is it not true? If we love men, do we not in the very act love God? He is loved in true love of men. To love man *is* to love God, at once is it and includes it; it has no need to be added. But we see the law which began with loving God was not the same; it had to add on besides the love of men. The love of God first is not complete in the same way; the neighbours might still be left out. So in that one command Christ summed up all; nothing is left out. It includes all duties; the love of God and every other command as well. All law raised to absolute unity is there, Love one another. And was it not a natural issue of Christ's life for Him to sum up His experience in a law which thus expressly omits reference to God apart from man? The work He had done was to break the bonds which came from thinking of God apart from man; to break mischief-rights, to put away nonsense-reasons; and here He sums it up in a command which says it all: Love one another, and have no other thought of loving God. All false rights fall off then. Do not talk of God; think of man.

Seeing the Sabbath among the Jews as having become a mischief-right, that is, a form from which the restraint had passed away, seems a starting-point for very much besides. Having become such a form, we see why it became included in the Decalogue. Among the moral laws comes a form. Why? Because these forms (emptied of restraint), these mischief-rights, even through their having become thus empty, are made matters of paramount importance; they gain for themselves all the feeling—nay, even more—of the highest duty. So is it not evident that if we now made a law of moral right we should certainly include in it, and most emphatically, a *form* of marriage; and the Hindoos the duty of not killing any animal? So we can understand why the Sabbath entered so into the Jewish Decalogue, and why also Christ's work centred so much around it. By the very loss of the restraint the form becomes felt so imperative. (If only because it seems that the overthrow of it *must* be for license: we may judge of the feeling in the other cases by our own.)

Besides, as we have seen, the Decalogue is not good; it *is* the law of things which "kills," saying not one word about not living for self; only do not do certain things—which yet may, and must, be done. Is not the contradiction curious, so close together, between, on the one hand: "Thou shalt not kill," and, on the other, the meritorious massacres?

In truth, is not the history of the Decalogue, the period of its writing, and therefore of very much more, clearly implied by the mere fact of the inclusion of the Sabbath? Is it not proved that it was written at a time when the Sabbath was to the Jews what monogamy has become to us, and not killing animals to the Hindoos—a form from which the restraint has passed? May we not know it was written when the keeping of the Sabbath had let the restraint slip from it, and so had come to be insisted on for its own sake, and had projected its own fictitious reason? If it had still been serviceable (in a true line, perfectly, with service) it would not have wanted any other reason. So we see the period when the Decalogue (and what was with it) was written; namely when the restraint had slipped away from the Sabbath, and after it had accordingly projected for itself a fictitious reason.

It is surely sufficiently evident that the reason given in the Decalogue *is* a projected one; and that the command was never introduced *for* that reason. Having it, and finding that it needed a reason, that thought might come; but the source of the institution was based on man, not on God. What a new light thus comes on Christ's words: "The Sabbath was made for man." Surely He was speaking not of any "making" by God, but of simple fact and history, speaking of the man who introduced it: "It was made for man." That was its design; it was not a thing man was to be sacrificed to. It was to their own history He was appealing. (And so how parallel to the appeal now made to the original Vedas against the superstitions of India.) The Sabbath, He tells us, was introduced, not for some reason about God, but for the good of man.

Was the original thought of the Sabbath, perchance, not of *mere* rest at all, but of action for others? (Think how well such an institution might have come from Confucius, for instance, with that intention.) Then could we not well trace it, and see the very same mockery of man's folly at the end? Acting and thinking wholly for others on one day in seven would mean of course *not-doing* for self; then the action for others slips away, and the form of it, the not-doing (how like the not-killing!) remains. And the whole process is involved, and it ends in taking care of their own interests, but refusing to help the suffering. And so what force there would be in Christ's words: "The Sabbath was made for man," if the fact He referred to was that it was originally meant for one day to be given up to man, to others' interests instead of their own. How absolute the inversion had become. (But was it greater than ours is?) And then how clear the process would be; the acting for others slipping away, would leave the "form"—the not-doing our own things; this would become sacred then, of course, and would project its reason (about God resting); and would become an abstaining from work merely, based on that notion, and then all would follow.

With the law of service all days will be truly Sabbaths. And so one lack in those first service-Sabbaths (if it were so) would have been that they were only one in seven. And indeed in this—in consenting to six days for self, and only one for service—was there not a negation that ensured the failure? It must have fallen, it was not true. A rottenness consented to in the foundation must destroy the superstructure.

And as we see of some mischief-rights, was it not of all? They are the great degraders of life, holding men under self; one and all they make it *duty* to hurt others, and so spread a blindness all through. Was not Jewish life degraded even chiefly by the Sabbath held against others' good? The needs of others were by it most of all deprived of power; and right itself forbidden to follow service, made to accept all license. And may it be that nothing so much degrades the life of India as the refusal to kill?

So the law of service is one perpetual Sabbath—the serving of man.

It is no real irreverence even to the Old Testament itself to speak of that reason given for the Sabbath as a nonsense-reason. It is right to feel contempt for that; it is to honour God, for that was dishonouring Him. It meant that the spirit had gone out of His laws. His own Prophets said the same; those laws of forms killed the nation, as they ever do; even as it is the same thing now destroys us. And Christ's own words repudiate the reason given in the Decalogue.

But though projected reasons are nonsense-reasons and must be so seen, yet they have their value too, and very possibly have a distinct and important truth, and one which could not be given us in any other way. Take the Sabbath for example; may we not say it is very probable indeed that the Being to whom God gave the task of making the "world" did "work" six days and rest the seventh? Is it true, and does it mean that God did give it to some creature to "make" the world, even as He gives it to others to make an orrery? Is not the universe itself most assuredly an "image" of some existence? Why may not God have made it through a creature, and a creature subject to the need of rest? We *know* no other "creating." But if the Being who made the world worked and rested, then we are told in that that He was a being like ourselves. This character is told us of the "Elohim."

In the Decalogue, again, we see a sign of a false thought of God making a false right in the forbidding of art. Does not the second command express a result of the false thought of God? And this false thought of God, and of serving Him as different from the service of man, was common to the Jew and Gentile. And so it had in both its effects; in the Gentiles it led to idolatry, in the Jews to the forbidding of art, and the other burdensome restraints; the two halves arising from one negation; from the thought of God as to be considered and served apart from, and even to the hurt of, man. So how truly these needed and waited to be made one. And their union came in the "new command:" Love *one another*, and nothing more. So it is true the Jews in one sense did avoid "idolatry," but it was at the price of refusing art.

Then if this be so, if it be a false religion that directs regard or service to God apart from man, or if Christ has expressly condemned it and given us a law which distinctly puts it aside (and our forgetting it accounts for our failure to be worthy disciples of His, and of Christianity to be worthy of its name), if this be so, then here what a store of power there is, of power available for man, for the renewing of our life. All the power, all the passion, all the human force and life, that go now into the devotion to God, apart from man, are wasted force; are really ready and waiting to do the things we count impossible, to make the new life we despair of. These emotions, grandest, most potent of all, perchance, that swell the human breast, these are bidden, God bids them, Christ commands, to take a new channel, to find one for themselves. And how human needs stand open to receive them! Here is a misdirected flood, cast back, and here an empty channel; each fitted, surely each (from the foundation of the world) prepared for each. Another waste of power here on a false duty; and not now a restraint but a passion. Both elements are given us, both powers are ready waiting to unite to recreate man's life; a passion of utmost intensity calling for a truer channel on the one hand, and a restraint (of passion only less strong, even if less so) demanding to be put away. All the forces that make strong human life are here united waiting for a new work to do; and the work, how it waits for them. Here is yet another duty we must give up, and all the power of it free for use.

And in this is there not an universal? See these emotions, so intense, so lovely, so exquisite, of devotion to "God" (and inevitably expressing themselves in mischief-rights; from whence indeed their value comes, because through these the want is supplied), these beautiful and mighty feelings, essential to the life of man, are given him first through error; are devoted to that which is false, and gain power from the delusion. Is it not always so? Is it not thus all good is given to man and must be? Through false thoughts, and false rights, all that is most valuable comes first into man's life; it is first outside, then brought within. For if this "devotion" is not to be, we are to have it *in its effect:* devotion to God comes also first in its self-form, and is to be perfected by being in its effect. It is only in its self-form that it is devotion to an isolated, separate God, a self-God, an Idol.

How quickly a change might come: children would only have to see it was not goodness lost but only goodness in another form. The difficulty with adults is that a change in the form of good—which is its ceasing in one and coming in another— is felt by them (and till the law is understood must be so) only on one side; they feel the losing and not the coming. They have to look through the ceasing to see the coming; but to the children it is different; it is a simple choice: Will you have the good in this way, or in that; at the beginning or at the end; in ways that restrain passion, or give it no reason for being restrained; that forbid good to be, or make it wholly free? The adult is so used to its absence at the beginning, he does not see the want; is not even aware of the vacuity, and so he clings to it so at the end. "A new and better righteousness" must be this seeming losing.

One of the chief hindrances to a true seeing of any of the moral relations, and almost the chief cause by which our thoughts of Christ especially are kept in a fictitious theological region, is the absence of understanding about self-virtue. We do not see that the "mischief-right" is a right which is *for self*, that is, to the hurt of others. So we seem to need above all to get to understand the meaning of self-virtue, that is, to see what putting self first is, and that that is wrong. But that *is* to be delivered from it. It needs only to see—for why should it be hard to do? How *can* it be hard to do when it means not cutting yourself off from pleasure, not making goodness mean restraint?

It may be said: But these duties you call mischief-rights are not putting self first, nor regarding self, nor do they come at all from thinking of self; they are obedience to God, and are done for the sake of, and out of regard for, Him. It may be added: They are not even restraints of passion, at least when they are truly done; they are the joyful expressions of love to God. If this be said, we must still look farther here. Granted they are done "for God," it is still self—that is, our own goodness—put against others' good. The being commanded by God and done for Him does not make it a different thing; what is said is: "God commands us to put self first," but it is none the less doing it. And the thought that God commands it, however honest, sincere, devout (as we know well), does not make it better, but rather worse. We can see this in respect to other errors than our own; a false right believed to be God's law is simply so much worse for being so believed; and the need for a truer thought is but so much the more urgent. Self put first is self first, and brings its fruits, none the less if it be thought to be a command of God. We must repent of thinking so of Him.

How totally false is that law: "Thou shalt not kill." It concedes all wickedness by what it omits, and what it affirms is false. It says: "You may hate as much as you like, but you may never kill;" while the fact is that we <u>may not hate, but may kill</u>. And so no wonder the Decalogue contradicts the truth about the Sabbath, affirming it made not for man but for some thought about God and in order to honour Him. And the basis of the other falsities lies in the false presentation of loving God; in the very thought of the isolated God to the love of whom it was necessary to *add* a love for man, and such a love! And this was betrayed by their prohibiting art to themselves: they had a monotheism, in some shaky fashion, that they had to forego art even to keep such hold on as they kept. And so we see the relation of the Greeks to them; they forewent monotheism but had art; and we owe not less to them for their art than to the Jews for their monotheism.

And here is revealed evidence of an intense relation of art to religion—to our thought of God. <u>A false thought of Him excluded art</u>. That is enough; it is even as a false basis of life—self-serving—sets itself against pleasure; it is the proof of a power and destiny of the excluded thing to put away the falsity; proof of an antagonism between them. Here is proof in the very fact of the Jews saying: "No art"—for God's sake and in order to worship Him aright—that art is destined to make true our thought and worship of God. Art must cast out the negation which seeks to cast it out. So we have yet to see more in it, to gain from it a greater benefit. Are we now beginning to see its power aright? So it will show itself to have a destiny for making our religion truer and completer, similar to that we already begin to recognise in science. If it had not it could not have been felt by the Jews in conflict with it so; that is the very same feeling as the self-based life feeling itself in conflict with the love of woman. Everything a false life assails is infinitely sacred, and has unseen spiritual power and significance. The falsity knows its destroyer afar off, and betrays its fear. Every such feeling we may understand thus; every asceticism means that something that has use and good is put away. There is a negation in the life that that thing will cast out. We may be sure of it always. Here, then, is a promise for us.

It may be that the Decalogue did not mean to exclude art; but the Jews had it so. Their thought of God did exclude art. Wherever there is a false feeling—that is, a lack—in man, there will be the endeavour on his part to put aside something that has value (that is, nature); and that good, when no more to be put aside, will cure that lack. It means that the two cannot co-exist. (So acting for self puts aside marriage according to service.) This is the law of the letter and of the spirit; of the letter the putting aside, of the spirit the coming back; and it gives life. So we see too the meaning of death: it is for life again to be made perfect.

Now, in this relation of Christ's to the thought of God, His putting away the isolated God who was to be loved and served apart from man, may we find a key to the difference of feeling on the question of His claiming to be Divine? Is not an appearance of such a claim, as if in a special and exclusive sense, likely to arise from such a feeling in Him, we not entering into it? So shall we find the true meaning of His words. And thus we may see better how the Christians were counted atheists.

Christ tried in every possible way to hold to the service of God apart from that of man. His soul tended to it, sought it, was only *forced* from it. But at length He was forced from it; and so in His new commandment how evident it is: *God is as if He were not*. Here at last is His true presence. The condition of truly reaching Him is fulfilled when He is treated as if He were not. Here we see religion become true, fulfilling the conditions of truly revealing God. The phenomenal is treated as if it were not.

Thus too it is visible why God had to be thought of, and entirely regarded and served with all the power of the intensest resolve, in this false way: it was that that might be rightly let go; might still be, even when banished in its effects. That false had to be as the true, that wrong as the right, in order that the true right might rightly come; the false God as the false right must be sought, loved, valued with all the heart, in order that it may be given up rightly. Here have we not the secret of Christ's strifes and tears? So every form is made to be valued; valued to the utmost, and held and striven for as the most sacred of things, that it may be rightly given up; may be still in its effects. (This is what we see in genius.) So is not this feeling of the infinite sacredness, the isolated God, phenomenal God, and of forms emptied of their life, the same, and for the same reason; that both alike may be truly and not falsely put aside?

And the reason that these are not and cannot be duties demanded by God is simply that there is not and cannot be such a God; that the whole thought of Him is phenomenal. There is no Being to make such claims or to be so served. That is to take the phenomenal as existing—our great error; to suppose our untrue imaginings to exist. Did not Christ feel that neither the way His fathers the Jews, nor the way His friends the Gentiles, served God would do? He could say *only*, Let His service be as if it were not.

Was ever such an adding by a minus as in this new law of Christ, such a doing by leaving out? What we see is the service of God vanishing and being in its effect. This too comes first in its self-form. Being in effect— or truly being—is simply being altruistic, and we have the type of all altruistic being in this service of God in serving man; a true service (to real needs) instead of an arbitrary, artificial one. Is there, then, something answering to these real needs of our fellows, instead of made up demands, in all true or altruistic being, in all coming to be in effect? And in every case of the "fluxion" is not this what takes place: that a mere phenomenal thing, arbitrary, made up by our "negation," passes, and is in its effect in a reality? So is there not a truth in the doctrine that the love and service of men must come from and by, must come *through*, the loving and serving God? True, if we see: it is by the passing of that loving and serving; by its being in its effect. That first, and through it the true; not by mere adding, but by the one thing *becoming* the other. So the saying is quite true: "Except through the love of God, no love of man;" only what it means is not known. Only through being forced with utmost reluctance and struggle to abandon that, could man have attained the true love of God. (It is as only through the "observation-true" does the true knowledge come, but it is not *joined on* to it. That imperfect is merged in the perfect.) And is there not another parallel here? It is said: "The love of man only through the family;" the home is the training-school for universal love. Is not this true also with an unsuspected truth? Is not our "home" even as that false serving of God was? (In truth, is not woman in it even so falsely served as God was, to the loss of her fellows? Is not the parallel exact?) The home, as we have made it, is the self-form of the love of man; and even so also to be in its effect; to be made perfect in seeming to pass away. As Christ from His new law simply left out God, and so gave Him for the first time true dominion; even so in woman's new law will not the wife simply be left out—left out, that serving others may have all the space? Hers is a throne, and she shall be a queen. For this is the true and only throne for evermore; the service wholly put for others; all claims foregone. So we see Him who sitteth upon a throne, to whom all blessing, honour, dominion, and power are for ever; the King we see enthroned for ever, and the sceptre is laid down, the kingdom disappears, and God is all in all. That is the King of Man; the pattern in whose steps all that is human treads. So also shall the wife rule when her dominion is made complete.

And how simply this putting aside the service of God for that of man *is* serving Him; it is done for His sake; is His service, recognised as the service He demands. It is fulfilling the two duties at once; man served *and* God; God in the heart, man with heart and hands as well. Both are done at once. The one is raised to a more perfect life by the coming in of the other. It is exactly the lesson of art; two demands fulfilled at once in the seeming giving up of one, the given up one therein made perfect. Here do we not see the bearing of art upon religion? That instinct of the Jews to put it away, owing to their false thought, is justified in this: the false putting of God's service first, so as to be against the service of man, must sometimes have demanded art to be put away; it cannot stand against its lesson of fulfilling two rights at once; the first right, the one according to the appearance, made perfect in being given up for the claims of other things which it excluded. For here is our first right—this self-service of God; the serving Him not in others—is the right according to the appearance; it is serving God according to the appearance of Him; to our thought of Him based on ourselves, and yet not really true even to ourselves; and not according to what He *is*. And so how simply also such service would be but the true service of the wife—the service of her spirit, that is, a spiritual service; a service "in spirit and in truth." (Have we yet read this aright?) Is not this the very thing that serving God as a Spirit is: serving Him in others, that is, *serving His Spirit;* serving Him as a giver, a lover? Do we not see, in the serving of the wife's *spirit*, serving her giving, the true spirit (or spiritual) service? When Christ said, "God is a Spirit," did He not mean simply, God is a giver, not a taker? He is not a negation, not a self to require you to think what you must render to Him, but a life who desires you as ministers of His service; that you too may live. He is a Spirit, and requires Spirit-service, service to those He loves, that He may bless and enrich them through you; so blessing *you* the most. Worship Him with spirit-worship; consent to be so enriched; give Him the gift of giving. He is a Spirit, and it is in that He lives, and so is woman too; only let her reveal what her being is. She wants spirit-service.

But how perfectly this question of service of God and man may be summed up in terms of art! Here is the law, "Love God perfectly;" then to that must be added: "Also love your neighbour; secondarily, as well as you can." It is as in art, saying: "You must draw the object, the outline, exactly, perfectly, with all your effort, all your skill;" then to that you have to *add:* "Give atmosphere effects, a feeling of motion, of fulness and multitude; secondarily, as well as you can." And in both, how the two commands are one! Serve men wholly, and God is perfectly served: give the true effect of Nature's fulness, and the object is perfectly served.

Through there being a phenomenal to us (seeming to us of course the existing till we have learnt) it must be that all truth and right, when it is truly gained, will be in a phenomenal false and wrong; will be against that which must first be felt as true and right. So worship in spirit will be phenomenal not-worship.

It has been urged (arguing for a moral centred on self) that this life of man's is as an embryonic life; very imperfect and with very ineffective functions; its chief business the perfecting of its own organs to fit it for a different condition, &c. Now this might perhaps be argued *a priori,* if there were no experience; but is it not enough to say that it means this life of ours, every one circling as much as he can of the world round him—"with limits?" Does it not betray itself as a projected reason? Here are these restrictions, &c., and the *life* has slipped out of them; and so the whole scheme wants something to rest upon. And see what mischief it is: this has in it all the thought of this life as only a preparation for "heaven;" it brings all that blinding influence of the fancied spiritual apart from this (which is indeed all one with the serving God apart from man); it turns the thought from this eternal to the imaginary future.

But how is this idea of an embryo related to that of this age as a chrysalis-state—a "dark" age? The conditions are essentially the same; it is true of man that now his chief work is the development for a condition that is to come; but then it is *in this world*, and one mischief of the other thought is that this "development" is not the bringing on, the working out, of the future condition, but is a preparation only for a change to come outside.

The thought of this as an embryo-life (in that sense of its being our business to form our own character) is a result of our having taken our pleasure, instead of service, for our life to centre round. Not that in fact it may not be true; and that our own development is the work of this life; but the question is *how* that is to be attained; whether by the life centering round ourselves or others. Is not the law of service the very means of man's development? Granted the perfection of its own organs is the end of an embryo, yet by what does that come? Does it mean that the thought, the effort, is to be put on that result, or would not that rather be fatal to it? May we even think of monstrosities as sometimes arising as if from such a misdirection of the embryonic powers? As if an embryo got it into its head, that its own internal development was its object, and so attended to it. What but an "arrest of development" could ensue? It would put on some undue restraint; check this, regulate that, bring to bear on them influences apart from the simple and only question of what was wanted. May we say of some monstrosities that they show us the effects of a "self-virtue" in the embryo? How should faculties, that are to be for service, be trained or developed, save through devotion to service?

And so, indeed, is not the very thought of the isolated God (the self-God) a "projected reason" from the restraint of passion that putting self first makes goodness mean? Not recognising the true reason for goodness being in restraint (namely, the regard to self), man has, of course, to invent another reason; and this is the self-God, the God who demands to be served apart from His creatures, the imagination, or "idol." We make that God for ourselves to stand as reason for the restraint; we (although we do not suspect it) having made goodness mean restraint. And is not the basis of it, in one aspect, this also, that we, having a phenomenal perception of our own being (not true, but resting on a non-perception), as isolated selves, suppose a God also, answering to our false apprehension of our own being?

And to begin by saying there is a God to be served apart from man, is sure to end in hurting man for God's sake. It must, for that serving of God must mean restraint, and restraint must come to injury. The result is inevitable: "May we not help others so?" "No; we must restrain our passions." It must go from bad to worse, and God's service first, apart from men, is sure to come to be against them. So the Decalogue, with God first, apart from man, is strictly idolatrous. And surely it is the worst and most disastrous untruth ever uttered to say: "God spoke these words, and said:" Put me first.

Then the serving of God and of self are two forms of the same thing—that is, of the putting away of pleasure (*i.e.*, the restraining of passion). This is the central point in them; the one that is common to both, and as forms of that they should be regarded. For is it not a law that whenever two things have a character in common, that is *the* character of them, they are forms of that unity? That should be seized as the point to be regarded in them.

This was the "pearl" Christ had "found:" the perception that men did and could "love one another;" that it was their nature, was real matter-of-fact common sense to expect it; that that command might be given with true assurance of obedience. It is not that men do not want to love one another, it is not that keeps them back; it is that they think they have to love God. So the sublimity of Christ's leaving out God from man's love. Put up a loving God that is not loving man, and man's strength is squandered on idle things and mischiefs; he has no power left to love his neighbour, and he avenges himself for his waste—makes an equilibrium—by not loving his neighbour. That frightful idol kills men's souls, and no being could stand against it—a God whom you can serve in drawing-rooms, and carriages, and by devout emotions on Swiss mountains, while your fellows are in cellars. It would kill any being to believe it, for it would turn him into the same image; he also would become a being that could be served so.

Christ also is to be served as a Spirit; and in our Christianity is He not served as a self? Is not this the key to the passages: "I am the Way, the Truth, and the Life," and other such? We misread them, thinking He meant, "Put me first." To live His life—not to be thinking of Him and His claims—that is to come to Him. He has set us an example, in His own revelation of God, how we should think of, and serve Him. Is it not thus Paul says: "If I have known Christ *after the flesh*, yet henceforth know I Him no more?" Paul's "flesh" is our "self." "Even Christ as a self I know no more."

If then in our Christianity Christ is served as a self, is it not, with all its good and beauty, waiting to be merged? Do we not trace well enough in it the effect of a worship of a self? See the hardness of external bondage that creeps over it perpetually. How beautiful Judaism had been, what Psalms it had prompted, what loving devotion cherished, sustained what sublimity of heroism! Yet Christ merged it. And so what beauty has not clung around the self-home, what tenderness and devotion it has cherished; yet shall woman merge it too. Shall Christ alone be condemned to be served as a self for ever?

The two forms of self-indulgence, Hell-fire and outer darkness, are the two punishments for those on God's left hand: Life's becoming; and on the right: Life perfect; a kingdom; pleasure made free.

The "body" raised in glory, the impulse put away with ignominy, comes back made one with Nature. The "raising of the dead" is ever the new life. So Paul says. But some will say: How are the dead raised; the rule of self cast out; with what passions then, what impulses, do they come?" (This would be the question arising in respect to a spiritual raising.) And Paul says: "With these same passions and impulses that have been put away in dishonour; these that were 'self' passions; they are the very spiritual powers themselves." They are buried physical self-things; they are raised spiritual.

And so when he said to his Gentile converts: "Stand fast," did he not mean, in your old Gentile freedom, which Christ has changed for you into a true liberty? If you take any law but His—of service—you come under the whole dominion of the self.

Why to be Divine should Christ not have had a truly human mind as well as a truly human body; why not limited in "time" as well as in space? If He truly had foreknown how His words about the unpardonable sin, in their vagueness to us (as reported), would have been a reason at least of madness, could He, who cured disease, have left them so? And throughout, though the things said are perfect, is there not plain evidence that there was not any superhuman foreseeing of the future; that what was not within vision then was not seen? That is, surely, that Christ was Divine in a true, human, real sense, and not a fancied one.

Has any curse been so great on man as that thought of "heaven?" It binds him in his contentment, and lets every evil practice and false thought rule unchecked. And it is an expression of the thought that "in this world" goodness must be in putting away pleasure; for heaven is to be pleasure, and so it must be in another world—the passions gone, not raised in glory. So it is not *self-not-first* to aim at, to work for, to enter into and find at our very doors, and waiting for us, the heaven that is not a dream: not this, but a mere passive change to be waited for; a falling off of passions and impulses, which even because they are to fall off may be left unredeemed from self. This is what comes of that fatal dream, which our holding to self-first, with its goodness in not-pleasure, imposes on us for our heaven. This is the palsy it inflicts upon our souls.

Shall we not have to teach that man's service must be to the universal (that is, to God; here is the true meaning of that feeling; made false by isolating God or thinking of Him as a self—a *not-others*): Man's service is to the universal; he has been trained to this through service to the individual in the false way—as *against* others. And this service to individuals was beautiful; it had exquisite characters that human history could not have spared—nay, that are beautiful and perfect in their place for ever, and shall always be; but the imperfection of it was evident too, was shown by what it became. It was one of the things that had to pass. So the service to the individuals as selves—or against others—stands midway as it were; it is better than serving and regarding self alone; though it is not the true form of regarding others, yet it is regarding them. It is as our "free-will" stands between mere passiveness and true freedom.

Looking at some self-restraining people, quiet, serious, earnest after good, consenting to the intensest sacrifices with unpretentious resignation, how one feels as if it would be quite good enough if all were but as these are. And yet, not only will not God have it, not only could not Nature be known at all if it were so, but these very people and their goodness could not have been if there had not been a man most intensely unlike them. They can be as they are only because Christ threw Himself with utterest recklessness of passion against the Pharisees; not caring what came to Him, to them, to the very religion He had loved.

And this life of Christ has made Europe new. Yet is it not strange? He was not talking of Europe at all, nor of anything that was in Europe. He was talking of things that existed only in a small section of the world, among a few people that no one cared anything particular about. To these He said: "You make void the law of God through your traditions;" with your ideas of goodness and serving God, you make His commands of no effect. And the life of Europe is the echo. Is not that the very central word of all Christ's teaching? "By your traditions you make God's law of no effect;" instead of this law of His revealed in human wants, you put words and thoughts of your own. (It is the very same as the problem of science has been: regard the things God shows you; do not set up your own thoughts;—and with the same conditions.)

Will not Christ's life be better and more truly seen by being thus seen as one with the bringing of man's thought up to the visible phenomena? Was not His great saying, "Your traditions," the very thing that had to be said of the traditions that put away learning from Nature? It was thought so much finer to invent our own truth. Did He not stand and call to man, for His *life* as well as His thought: "Take *Nature* as your guide; hear God's voice there?" And there is in both the same seeming descent from the grand and noble and supersensuous. It is in the intellectual as in the spiritual life. In both humbling is exaltation.

Christ said: "Not your *goodness*" (traditions must mean man's aim at goodness), "not your goodness; do what God wants doing." This is the power of traceable service: it brings man's life (as observation brings his thought) under Nature's hand, to grow thereby. It is one call: "Learn from *Nature;* God speaks to you there." And thus we may see quite afresh His reference to the Holy Spirit and His mission. It joins itself to this work of His in bringing man's *life* under Nature. Did He not feel that in this He had given man the guide into all truth? Here was man's guide, Nature herself, in the form of visible service, and he had turned aside from her —the Holy Spirit, as Christ called her. This makes it simple fact; Christ thus did bestow on man his guide into truth. Of course it is not merely the visible service, but that to which it leads; as in science not merely the appearances, but that which comes of studying them. (It is better to say *traceable* than *visible* service.)

"Not your own goodness or virtue, but human good;" this is, goodness for the bad. For the tradition is sure to be a hard thing (it is this alone that commends it to the self), a putting away pleasure. So sweeping away the "traditions" is goodness for the bad; it brings the outcasts into the fold. "You condemn people, and cast them out from the power of good for not doing certain things, and God never commanded them: you *make* them bad."

By giving to man the "right" of real demonstrable service, Christ delivered him from the need of having to put away pleasure; that is, from the necessity of having his regard upon himself. So Christ gave man a pleasure-religion; a religion with pleasure free; the old impulse, sown in dishonour, raised again in glory. Christ gave men this, and if it has been lost, is it not clear how it has been? We have consented to come again under the yoke of bondage; and (putting theological meaning in His and His disciples' words) have made for ourselves again the goodness that is in putting pleasure away. Then for a time men strove for it, and then they gave it up; but the longing remains unsatisfied. This is what is amiss: we have lost Christ's gift of the religion of pleasure; the religion which deprives pain of its power to be better than pleasure (a power it cannot but have while self is the regard ; that is, while others are anywhere, or to any degree, left out). We have lost Christ's gift ; or may we not express it as the guiding of the Holy Spirit ? We have lost the leading of "Nature," of real demonstrable service, for these are one. So we have lost that which is "heaven," pleasure no more worse than pain. Christ gave man that.

The coming of sense into man's intellectual life determines that he should have the life to which the free use of sense (even the insistance on its being used to the utmost) belongs. Now, only in Christian countries has this change taken place ; is it therefore truly part of Christ's bringing man to the guidance of the Holy Spirit ? For is not man's intellect coming to rule sense—through Nature being forced upon him—a true fruit of the work of Christ in giving man the law of traceable service ? Since He brought man to Nature and observation, does not the scientific process owe its true parentage to Him ? Was not the old thought of a truth that was above sense one with that of a goodness that was above traceable service ? These are but two expressions of one falsity. And in sending man to look at the real sensible wants of his neighbour for the guide of his actions, He really set in motion the powers which led to his taking real sensible appearances for the guide of his thought. (And do we not thus feel a sacredness stealing over sense and its use, over all the sensuous ? We begin to feel that it is in very truth the guiding of the Holy Spirit, and what a new thing it might be to us. And it ceases to be a wonder that by a thing called sensuous, nay, most despised and degraded, should come man's greatest good.) So by bringing man's life to traceable service as its law, or means of guidance and development, did not Christ really bring his intellect to traceable truth as its means of development? He bound man to Nature; by bringing his heart to her He brought also his thought.

And so may we see in part how it was expedient for Christ to go away? Could the dark age have come with His continued influence? For it was necessary the dark age should come; that was the essential means of bringing man to the guidance of Nature; the inevitable form of the coming of life. For life must be given according to the nature of life; must grow as life grows, cannot be given from without. And the bringing man's *thought* to Nature (the life of his intellect) could only come by sense being compelled on him, even as it was. So that (intellectual) dark age was a true and a visibly right fruit of Christ's life and teaching; of His bringing man to Nature. It was the inevitable process in respect to thought, even as the morally dark age—the having pleasure forced on him before he has accepted the life to which free pleasure belongs, and as the means of bringing him to that life—is the necessary process in respect to his spiritual life. What we see in both is the becoming of life; it is Christ giving life to the world; life growing. And He did it who said: "Make not the commands of God of none effect by your tradition;" He who said: "Do not fancy about good and make up your own goodness, but look at traceable, demonstrable needs." He gave us Nature and her freedom, the kingdom of *Pleasure* and its righteousness.

Christ's law was simply genius asserting its right as the universal right, even as genius was sure to do. Was it not certain always that the genius-law would be affirmed as man's, and that men would recognise it, even though they misconceived it? So it is affirmed, and then lies latent for a time, and works till the whole is leavened. Is this the meaning of the "leaven?" It was hidden, as if lost; but suddenly, behold, the whole lump is *so;* prepared, made ready for that law. (Was there in history a "leaven" through all the dark age, working and making ready the human mind for knowledge?) And, indeed, is this—the affirmation of the genius-right as the right for man—*the* thing that man recognises as divine? Is it by this that every divine book has had and held its sway?

"The kingdom of heaven and its rightness;" the law of service which makes pleasure free. So do we not see a meaning again in: "Seek first . . . and all these things shall be added?" If the law of service rules there will be more good, more enjoyments for every one, than any one even desires. To get this law accepted is the only need; with it all good will come; without it really and truly, none; only labour that mocks itself. And thus the opposites in Christ's sayings are clear: have the law of service ruling and all good will be; it will be the rule of pleasure and its rightness. But those who try to bring it must accept the loss of all things and become the scorn of men. Here are the two things: the law of service which will bring all good; more to all than any have yet dreamed of yet; but you who go to teach it, you shall be counted vile, and men will think they do God service in killing you. That law answers perfectly to these characters; it brings all good and is counted bad—the law that makes pleasure free. This comes by God having joined service and pleasure; by the self for goodness having put pleasure away. The man who preaches God's righteousness must be accounted a sinner. Here it is: *all* good; the one simple thing that will do all things and relieve from all other need to care; and that must be taken up at that price and no less. "Seek first"—that which puts wholly away making pleasure worse than pain.

So again, when asked about the kingdom of heaven and what "marriage" would be there, He replied at once: It will be impulse perfectly free; the rightness which makes pleasure wholly free is there; there will be no sign of any reason for pleasure being less good; they will not marry there, but will be as the angels of God which are in heaven—in *Nature*—obeying their impulses perfectly. In "heaven" there must be no touch of the feeling that anything is better not to be because there is pleasure in it. All source of that must be abolished utterly.

For the kingdom of heaven is the kingdom of Nature. The law is: Be Nature, that is, *grow*. Is it not rather strange that though we know how we give law to children, which we know they have to "grow" into truly obeying, and that all their failures and even false attempts are real obedience and the very right things, yet that it has not occurred to us to think whether God's command to man might not be one of the same kind, that is, not Do this, but *Learn to do this?* Two errors, which are really one, have prevented us; one that we did not see that God's true command was one which might be thus prepared for, was one which meant doing *automatically* (though its very words mean this), and therefore was one which was obeyed in failing, which supposed preparation; and the other was that we were not thinking of the law as being for *man* to grow into. We were thinking of the individuals only; from which point we can truly see nothing.

The instant reaction of Christ's mind, when the question was raised about marriage in that world of which He had spoken, the world where service was the law and pleasure therefore was free ("Nature and her rightness"), the instant reaction of His mind when it was asked: "How about pleasure in those days?" was, "Anyhow" (even as the artist paints), as it is in Nature. Now this is the very same with Paul's "raised in glory." It is one thought. In that life with what impulses do people come; how about pleasure? "With the very impulse they had put away with shame," says Paul. And Christ before him: they ask no questions about marriage.

So man's experience is a revelation—by a minus—of what is in Nature. He learns so what Nature is; gains experience of her, is made capable of being one with her, for what is in her has also *become* in him. And here again appears an identity of "heaven" in Christ's words with Nature; these things have to be in man as they are in Nature. Is not this one with: "Thy will be done on earth as it is in"—Nature? (Again: man's life is a revelation of Nature by a minus: but that is what art is. Has man's life the same meaning as an artwork?)

How beautiful is the use of a superstition, or feeling that a thing may *never* be done; ignoring the question of its use. The problem is to have the regard on others, instead of on self. If the regard is on self, it is wholly unsuspected that it is evil; nay, it is felt that it is quite right, only certain restraints must be observed. (It is exactly trying to make up a right by two wrongs.) Now, to cure it, see what is done in superstition: a thing is taken which when done for self becomes evidently and obviously bad. So, the self being still first and being taken for granted, the feeling arises that that thing must never be done. There is the superstition: it is the feeling of right with self assumed first. The *thing* must never be; even though human good be sacrificed for it. It remains only by urgency of human need to break through this law (mere forgetting is enough) and the work is done. Then the regard is transferred from self to others; the thing is done when good demands, refused when good refuses. The law, which was impotent because against service, is mighty because expressing it. And the problem is accomplished; the regard which was on self is now on good, and superstition is the means.

Now with this thought can we read back a little into history? Were all laws—those which with us are laws of action, such as killing—once laws of things? Were they not first *all* the subjects of superstition? So does the Decalogue, for instance, reveal to us the existence of a time when the law: "Thou shalt not kill," was a dead law, as ours now of marriage? So has all the advance of man been through the change of laws of things into laws of action, by aid of superstition?

Do not the strange superstitious usages everywhere, especially in the earlier civilised East, indicate this, the even universal tendency, to make laws of things? And so, by the by, if Europe is more "advanced" it may be to some extent because it was later; and so escaped in part this necessity for a superstition for every right; that having been borne for it "vicariously" before.

Then do we see in the universal prevalence of laws of things the reason for the true laws having been so often of no effect? Was not that the result of the false laws? When we look back we see such lawlessness, such violence, murder, robbery; we are astonished; but did not that come, even as our lawlessness in respect to chastity comes, through false laws of things, confounding service and disservice in one common condemnation? Should we not truly see the former lawlessness in our own? Other laws were to them made void as the law of chastity is to us. So we are not different from them; only we have escaped from *their* superstitions. Laws, that were impotent to them, are no more made impotent to us by a false right ignoring service, but when that false right still exists we are even as they.

Did not Christ, at the confluence of the Hebrew and the Greek spirits, naturally speak of Nature as the Holy Spirit? And if so, may we thus understand the blasphemy against the Holy Ghost? The man who refuses Nature and her guidance says of that which service bids that it is still evil, vile, wrong. How can he be led aright?

Mahomet seems to have been intensely a theological man: his thought was of God, and everywhere he made that a turning-point of the true faith. Is this a chief difference between him and Christ? Christ was emphatically not theological; His new law simply omitted all reference to God. And so does Mahometanism come as the bringing in again of theology?

May we not see clearly the basis of Christ's relations to marriage in His demand for a true rightness, a true purity? Our wrong is that we consent to *some* impurity; to an impurity that forbids good. We consent to this: man need not be so pure that service may wholly rule. He may have and keep so much lust that

that would be impure. That puts all wrong, all into mere confusion; turn good itself to evil. But Christ did not consent to this; the key to all His sayings here is given in His express forbidding of it. His law was on the desire: man must not "lust," *must not desire against service*. (Is not that the true meaning of lust—desire against service? Could it be more perfectly defined?) So all was simple: He forbade that which alone could make right mean anything else than whatever was for good. So, when a problem respecting the form of marriage came, He put it aside as a thing that could have no meaning in man's *life;* it would be what was for good; there was nothing more to say. And when the woman was brought to Him, was not His action essentially the same? These things need no special law; with *life* they will be right. "Have traditions made God's law of no effect with you? Feel it more truly for the future. I do not condemn you, but *sin* no more." Then when He spoke of divorce, was He not speaking against the habit of refusing the obligations that union with a woman brought in Nature?

The point is to desire a thing if it is good, not to desire it if it is against good. The difference is between a rule over the desire and over the deed. What we seem to take as of course is a desire always for the same thing (the pleasant thing) and a control over the deed, an abstinence from it. This we are familiar with, think of as goodness, rightness, &c. The desire for the pleasant thing is always supposed, whether it be for good or not. Thus the abstinence is sure to become quite irrespective of good. It is the *rule* of pleasure which comes inevitably with the concession that the *desire* need not follow good. One comes to the very heart of the question here: may or may not the desire be exempted from the law?

Surely one would think it was easier to do a thing when it was for good and not to do it when it was for evil, than always not to do it; easier to desire it when for good, and not desire it when for evil than never to do it whether for good or not. No law can be easier than the law of service except one claiming *license* for the desire.

But at least may it not be said that under certain circumstances we do obtain results by abstinence which we cannot by any other means—where a law of use according to service would be unavailing? May it be that man "in this world" is in such a condition as that to which an individual reduces himself by drunkenness? The true law is beyond his power; and he must have one that ignores service, and is based upon his defect. But then let those who think so give up Christ and His prayer. Every day that I live I grow more thankful to Christ for the things He said and did. It is upon *our* problems those passionate lips pronounced their verdict, which the world—no, not even those who most claim Him as their authority—cannot set aside.

Also how easy it would be, how simple, to make the *demand* upon the desire, to bring the law on it. Simply have no other law; have that the right, the only right; let there be no other, and man is compelled to attend to his desires, and make his rightness be in them. But the outside laws apart from service prevent this; they forbid the desires being upon service. And so they make it seem natural, and a thing of course, that the desires will be on that which is our own pleasure, and that right must be in restraining them. But how simple it would be to have a right that must make the question be of the desires. And why should it be harder? Is it hard to desire good? Do we not often say: "It is easy to desire; the *doing* is the hard thing." And we let the desires go unregulated, and insist upon a doing which not only is restraint on our desires, but is less good for others.

By this means there would at least be brought to bear upon the desires all the power that is now exerted on the deeds (all the moral and other feelings); and do we really need anything more? But besides this there would be at once added all the power of "good" or service that is now excluded. And it would be all in one direction; not interrupted or made to contradict itself; it might be constantly felt and regarded and rested on, as it cannot be while there are rights that, on any ground, contradict traceable service. The whole power of that is lost, for to give it sway would be to be led wrong sometimes.

Is not the false thought of the Jewish life summed up in those words: "Fear God and keep His commandments?" This Christ put aside. Nor did He say that the true service of God is in the perfect love and service of man. He adopted the other course, letting God be as if out of sight; He said—not, Serve God by serving man; Serve man for God's sake, &c., as is said now—but simply: "Love one another;" *think* of men and their needs.

And when men say: But we must love God first in order that we may love men; we cannot love them enough if we do not; they are not lovely enough: that is a distinct refusal of Christ's command. Christ's command is: *Love one another;* no easier thing, but that. No loving some other Being in order that we may do by men *as if* we loved them without really loving them.

How we tend to go back to that law—that "whole duty" which is not man's duty, and proved itself not by its failure. And we reap the fruits; for this thought is one with not seeing that claims are *always* to be obeyed; it is one with having our right in things—the things we fancy at any time that God commands. Thinking thus, we necessarily make our right in fixed things, and the not-regard to claims is sure to come upon us. We have bound ourselves under subjection to self. In truth, this thought of "God and His commandments" is only another form of that not-regard to claims which is regard to self.

Is it the fact that the needed becoming "better" is done at certain stages or periods in man's life—answering to the process of the working out of a correction of the premiss—and that then when this, the hard part, is done, there comes a time when what is wanted is not more becoming "better," but the truer use of what has been gained, a different way of thinking or beginning, in a word, *knowledge?* The time when Christ came was one of these, and so it was that He insisted so much upon *knowing*. And these times are necessarily marked by license and relaxation of bonds; seeming failure of the power of good; a loss of what had been the former good.

Here we see perhaps one reason man has thought of the claims of God instead of his fellow-creatures, namely, that so his rights could remain fixed. "God's claims"—as so imagined by man—do not change; so his rights can be in things. Truly seen, indeed, should we not see that not God's claims but the idea of a fixed right was the cause here? Man finding himself with such a dead right—necessarily ceasing to have a true reason because Nature changes and her claims—*projects* these claims of God; they are a projected reason. Then also we can see that God's claims rather than his fellows— that is, God's claims as a self instead of in others— would have fixed themselves on man's thought of duty, while his eye was on himself; because he would make them demands for putting away pleasure (as our fathers thought), or at least for taking only quite refined and elevated ones (as we think); in a word, God's claims as thus thought of (as desired and imagined by us instead of as revealed in His works) would be sure to be things man could with self first still feel right and good. Regarding God's claims in man would demand things which with self first were brutal and impossible. We can see, evidently, why man has put imagined claims of God in place of true claims.

This thought of God's claims—imagined instead of revealed—is the child man's contrivance for nailing down his compass so that north may always point the same way. Can he have a *varying* compass?

Nature—in human wants—is God's revelation. We, not dreaming that *they* could be rightly taken as our guide (since if they were would not "right" be constantly changing?) have of course had to suppose other revelations to guide us. For assuredly we need a guide. And now in this thought is there not a light upon words of Christ's? Is it not plain that He looked forward to a guidance by a "spirit," not by a book? What sign is there at all that He contemplated in the least any such revelation or inspired guide as we have thought we have in the New Testament? He referred to a wholly different kind of guidance. And so again does it become clear why He said it was expedient He should go away? Conscious as He must have been that He was making all things new to men, did He not feel that it was essential He should die and leave them in order for their own minds to operate spontaneously? Their souls and thoughts also were to come into relation with Nature—the Holy Spirit was to come to them—and it could not be until the overmastering weight of His thought and feeling was removed from them. He had stood to them as Nature herself, and His words had been spirit and life to them, but it was to Nature they were to go.

This is true of every great teacher; indeed, every teacher says so: I must leave you; you must go yourself to Nature.

So in this way, in his *needs*, man is part of Nature; in this perhaps most of all; in these the Holy Ghost speaks to men. Here, above all, *to us*, is Nature; to us, the Holy Ghost.

Have not the "temptations" of Christ a visible meaning? "Worship me"—how plain it is, as Christ became conscious of His power, and His desires grew definite: "You see, how, if you insist on the perfect right, the right from the beginning, you will fail, will have before you simply more exclusion and loss of all power to do anything; but if you will say nothing of that, but let the central evil remain for the present, doing what you can to remedy the immediate evils, and trusting to the general advance of human nature to bring a better state in due course of time, what is there that you will not be able to do? See your power: you have a new vision of the world, a persuasion none can resist; all the kingdoms of the earth are yours, and their glory has grown but for you to reap; you have within you Jew and Greek and Roman; you unite them all in your thought; in the fire of your passions they have melted into one. You can do infinite good; only do not touch the central wrong, and what mischief is there you will not remove? But touch it and a black veil falls before you; there is nothing after." The echo of that temptation was: "I saw Satan fall as lightning from heaven."

Then the other two temptations also have a meaning. If Christ brought man away from the imagined will of God to His revealed will in Nature, or in needs, then the temptation to cast Himself down exactly expresses this; it was: "Go not according to steps of fact, of *traceable* order and need; do not look at *Nature* for what God wills you to do; but apart from that, be thinking of what God wills in untraceable ways; trust to them and follow them; look away from the visible to the invisible; serve God, not man. Never mind that it is against the visible order and demands. Has not God angels? And are there not written commands? Is not this the very spirit of Scripture: Serve men *through* God?" And do we not see the refusal to throw Himself down when He healed the man on the Sabbath day? He would not trust to God's untraceable purposes of good; He would use the visible ones. To refuse traceable service, because "God can overrule," &c., is to throw oneself down because God has angels.

And so we come to the question of the rule of traceable service, with its one emphatic demand now. And is it any wonder; must not everything rest on that? It is felt that it does. If the law of service is to rule there our whole life must make itself anew; it has this power.

Is it any wonder therefore that round it all turns? What a gladness it is that the proof so multiplies; the demonstration becomes so clear that it may be used.

Then has not the temptation to make stones bread a similar meaning? Was it: Put away ordinary things; attend to spiritual ones; never mind earning your living? And the reply: That is not truly following spiritual things; we must follow God's *revealed*, not His imagined, will; it is expressed in facts. Every word that proceeds out of the mouth of God—*every fact of Nature*—these *are* the very spiritual life for which they would be forsaken. Both show Him clinging to the facts of Nature; the traceable demands. They are the expression of Christ's bringing man to Nature, His "sending" to them the Holy Spirit. He would do in Nature's way. He could "send" the Holy Spirit to others, for it "came" first to Him.

Christ refused to look away from Nature—the traceable—to trust to and follow the invisible; yet is not science, every knowledge of Nature, looking at and following the invisible? It is true, but it is with the conditions fulfilled; it is not looking *away* from the traceable. So is not science the condition for that looking to the invisible to which man is so prone? And so, too, when Christ said, "Greater works than these shall ye do," did He not refer to science; that men should come to know her, and avail themselves of her power even more than He, when they had learned not to look away from her?

Is it not the union of opposites? Looking at the invisible and not at the visible, one of them; at the visible and not at the invisible, the other. Science is the union, up to a certain stage; but then again comes the same opposition, and the same demands. (It is the union of sense and intellect.)

Thus too, through yielding to the traceable, shall not men fulfil the conditions of also knowing, and following, and trusting to the invisible in the moral life? Is not the law of traceable service like the coming of science, bringing in to do their part those low and despised things that man has thought he has been most like God in being blind to?

The intellectual used to despise those whom the senses held; but knowledge has had to take them wholly in; to find them even its foremost workers. So how the moral have despised those whom the senses have had power over; yet shall life find them chief among her instruments.

Christ refused to break the order of Nature, and turn stones to bread; because He was hungry was no reason. But then suppose He had refused when hungry men were around him? And did He not eat Himself when He multiplied the loaves? (Who put all this meaning into these little narratives? Was it known to them?)

How plain is "You strain at a gnat and swallow a camel." Here it is: throwing bad shares upon the market, and setting laws on thieves. And so devouring widows' houses, of course: twenty widows may be ruined so at once. Is the difference between Christ's day and ours, that then the devouring was done openly, and we have "advanced" to insisting on not seeing what we do? We will be able to shut our eyes, or so to close them that all the things *we* do shall be all right, and we won't look beyond. We will not be thieves any more; only buyers of what is brought to us. And this is

F

wonderful; though it is worse, and more cruel, yet also it is a real advance; even in that a step is truly gained, for now we are compelled to see.

Christ *has done* His work; He has put the regard into man's heart; put it fully. The work is only hidden; not less done. Touch the world and see; call it to show itself; bid the grub reveal what is within it.

We do not *use* the goodness there is in men; do not arrange our life on a plan that is proportioned to it. We act on plans which imply, I suppose, much more of not-regard than exists; on plans which perhaps might have been necessary, have been true to the not-regard which existed when they were introduced, but are certainly not truly related with it now; which imply man to be worse than he is. So was not this one thing Christ did for men? He gave the pent-up goodness—the regard that had found life planned *against* it—freedom. The affirmation that charmed and delivered man, was: You *can* serve God as a spirit and in truth; make it your law and try; you do not need any more those outside restraints. Man's regard had been growing beneath those outside rules and forms which expressed its absence; and Christ said: Let it come forth and rule; act now, O man, according to your nature. To the long-crawling child He said: Arise and stand upon your feet.

And the parallel shows us how much *easier*, when the time is come, the life true from the bottom is. It seems much easier for the crawling child to crawl (it *was* the only thing possible); but when it wants to do anything how much harder it is; it cannot use its hands without such trouble. Is it not so with us? It seems so much easier to let self-interest be first altogether; but then what trouble to *do* anything. And is not man's last consenting to have self-interest first, the very same as the child who has instinctively tried to run, coming to perceive that *he* must crawl? "I thought I was a walker," it might say, "like those other beings, but I perceive I am not. There may be, must be, surely, another state for me, when I also shall be able to walk, but not in this state." Then there comes a doubt about that "other state;" it is not altogether so clear; but this very doubt means that he is to be a walker *here;* in spite of experience, in spite of difficulties, difficulties that have even made him give up.

And does this new liberty to goodness—the life planned upon the true nature—always come by regarding fresh claims before excluded and made possible to come, indeed, only by these? As if it were said: Your goodness seemed to demand these claims to be put aside, because your not-regard demanded restraints, but it need not be so; it is not true any more; you can regard them, and you must. So it is plain how with the growing regard we add more and more outside things, leaving the plan unadjusted.

"Not having my own righteousness, which is by abstaining, but God's own righteousness, which is by the *passion* Christ has given me." Is not the true thought for "faith" the very thought of Prometheus's *fire;* that is, light and warmth, knowledge and emotion? That is, the passion that comes with and by a seeing. And with this how well agrees the explanation of faith; the evidence —the coming into appreciation or regard—of things that were absent from it.

We must learn to see Christ's *intellect* better. When

He said He would "send us" Nature, was there not the consciousness in Him that He knew her intellectually as well as morally, and that He had really given man's thought the key of knowledge as well as his heart the key of life? When we look into His sayings do we not see that there is all science in them, the conservation of force complete? It is expressed on the moral side, but the physical and the moral are one fact; and as when we see it physically we feel it at once to be the moral also, so must it not have been with Him? Perceiving it with such clear eyes in the moral, must He not have felt it in the physical too? In bringing men from fancying about the moral will of God to His revealed will in Nature, He had also, virtually and truly, brought them to the true means and mode of knowing.

So is this too a key to: "Greater works shall ye do?" Does it refer really to the works of science? The Holy Spirit would "come" and make them possible. And then this may be the real significance of His miracles: that by His true feeling of Nature He could do things no one else could, even physically; but that He looked forward with some true vision to our science, and felt that men, by knowing Nature better still, would do much more.

The law coming on the heart must fall off the hands. This is what men wish to avoid; they say: Let it be on the heart, but let the *things* still be done. But it cannot be; for that means others' hurt, and that *is* the law not being on the heart.

If the Holy Ghost in Christ's mouth meant Nature, the unpardonable sin is clear. "It does not matter how you regard me or what you say of me; I shall not mind;

you will be forgiven. But if you contradict Nature, and will not be guided by her, how can good come to you? There is never any forgiveness for that. Who can forgive you? Can you get to a mountain's top by walking down it?"

Is there the least sign of any thought in Christ's heart that His followers would ever be paying special regard to a book? Expressly He looked forward to, and bid us look to, another guide altogether—the Holy Spirit. Being guided by that, then, we are obeying Him. And so looking simply at His words and actions we can see what mode of action in us would best fulfil His desire. Assuredly, first and chief of all, that we should take the Holy Spirit and not any writings as our guide. And see how emphatically He said it: All blasphemy against the Son of man, even refusing *me*—not only a book about me—shall not matter. But keep close to the Holy Spirit.

What a sight of *sin*, of scorned and broken *law*, the world presents! But it transforms itself when we see. It is not of broken law, of disobedience,—that is the appearance merely,—it is man imposing false laws on himself. (And has he not all along done the thing that was the true right, the thing that served?) What a different sight it is! Of course there has been the appearance of disobedience, the phenomenon of sin. The disobedience was that he was obliged to make these laws.

Genius always is not wasting. By this it has its new power and does things without means; using power that has been wasted. Now, by the light of this, look at the loaves and fishes. Genius does its miracles by not wasting; that is, by ceasing a waste. Christ was conscious of this; He felt that He did. May there be here the very secret of that story? May it really express, not a thing He did, but a thing He *said*, with that consciousness of His power to do by not wasting? So should we read the end first and hear Christ say: "Gather up all the power God gives you; let nothing be lost, and a few loaves and fishes shall feed five thousand men." Are those "miracles" the expression of Christ's consciousness of the power of doing without doing?

The central nucleus of truth in our thoughts respecting revelation is contained in our thought respecting the Old Testament as an imperfect and adjusted revelation, truly from God, yet partial and needing to be carried farther. This thought needs to be applied to the New Testament on the one hand, and to the sacred books and beliefs of other nations on the other hand. It is *a* true thought of revelation (as the most sincere Christians avow); it is the only one which will apply universally. It is not *a* true thought, but *the* true one. And what difficulty and discord cease when it is made universal. What liberty it gives us to embrace what we have excluded. And did not Christ expressly claim this thought, promising a Holy Spirit to guide into all truth?

Seeing how distinctly it is by that which is accounted "badness," is despised and trodden upon, that the true work of the world is done, the true law written, may we not see the fact in Christ's coming from Nazareth? Do we not see a spiritual fact here again reduced to a fleshly level? And this is a thing we must always be prepared for; to see in the fleshly statements the spiritual facts that have been sunk into them. Is this a chief key to "miracles?"

Christ's references to Himself strike us as if they must have meant in His mouth that He was to be regarded in some special light, and intended to claim some special—even superhuman—relation to mankind. But was it truly that in His simplicity He spoke simply as He felt, said what He perceived was true, it not being anything to Him whether it were of Himself or not? And so we, with our self-regarding reticence, misapprehend Him, and think that He must have meant to claim some super-human place and to fix mankind about Himself. Whereas He said plainly that He wished to lead them to the Holy Spirit to be guided.

When Christ said: "Seek ye first the kingdom of God . . . " was He simply seeing the fruits that would come of a perfect regard, not meaning the persons to whom He spoke (knowing they would lose all), but of the future? "When the true right is sought—God's right, the nature-law—then there will be no more *any* want;"—a fact simple enough, and that needs no prophet-eye to see it now, even if it did then.

It may be that that which really constitutes a *religion* is a new intellectual vision, that is, a truer apprehension of man's life and of the world. And is it *thus* truly a "binding," that is, bringing into one of the bad and the good? That is, a religion is ever a cutting out of self-righteousness; for that is the union of the good and bad, and only that. And it comes only by the being compelled to abandon a restriction.

Had not Christ the consciousness of relation to other Beings? And is it not one that becomes obscured and as if lost sometimes? And so this may be the meaning of the words, " Eloi, Eloi, . . ." not that God had seemed to have forsaken Him, but that Friend, that Lover, that Being who guided Him seemed to be no more present. This surely befalls sometimes all who have that consciousness. See the word used, " Elohim," the beings who are Nature. " O Nature, O Guide, why cannot I hear your voice ! "

Assuredly the work of genius is done with a feeling of wrong, that is, the *laying down the life*. And here is there not an instance of Christ's disciples giving a physical meaning to a spiritual fact ?

Here is the good thing : the law-breaking blood is really stronger than the law-keeping, however much it may seem the contrary at any time. For all that is genius belongs to it, and Christ above all. And thus do we not see how Christianity has come to mean so different a thing. It has fallen into the hands of the law-keepers. What we see is the law-keepers trying to represent a law-breaker. This accounts for the contrast, and surely for the inventions too.

When Asia and Europe join hands again will not that be life renewed ? What made Christianity such a source of life was its union of Asia and Europe. Not that Christ was more or better than Buddha, but that through Him Europe and Asia were joined in one.

And is not one chief good and necessity of the Asian life this very hold to the free joy of man in woman ? Is this a chief thing she will give back to Europe—with the conditions fulfilled ? Is not Asia's power and gift this passion of unrestrained joy compelling us, who cannot have it without its conditions, to fulfil them ; they learning also how not to have to give it up? And even in its falsity, even in its utmost corruption as now, still does not that free joy keep life heroic there?

When we see how intensely ascetic the Buddhist religion is, does it not become visible that Christ really stood against it, that is, as adding to it? His was—perhaps consciously—a reform of what was, essentially, Buddhism. So the New Testament is so emphatic against self-righteousness; and He was called licentious.

Love and Faith—we treat them both the same: they must mean loving and believing in no one else but one. That is *the* demand we make: the quality of the faith and the love may almost pass unquestioned if only we will be quite sure that for any one else to come in would be to spoil it altogether.

We need never wonder at any sinking down of spiritual things into physical; we have it in its utmost form in the thought of the resurrection of the dead—even apart from the idea of the body rising. The resurrection of the dead is the making man alive; his acting for self no more. What is the thing to be hoped for above all others, the one hope worth our having, worth God's giving, what but man's life, his deliverance, his being brought to have self no more at all the ruler, what but the "resurrection of the dead and the life eternal"? So Paul said: "For the *hope* of the resurrection of the dead I am called in question." All his life was folly if man could not be trusted to become able to act not for self. This was his faith, his vision rather of the things not seen, and that seem scarcely visible even yet (nay, more obscured than ever) though Christ had revealed them. His grasp was on the fact that the appearance of man is not the truth, and that to know him we must go deeper than the surface.

Poor Man, how hard it seems! As if he could not get right any way; neither by refusing pleasure, nor by accepting it, nor by adopting any law. How earnestly he has striven, and how cruelly he has been baffled, as if wantonly, pitilessly! But how could it be otherwise? All the while he has been trying to keep a not-regard within him; he has been trying, *with this within*, to become true to Nature. How is it possible? Keeping a not-regard, an untruth, a dissonance, a non-conformity, how could his life go on aright, how possibly be one with Nature? So he comes to think of course—being by his firmly held not-regard out of harmony with Nature—that he wants "another world" to be good or happy in. Of course he feels so while he refuses to be according to this. But how could he be right to any world if he keeps a not-regard within him? It would make him as false to any other as to this; it *is* falsity and nothing else. And with it no goodness and no aspiration are of any avail; they are not to the point. What is wanted is, not goodness—not first at least—but conformity to the fact; without which all goodness is turned wrong.

And then with this not-regard yet in him how false becomes his religion too! He looks to "God," and tries by a regard to Him and thoughts of Him, &c. to make up for the not-regard within; to put a regard to God as a substitute for the regard to facts around. It is inevitably vain; how can it do as a substitute? The very regard to God built on that not-regard becomes a falsity. So is there not a light on what is wanting in our religion? It is put wrongly; made a *substitute* for another regard.

And thus how perfect was Christ's new law: "Love one another"—have no not-regard; all else will follow. With the foundation rightly laid the builder's work is secure. But think of building regard to God on a basis of want of regard for man! How could it but run into every form of monstrous error and cruelty?

Is not Asia worse than Europe—in so far as it is worse—because Asia holds to a tenser, more passion-restraining goodness; therefore failing more and running into more unrestrained excesses? So do we see that Christ relaxed for Europe this tenser, harder effort? He brought in more regard for man, less tense effort on putting away pleasure: which are one. That is, it is not a relaxing, but the casting out of a not-regard. Perfect regard is the true Nirvana, and so had not that also its negative image? And so was it suppressed, and self-desire accepted? Christ united Europe's regard to the phenomenal with Asia's restraint.

As the New Testament is so clearly related to Buddhism, so is not the Old with its ceremonies and sacrifices to Brahmanism? Are the two books, indeed, simply the form in which that great universal crisis has come to us? A chief thing Buddha did was to abolish caste, and Christ's work also was abolishing caste. And it was regard to men's condition which moved both Sakya Muni and Christ, and moved them both in the same way to put aside the outside laws and insist on the desire.

Think of the greed of our beautiful life. Can one not see Christ in His story of Lazarus? *Because* he had his good things here the rich man shall be tormented, and Lazarus, because so poor and wretched, shall be comforted. Does not the whole man stand before us with His quivering passions ? "*Because* you rich people cannot see—look out." Even the very limits of His thought bind Him to us. We love Him the more that His soul could not endure the contrast; could not even wait to trace the reasons, to weigh the excuses. And do we not see Him in that passionate story, see Him in His limitations ? Was He as profound and wise a thinker as Sakya Muni ? For one thing, did He not die too soon ? But He had felt the make of Nature, and saw that man would come to know her. He had said (it was all): "He that will save his life must lose it." And did He therefore feel it was better He should go away, that He should stand less between his friends' eyes and Nature, should bind them less ?

"Can we not have this good [killing the sick] without waiting for Utopia or the millennium ?" No, surely. Here is the meaning of " Seek first the kingdom of heaven . . ." That is Christ's reply to this question. The key to the passage is that it refers not to the individual, but to man, of whom Christ was constantly thinking. Let man gain the true law, the " right " of the kingdom of heaven, and all those good things he vainly aims at and longs for will come. Christ was thinking constantly of man ; as every one must who feels the real problem, and sees how it depends on having the right aim and law, and how, till *man* accepts the true aim, he must make false laws, which set good absolutely at defiance.

For this is one key to the mystery of life : we take a wrong point of view ; that of the individual instead of man. The reference and meaning of experience is not to the man as we term him, but to man truly so called. (May it even be that this is the truth of the feeling that man, " in the body," is in an essentially evil and imperfect state ? The individual alone is in the flesh. *Man* is not in the flesh.)

The creation of the life of Man *is* in this individual experience, in all this individual failure and ruin ; to understand these we must see them as the expressions of that fact. And does not this involve that we shall have a "consciousness" that shall be of Man ? Our deliverance, our salvation, our fruition, that shall compensate for all, shall be in feeling truly to the fact. This would give the very thing that is meant in the thought of heaven. How can we think any external change is necessary when a change to a truer consciousness would give it ?

In reference to killing the sick, it is argued that it must not be, because of what life and death are; that is, because of *our thoughts* of life and death. But there is another issue to this; the other end—the assumption— may move. If killing the sick be a duty, then may not that change our thoughts of the meaning of death ? We may have to find a thought of death which will suit the rightness of killing the hopelessly sick; this new perception of right may call on us to alter our theory here. So we see two things in respect to thought : one, how *moral* changes influence it. (Might it not be truly said, indeed, that the intellectual life of man was an offshoot and result of his moral life, moral perceptions always giving the impulse to truer intellectual ones ?) And the other fact in respect to thought is : how always we must remember that the movement may be at either end (as it were) of the force; it is as if we had a "pole" of force or "line of action." An assumption at one end, results at the other; the assumption may change as well as the results be maintained or modified. We need to keep this enormously more in view. And surely the laws of the process, the conditions under which the assumption must move, may be more deeply expressed, some general answer given to that question like a general solution in algebra.

How far it is from putting Christ aside to see all things as the bringing of man's life. That is what He thought of, lived for, revealed, and made man's possession. To see it in all things, therefore, what is it but to lay them at His feet, to read them by the light that He has given? What but to see even in Him a new glory, a true revelation of His divineness? For that exclusiveness, whereby we have sought to do Him honour and hedge about a divinity too weak and poor to be otherwise sustained, refuses any more to be bound about Him. He has broken the bonds of that sepulchre, cast off those swathing graveclothes; that death also cannot hold Him. Why any more seek we the living among the dead? Behold, He is risen into His true glory. Because the true *universal* Godhead stands visibly revealed in Him, He is no more ashamed to call all men His brethren.

Has not every great religious teacher (from Confucius downwards) *put aside the service of God?* That was what Christ did. And it is necessarily so, for whenever a cruel and foolish superstition comes into man's heart he instantly connects it with God, and says He commands it. All religious teachers of men have come into a world where they found people saying: I love and reverence this Person so much that I shall hurt my fellow-creatures for His sake. And this has determined their action, has *made* their vision. The secret of their lives is given by it. They have *known* that God did not will that. And so they have spoken in His name and " with authority," an authority needing no external source, because conferred in the very act of hearing by the hearts of the listeners. What they have done has been to give to man a different service of God—a new heart-service—by putting away a service of hurt, that is, a service in things. The truer service necessarily comes with that. Without that injury to their fellows, proving it could not be the true law, they would not have been delivered, but have gone on thinking that law the true one. Every putting aside a law of things is bringing the law anew upon the heart. And that is done through the injury it inflicts, making men know that God cannot have commanded it. So this evil wrought for God's sake upon their fellows has wrought their deliverance and been needful for it.

And thus we see a light in part on that terrible mystery, why *so much* pain is inflicted by men upon each other. These cruelties have been the means—they are the only means—by which man can learn that the obedience God demands from him is an obedience of the heart. These cruelties alone compel him to leave off serving Him with mere fixed outside deeds which kill. The latter would enslave him for ever if it were not cruel. Its cruelty has made—has inspired—all the men who have delivered him.

Now, how far have all the great religious teachers put aside service to God because cruel? It is clear in Abraham, but was it so of Moses and of Mahomet? These are surely instances; they spent their strength in putting aside idolatries which were doubtless cruel.

So we see how the power was prepared and stored up. The only way in which God's law has been, or could have been, brought upon the heart and made a heart-service, has been by its falling off from things. For man's service to God does come first in the form of things, as we see in the question, "Why does not man restrain his passions?" That means, "Why does not man serve God in pleasure-restraining things?" So it is only in transferring the service from things that the true heart-service comes. And in order that this transference may be made it is necessary that these things (the pleasure-restraining things in which man first seeks to serve God, putting absence of his pleasure to do duty for another's good) should be cruel. This is the power by which, the things being for that reason put away, the service of God comes on the heart and rules the act; and so the whole life is altered, and serving God is no more things added on to it, but the *act* that constitutes it altogether. And this injury to others, which is thus necessary for the deliverance to be wrought, is of course necessary also in Nature, as it visibly is. By the perpetual change rigid things must be cruel, must destroy. And so also it was necessary that man's sense of right should lead him to cruelty also, that the false rights offered to God should be avenged with torture. This was also a needed force, and it also was inevitable. When man had made a false worship of hurtful, pleasure-restraining things, he was sure to make torture his means of enforcing it; so giving the other element of cruelty which should break the yoke.

Thus the true religious teachers and deliverers have been simply those to whom it was an axiom that God could not be truly served in that which hurt His creatures. That was enough. They did not need to be great, not even probably to have any very special gifts; only they needed it to be absolutely clear that putting our not-pleasure instead of another's good was mocking instead of serving God. Any one who sees that can deliver man, can deliver him from himself, can say to him, and in a voice that carries with it its own fulfilment, "Put your fellow where yourself has been." That is—it is nothing less—he can raise the dead. But only because the life has already been working in them, and is ready to be revealed.

Now how does this perception come? What will enable a man to see that it is true, not only of other nations' cruel laws of things wherein they sacrifice men to their fancy of God's will, but of his own nation's and the things he himself has thought most sacred? If we could only tell *what* it was that enabled a man to see that his own accustomed and accepted and revered laws, that had meant purity, reverence, piety to him, because they meant evil to others were not and could not be commands of God, nor any welcome service—if we could see that, perchance we too might gain deliverance. A true heart-service might flow in as *our* cruel laws of things also vanish for evermore.

What is wanted to make it an axiom that a thing that hurts our fellow *cannot* be service to God? Is it anything but pity enough? Or is it that what is needed is not more pity, but rather simply a power of seeing one thing by another, so as to be truly led by Nature; to be able to see the truth of that which has most bound even ourselves through being able to see it in another thing? Is it the power of seeing that a thing is one way even while we *feel* it in another—the *emancipation* of the intellect? Evidently this would give the power of seeing that a thing was different from what we felt it.

What is wanted is to see that *the* cruel thing which we identify with religion and purity and always have identified, and still *feel* sacred, is the same as the cruel things which our forefathers identified with religion, and felt towards in the same way, and which we see quite easily to have been evil and false. Now this is given by seeing one

G

thing in another. And is it not visible that Christ had this power eminently? He was always talking in parables. What was it that above all showed Him that the true law was not a law of things, and so must be on the heart? Surely it was in Nature He saw it, the feeling of her self-less freedom. He saw God made the sun to rise on the evil and the good, and so He did not condemn the sinner.

Was it not the cruelty of idolatry that introduced monotheism? And so is not every purification and intensification of religion really due to the power of service, arising from a refusal to persist in supposed obedience to God which meant hurt to man, and was really only man's thought of himself? So Moses and Mahomet, the great insisters on God and His laws, would be included among those who put away the service of God, that is, the cruel service rendered to idols, and by putting away that service had a truer thought of God revealed to them. So we see in Christ putting away the toilsome ceremonies —(for were not those long journeys to Jerusalem, for instance, often disastrous? Had He perhaps known His mother suffer, and seen how hollow they had become?) —putting away the toilsome ceremonies and journeys, He could not but see that God was a Being who demanded spiritual worship. And so, putting away the hurtful "restraints of passion," how can we fail to see that God requires a life with self not first, and must be worshipped so? If He does not require a journey to a sacred city, He demands a heart-service, which can be rendered everywhere: if not these restraints, then a true ruling desire for good.

So contrary to Christ is loving God first, and men

through God, and for His sake. In fact, do we not love the persons whom we do love best, and Him through them? And do we not see this in Christ's urging that men should love *Him*—Him, a man, and other men for His sake? Is it not as if He had said, " Love them, for I too am a man; for my sake love them?" And how far is it from being true that to love man we must love God first; it is as a man we must learn to love God.

It is plain that if a certain order or law is made necessary by a condition of men, then if there came one in whom this condition is not, the necessity will not exist to him, and the order will change, the law will become new. Then here is a key to the change, the renewal, the deliverance that shall come. We may know the answer to the question, " Art Thou he that shall come?" Does the law alter in his person? For evidently, if there be a law which is necessitated by a condition of men, there is a possibility of deliverance in another way besides that of obedience, namely, by change of the law. And if that condition be the relation to self, then a different relation to self will give the different law. Here is the whole secret of genius.

Here there are two laws, resting on two different people; a law that rests on a condition that is present in the one, not present in the other. What shall ensue? Shall there remain permanently two different laws? This, too, has been tried. The traces of this idea are very visible in the social order, especially the older forms; in monarchs and castes with a different law from the rest of the people. And one may see that Christ most emphatically put that aside. Then if there are not to be two laws, which is to be the universal one—the one that is made necessary by a condition of men (an evil condition, or at least a less perfect one), or the law which comes when that condition is not present? One person must give up his law, and take another's; the question is which.

And it is assured beforehand; for the arising of the person on whom the new law comes is but the sign of the readiness to cease of the condition which has made the other law necessary. The law which does not imply that condition of men's is the law that becomes universal; one can see how it must. It puts nothing in the way of Nature; it is easier; it ceases to refuse to let good be.

In Christ's "new law" we see the service of God treated dynamically as in the fluxion; made a power, held in its effect. Do we ask where the service of God is? It is here, in having brought, and in maintaining, this perfect service of man. Here we have it in its effect, in a living form, as a spirit. We have it as the astronomers have the observed motions of the heavens; which it was their first duty to hold as dead burdens, but only that they might become living.

Poor Christendom, like all the rest of the world, has been trying all these years to persuade herself that she knows. May she not, at last, confess she does not, that she has been but like her fellows? Has not *her* genius-time come?

Can it be that the God of the Jews was Nature? Evidently they are constantly identified. "The Lord uttereth His voice"—in the thunder. See the law "written on stone:" that is, Nature's law; it *is* written on every stone. And it is *one* law, one God; this is the most essential thing. Was it not the very feeling of the oneness all through Nature that we have learnt again to see, the unity of force, the very keystone of science?— At least if it be not this is there not a most true parallel?

Why Christ put aside "loving God" is clear. And how much we need this too; for what do we do but make Him an excuse for keeping away from us Nature's demand for a right that should be in the way of doing and not in things? We use our fancy of His will against His visible law, His audible command. Every superstition which our acting for self makes us put upon ourselves we hang on Him, and profane His name to consecrate. It is inevitable we should. (Is not this a true meaning of superstition: thinking that things which may not be done for self may not be done at all?)

We have not been capable of receiving the privilege of loving Him, for we have made it an excuse for hurting our fellows, and keeping hold of that which makes mischief—rights. For, indeed, loving God is a privilege, and demands conditions to be fulfilled. It cannot safely be undertaken with rash hands. See here the ancient thought, Jewish and Pagan alike, of not suffering *any* to touch or approach divine things. Christ made them free to all: true, but by fulfilling the conditions of having the law upon the heart. With that, it is true: but has this condition been retained?

Loving God is a privilege, and demands a condition; with self first, and the false rights that that brings, it is a fatal danger, for it binds with all the authority of God's will upon men restrictions which their bondage to self— that is, their not-regard—alone imposes. So it was inevitable that Christ should put it aside; it is visible as a necessary thing. For, to a being working out a moral *reductio ad absurdum*, it is evidently a most dangerous thought; to a being subject to *false* rights, which therefore instantly stretch out their hands to cling on to God, and the more tenaciously the more false, and merely imposed by self, and therefore opposed to human good, they are. It is inevitable that a being with not-regard and false rights must abuse the thought of " God's will." And so long as not-regard remains in him, he must go on to abuse it to the utmost hurt, the utmost consecration as divine of evil things. So how simply Christ said: " Leave loving God for the present, and fulfil the condition of its being safely done ; put away all not-regard."

And so in this love to God, and trying to serve Him, do we not see a use also ? For by it the power has been given to the false rights to remain. And has it not been only as much as was needed ?

Here is a most palpable way in which we lose intensely by thinking of Christ as different from ourselves. When we say that He did not argue against false laws, but broke them, and so on, it is replied : But He had knowledge, and power to make laws. . . . And so we are deprived of the value of His example. Suppose, instead of curing the sick people, Christ had left us " Discourses on the right way of keeping the Sabbath."

A thought half appears respecting the idea of monotheism as parallel with that of one law. Thus, it is so probable that the chief insistance was not so much that God was one, as that this one God was to be recognised and served. The heathens recognised " one God " in an abstract way, but *their* gods—the gods to them " in this world," as they might have said—were the many special separate gods, each relating to its own thing, " gods of things," as it were, instead of the one God of the action, one in all things.  The one God was recognised even as we recognise the one law (of service) as if for a higher state, a different condition from ours; and the many "gods of things" were put as their gods, even as we put the many *laws* of things.  So that we might read: This one God, put so far off, this is the God for you; your only one; you may not have, nor seek to serve, the others; they are "idols" only; and the serving them, holding them as God, and as having authority, means hurt to men.  You must not obey them; it means cruelty.

A sort of insight may thus be gained into the intellectual life that was and had been then.  For in putting away as above and beyond them—as only for a higher state perchance—this one God, do we not see the clear traces of a sort of Positivism, a restraint, saying: That is above us, we cannot know; our business is with these things.  We know how that comes.  And there is a beauty in the subsequent course.  This deeper "one" was bidden to be taken as the God, and not the "things" that had usurped His place.  Most true and good; and yet see what Christ did.  He, as it were, retraced these very steps; putting aside that which was so great an achievement, and bringing back, only in a different form, the very kind of thing that had been put aside; coming "down" to the present physical things in the form of human wants.  This one God, who had come in to put aside the false idol-gods whose service meant cruelty to man, Him also Christ in His new law left out, and said: "Love man."  How perfect it is!  And yet again shall He not return to us?

Our thought of Christ's enormous superiority is not false, but it arises from those with whom we compare

Him. It is the glory of Asia that dazzles us in Him; it is true Europe has never given us His like, but He is one of a long series of Asian men. Buddha also sacrificed himself to deliver the world. That was an old Asian thought that lived again in Christ.

Is it not true that every man who has had power to found a religion or do anything like it, has always had a strong feeling of other beings around man; finite intelligences, but not merely human? This was the case even with Buddha.

It is easy to see how Christ must have foreseen His crucifixion; it could not have been doubtful in His view. Distinctly He refused the things the Jews thought right. He knew He made it impossible for them not to kill Him. It was even as now a person killing the hopelessly sick, and avowing it, would certainly be hung.

It is indeed really the same with women who give up their virtue for love. Society deals really with the same problem in that. So in what wonderful relations this stands!—And in truth how *all* law-breaking stands in a new light through this sharing of it by Christ.

That was "the glorious liberty wherewith Christ made free:" If you want to know God's will, look at your neighbours. The Sabbath was a little thing—a very foolish superstition as men thought of it; but it sufficed to show to the world that God's will was to be seen in your neighbour's wants.

How should one possibly say—and now too—that Christ knew all things? One must know all things oneself first. And why should He? He could not have told us. Was it not enough for Him to know as much as He could turn to good?

Is it not plain how simple and daily a thing the New Testament is speaking of? There had grown up the greatest system of self-virtue, a pursuing of " goodness " apart from others' good, and crushing it. Now, the putting away of that, the recognition that the claims of others are supreme over our self-virtue (the very coming of *art* into life), was enough to account for all the enthusiasm. It justified the expectation that the fruition—the " end " and object—of the world had come. It was justified,— nay, it was true. It needed only that the light should be perfectly and fully seen. Might we not almost say that if it had not been for the physical relation of man and woman everything had been done? But that had still to be brought within its sphere.

Is it not curious that Paul, who so puts aside self-virtue in respect to Jewish things, when he comes to speak of women goes wholly over to it, and gives no sign of recognising the other righteousness? Does it not show how this subject had still to be brought wholly within that domain?

Whether it is possible for " a man " to be " more than man," to be the incarnation and so the revelation of Being that is more than man, depends entirely on the relations man bears to other Being; on what the constitution of Nature is in this respect. Now clearly we do not know this; we are not able to say whether it is or is not. Why should we think it more impossible to be than not to be? If some man, then, evidently distinguished from others, and having power more than is usual, says that this is the case with him, is not his opinion by far the most likely to be true, the very best evidence we can have, and with no presumption whatever against it? Especially if there should have been a series of such men and they should have agreed in this representation, were it not most irrational not to hold it extremely probable?

Christ established a law of service against self-virtue. That was how Christianity made a new thing of human life; it was the overthrow of self-virtue. Now, even from His own recorded words, apart from all other reasons, it seems certain that Christ included in this overthrow of self-virtue and establishment of service as the law, the relations of man and woman. But His disciples (at least those who led the van) did not do this; their eyes were (as was natural from the conditions of men's thoughts then) on theological relations mainly, on questions of man's "direct" relation to God. And probably questions of service in respect to women had not come much into prominence then. And so in the relations of men and women the very central idea of their life and work was wanting. So we see that Paul, when the question arises, has not a word about love for man, but is as theological and self-virtuous as if he had never left off being a Pharisee. So has not the history of Christian life been inevitable? See what a history of wretchedness about woman. It was self-virtue and its fruits all through our fathers' lives and our own. If Paul had but said, thinking how his Lord had dealt with every claim of human good: "How can any man who is a member of Christ consent to be the instrument of a woman's hurt? How treat as a wife any woman whose injury it means, or how refuse any marriage which would mean her good?" If Paul had said this would not Christianity have had a different history? What evil did not his self-righteous thoughts here bring after them?

But we can see why this long course was needful. Such degradation and evil had to come that service should have power to compel man's regard from himself. And also the power of asceticism had to be developed too, the hand to be pressed firmly against all self-pleasure. And for this, too, the self-virtuous thought was needed.

The New Testament (where Christ truly is its centre) is a great pæan of Art. This is how not to have to obey that law that has been upon us. That law is fulfilled, its meaning revealed, its end accomplished. Behold the law is fulfilled, fulfilled and blotted out. And with that comes, of course, the perception (so glad a perception) that a wall of partition is broken down; that men are no more divided into two, but are one in God's sight; included all alike in sin that alike on all He may have mercy.

If we could but regain this perception, this gladness, that a wall of partition again was broken down, bad and good visibly one again, with one condemnation and one mercy! At least we should (if we had not all things) have regained the thought, the gladness of the New Testament; we should be again where it put men; and its fire too would be kindled in our bosoms. If we could regain that feeling, of a wall of partition broken down again, of those that thought they knew God and obeyed His law, and those who did not or would not, being one before Him, needing a common mercy, then we should know at least we were feeling as Christ had taught Paul to feel. What gladness that sight would be! And it must come with every correction of a premiss.

Here is our thought of having the best good we can get: to draw hard and fast the line between good and bad; to keep it clear, firm, and strenuously enforced. Here is the thought of Christ: to break down the wall; to see them one; to treat them with a common mercy. Here is the contrast. And it is simply that which must come if man begins with incompleteness in his starting-point. The one plan is carrying out rigidly the right upon the incomplete basis; the other simply the correcting it. All the characters of it are implied in that. It is saying simply: These elements we have tried to put aside are also included in God's world; it was the imperfection of our apprehension of it made us try to put them aside.

So again one sees that what man was commanded to do was not only not to divide things into good and bad, but not to divide *persons* also into good and bad. Finding the right that makes things no more good or bad is one with finding the right that divides persons no more into good and bad. When once our eyes are opened how plainly is the whole attitude of the New Testament one with the other corrections of the premiss in human life.

Could Christ's meaning in saying: "In me you see God" and the related words have been what we might mean by saying: "In me you see Nature?" Might we not, with a certain feeling of Nature's Being, put the name of Nature for God's name, and so perceive and feel more truly the real thought? For had not Christ a feeling of life—of conscious life—where we have it not? And we must discover that before we can truly feel the meaning of His words. And it must be *felt* in order to be truly known, not merely thought. Can we not well think of a man saying with distinct consciousness, "In me you see Nature;" he that has seen me—seen the passions, promptings, forces in me—has seen Nature? Nature is revealed in me; the forces which are in her are those which you see in me. See her through me, you do not see her otherwise." For it is so: some men do reveal Nature in their very being; in the even terrible strength and power and control, yet without effort, nay, with perfect yielding; one may see in them what is in Nature, passive and quiet as she looks.

Look at the whole tendency of the New Testament throughout. Here is Christ's very first description of the living man: "The wind. ... So is every one that is born of the wind. ... The Spirit shall guide you." And Paul's answer: "Be led by the wind." Can "born of the wind" mean self-regard put away and so impulse made free; made as genius, a little child? Might there have been a doctrine and mode of speaking that Christ had heard, of right being in having the impulses free, and this expressed by "being born of the wind?" So did He not quote it to Nicodemus as an expression he should have known? As a man of intellectual activity Christ must have joined Himself to some religious current among the Jews.

And again the condemnation of self-righteousness all through; and Paul's words: "Where is boasting then?" Boasting is excluded; no one can glory in a right that is simply not putting away pleasure. Being good is to mean nothing to be proud of. Then that Christ Himself turned to Gentiles, and even His followers left the rigidly righteous Jews and turned to the impulse-led Gentiles. And might that saying, "So is every one that is born of the wind," be taken as Christ's expression of His own law and choice of right, His avowal that He acted on His impulses, and that that was His law? And was not His life that?

Men say: "For that you must make men different

creatures." But that is the very thing that Paul found needed, and affirmed was to be. And Christ's first words were the same: "Be born of water that we may be the children of the wind."

At the beginning of the Old Testament comes the command not to know good and evil, not to have a different law from Nature. At the beginning of the New: "Except born of water and the wind (fulfilling the condition of obeying impulse) you cannot enter. . . ." At the beginning of each the same thought; and did not each undergo the same fall? "Be able to obey impulse," Christ said. "Think of your own salvation and restrain passion," replies the Church.

So it was assured what Christ would say when He was asked of marriage in the true human life. He *had* answered before; it was included in: "Be born of water and the wind."

It is true Christ said: "He that loveth father or mother more than me, is not worthy of me." But see His parable also, where those who had truly served Him had expressly *not* thought of Him. Does not that mean that serving Christ is serving *all*, is having the eye and heart on every need, and that putting the "home," the immediate circle, before this is turning away from Him? He has told us plainly what the only "doing to Him" is. That love of home and family too must lose its life to gain it.

Christ (as He is presented) was for some reason in the habit of speaking of Himself as of all men, of mankind. He had so deep a feeling of this that it moulded

His language constantly. In His parable He says: "Ye did it unto me." Is not this then what we should think of always? For instance: "He that loveth father or mother more than me," than all who have needs. Is the key to His words in the *identity* of God as a Being who can be served with men who have needs? "He who has seen me," the men who need his aid, "has seen the Father." Is this then the truth of the thought that Christ is Humanity?

I have felt before that our feeling of ourselves as isolated individuals is a diseased feeling, a paralysis whereby we are not conscious of that which we are. So that this would mean that Christ was free from that disease.

Again: "The pure in heart shall see God." To be "able to do anything," is to be pure in heart; that is, it is to have the regard on needs. Through regard to our fellows—which alone can give purity of heart and make us able to do all things—alone we can see God. Except through man you must not think to see God. (And indeed otherwise what is even desiring purity of heart but another thought about ourselves?) In truth, the words are again: "Born of water and the wind." Be pure in heart, with no not-regard, born of water—and seeing God *is* the impulse free.

We want to aim at a lower good for man here; we think we must be content with that; but we cannot get any good so, and here in this great foul city we must at least seek for the better. So when we read "wind" for "spirit" instantly a real, human, and how inspiring a meaning comes into the words; they mean instantly the *better* goodness, and challenge us to it. We must be, and must seek for all to be, able to be "children of the wind." Their meaning rises so; and thus we see that all that great sacerdotal system has come from not seeing the simple meaning, this real, practical thought. That is, it comes really from aiming at too low a good.

It may be hard to be "a child of the wind," but it is inexorable; without it we cannot enter into the kingdom of heaven. And now is it not plain what the kingdom of heaven is? A change must come to us ere we enter it. Now what must we be ere we can be one with *Nature?* what but "born of water and the wind?" that we are not is what separates us from Nature; what, therefore, is entering the kingdom of heaven but *entering Nature?* (And becoming as a little child is the same; the child is part of Nature.)

So man has been right in the feeling that there is a different state, a different *world*, for him; and that to that he must look forward. That has not been a delusion. It is his not having any more a different law from Nature.

Any one who sees what true good is, sees that it will assuredly be done *here;* that this world is the place for it; a place to which it is suited and alone is suited, and which is suited to it. Is not that what Christ saw, and why He bid us pray for it?

Has there been so much that is bad in human life? Is there anything of evil, or has there been, but not-regard to the facts? And we see that that is compatible with exquisite goodness. Yet that and its fruits—are they not all? And has there ever been a worse thing than that which is so tolerable to us now—the life expressing not-regard and feeling itself good and pious?

It is striking also how Christ, whose command was to fulfil the condition of having the impulses free, affirmed that a " spirit " (a wind) should come that would be a guide into all truth; a guide above human knowledge, unimpeded by human ignorance. It is the very fact of impulse when the conditions for obeying it are fulfilled. We see it absolutely in respect to food. There man has, if he will fulfil that condition of letting impulse guide him, " a guide into all truth." Now, is not the real meaning clear in this? Was it not this *fact* that Christ knew and spoke of? Having bidden us be " children of the wind," how could He help knowing also that this " wind "—the impulses of man—would be this perfect guide?

The "wind," the guide to truth, is man's impulse when the conditions for obeying it are fulfilled. Be born of the water, and the wind will guide you beyond all human fallibility. So there was necessarily the insistance on this condition. (And so we see in the Church the hypothesis set up which comes always from not seeing the fact.)

Christ was the man who bade us fulfil the condition of having impulse free; and He also made the promise that a spirit should come and guide us into all truth, a spirit not fallible, unaffected by human ignorance. But these two are one. To be able to obey the impulses *is* for them to be a guide " into all truth; " the very voice and hand of Nature, unaffected by human ignorance, guiding us where our knowledge does not go.

It is having our moral nature, our souls, work as our body works now. And is there not here a light on the true nature of each? May not our present experience be a " becoming " of a moral or spiritual " body? " Is not " spiritual body " a perfectly instinctive spiritual (or, as we term it, " moral," but then " moral " no longer) life? I have seen before how " a body " of impulses, desires, and feelings is even now being created.

H

So in the very command to be able to obey our impulses, the coming, to those who obeyed, of this infallible guide is implied. The promise of this wind to guide into all truth means that Nature, so allowed to enter, being in man and dwelling in him, would be an impulse, guiding him and unaffected by his ignorance. How could Christ have preached that law and not seen and announced the consequence? Being Nature *is* having the Holy Spirit. And it is what we see and have so simply realised in respect to food. There man, having become able to obey his impulses, has received the spirit, an instinct that guides him into all truth.

It may well seem absurd to think there can ever be this impulse true and perfect beyond our knowledge. But Christ believed it was sure, affirmed it positively. Yet it must have been harder to see it then. Paul learnt it from Him also. And the loss of it brought the Pope, an artificial substitute for the misapprehended fact.

And is here the true significance of the feeling that makes people cling to "intuitive" morals? Is it not the maimed expression of the thought of instinctive or automatic morals? The demand is for absence of external guidance appealing to judgment limited by our knowledge, for an impulse, an infallible instinct beyond our ignorance.

The deliverance of man is from laws he cannot obey, because they are not good enough, having too much accepted not-regard in them. This is the deliverance he craves for now, and must have. Christ delivered man from disobedience and put obedience in its place; but it was by *altering the laws*. He did not teach him or enable him to obey the laws he had; He taught him how to have other laws. And by means of a new thought of God; He is a Spirit; serve Him not with deeds, but with *motive*. This is not putting away the service of God; it is His most perfect service.

Having self first makes an impossible law, kept by no one; and where even externally it is anything like kept, it is only by means of such contrivances and aids, such an elaborate system of means. And what a light comes on the curious connection between superstitious or false religious opinions, and " virtue " or obedience to law. That the law is a false one explains this; false and superstitious thoughts are needed to keep it. And so, indeed, has not all superstition arisen chiefly from the false laws that having self first (so needing a self-virtue) imposed? Are not superstitions, and all the fictitious theology, the nonsense-reasons projected by self-virtue? And so their source remains, these superstitions cannot be really put away,—for the facts cannot be put in their place. To put aside the service of the false laws is the deliverance from superstition.

This fact that the evil and sin in man is not his *breaking* laws (as we take for granted), but the making false ones, accounts for the false seeming of men as so divided and contrasted; as if some were good and others evil. It is evidently not truly so; but the wrong and sin are the wrong and sin of man, and not of some; all the wrong of all exhibiting itself where quite extraneous things determine.

How plainly the knowledge of physiology and medical science are the centre and key of all life. And at least to a physician it may well be the chief fact in Christ's history that, against all that was deemed divine law, He cured diseases. Nay, is it possible that in truth Christ was a wonderful physician; that He had learnt of the human body, and of remedies, and with marvellous intuitions had gained unexampled powers of cure? So one would understand the saying: "Believe me for the works' sake;" that is: "Indeed I do know Nature these things I tell you are true; could I make these cures if I had not learnt to understand her?" And again: "Greater works than these shall ye do;" that is: "Nature shall be understood still better than I understand her."

There is another passage that connects itself with "This people . . . is cursed" (as meaning: "We know the true law; that it is spiritual, but these ignorant people must be kept under the letter"), this, namely: "We are Abraham's children, and were never in bondage to any man." Abraham was before the law, and was not under it. And the passage may mean: "We know a man may have freedom from the letter of the law; that he may live in the spirit; we are free as Abraham was; we were never in bondage to any set of literal rules."

The important thing in Christ's day—that for which human lives and souls were sacrificed—was not, as it is with us, marriage, but the Sabbath. And He struck at that. So we have long narratives and discourses respecting the Sabbath, but respecting marriage only a few transient allusions: the law that men must be able to look on a woman and must not make their right in refusing to look; the quiet putting aside of special marriage in the true life; the not condemning the adulteress; the quiet mention of the facts, unreproving, to the woman of Samaria; and, finally, the forbidding of divorce.

Now, what is this last? It may have meant this: " If you have reason for another wife, do not turn your back on the one before; remember that it is a permanent obligation you have undertaken. You must not turn away a woman just for your pleasure; it is her good you must consider." Never meaning for a moment to imply that at the mutual wish, for reasons true and really good, there might not be a parting. But that sending a wife away, *not* at her own choice and for reasons of mutual good, but against her will, was to be justified (that is, *generally;* it being as all laws of things are) only by adultery; that there only a wider good could overrule the wife's desire. Was this it?

But so—because relatively of less importance then, and so less fully spoken of—did not even those who most entered into Christ's spirit fail to recognise it here? And here, therefore, the false law established itself, and our history has been learning to see *here* what Christ told us.

How should those who do wrong be met? How did Christ meet the Gentiles? It was not by enforcing on them the duties others clung to, but by bringing both to recognise new duties they had alike neglected, duties which took away the need for the others that had been partial and refused. Part of that which the Jews called wrong was true to Nature. And so will not every division into bad and good be made one?

It is no contradiction that the same man utterly repudiated any thought of God's will which was not one with service, and was the man of all others most filled with the feeling of God, most carried away by absolute devotion to Him. The two things are one. He could not let God's law mean hurting a man, because He had thought of Him earnestly, applied Himself with all His heart to know Him. The reason the others could think of His law as being hurt to man was that they had not thought of Him; had not seriously and deeply pondered on Him and sought Him and searched Him out. Even when they had thought they were thinking of Him they were thinking of themselves. How could a man who had ever seriously thought of God at all think of leaving a man sick for His glory? (But we think we must leave women sick for it.)

Is this why Christianity seems so little; that the harvest is absorbed in a larger seed-time; that it is a preparation? Now of what? Is it that it has *initiated* the great deliverance from self; the putting away of the (need for a) law of things in respect to woman? Did it not clear the way for that and put man's energies upon it? Christ put away that which had made necessary laws of things in respect to God, and so prepared for the work of putting away that which made laws of things necessary in respect to woman. So this then is what we owe to Christ. He has brought us to be able to have a law of service—a spirit-law—even in respect to woman. This law was not possible perhaps either for Greek or Jew—made by them both a cruel indulgence—but Christ has made it possible for us. And naturally; for see how He turned our eyes on our fellows' needs, commanding us to make even the service of God mean that. So as

Judaism was, we may say, the correction of the premiss in respect to man's relation to God, so has not Christianity been the correction of the premiss in respect to man's relation to woman?

Would it not be beautiful to see Christ's work thus in its historic place? We have to see *the thing* that He has done for us. And could any gratitude or homage be deeper than man would give Him who had done that for him, once he comes to see what it was? Would he not well see that all the other things supposed were indeed but shadows and images compared with that living fact: a true law of service in respect to women *here?* Man at his utmost dream has never dared to think of such a heaven as that. He would indeed, if that were true, wake up to see that Christ had given him more than his heart could desire.—I stand here as affirmer of the greatness of Christ's work, that the thing believed impossible *He has done.* He is robbed of His glory. He can make man pure *here.*

Christ healed the body and was the physician of the soul. Then what was the disease in the soul? It was that which made men think of God as commanding a thing, instead of as revealing His command in the good of men. Was it not clearly that in their goodness they found a need to think of themselves and of what *they* did? And from this did not He show them how to be delivered? Or we might well say that their disease was inventing a God. And that is simple. For needing to have their thought on their own action, they had of course to put their good in restraining. And then they had to invent a God to command the restraint, since man's good did not command it. And this is the evil of having our thoughts on our action; we make restraints that human good does not command, and then we have to invent a God to command them. So that the disease was really inventing a God. Is not that *the* disease of man?

Christ had a most peculiar and emphatic mode of serving God both in deed and word. And it is striking that the man who, above all, thought of God and felt Him, lived in and for Him, He, above all, took as His absolute service of Him the needs of men. But indeed this must have been. Only lack of the feeling of God's presence makes us feel anything else as His will. The two are not opposed but one. He it is who speaks to us in these. And indeed, is it not only by feeling the needs of man to be absolutely God's voice, that they can be made the absolute rules, and the law of service enthroned? (The invention of another "law" of God, is the result of the non-feeling of that which *is* His law.) So long, doubtless, as there is any feeling of the needs of men as being not the absolute and simple expressions of God's command and guidance, so long doubtless there must be a feeling that prevents these being taken as the absolute law; there must be some latent feeling of antagonism, and so the action be disjoined, more or less, from the needs. And surely it is striking that even when no God at all is recognised, still the simple law of service does not rule. Only with the feeling of their expressing the law of God and His guidance comes the perfect rule of human needs. And, perchance, this feeling of their being the very voice of God *can* only come with the perception that through them false laws must fall and a new life come.

But they must be seen to have this virtue before God's voice can be absolutely and wholly heard in them. Till then do they not inevitably seem to be contradictions, in part, of His will? And so man's thought inevitably turns *from* them. Thus we see how Christ must have felt man's needs to be God's voice, and alone His voice, because He saw that by them the false laws fell, and the new life was brought. It is evident too how their real value is in their power to make life new. It is not merely for the relief of the needs, but for that work on the life, that their value is. So they can only be truly seen to be God's law when this power over man's life is seen in them. It is the use and meaning of them: till they are seen thus they could not even truly be seen to be the voice of God. There must seem to be other and worthier guides, because worthier and better ends.

Only when the external and material is seen—by the regard being on others—to be the very highest and most perfect means of attending to the internal life, can we escape from thinking that we must turn away from it to the internal. For it is a true and indispensable feeling that our own life within *is* a thing of infinite value and necessity. And so the needs of others can be seen in their true meaning and value only when they are seen to be the means of creating this internal life. And what we need to see, and have not seen sufficiently, is that those needs of others which are our pleasure have this function, as well as those which put aside our pleasure. We have recognised this value in the needs of others only in the latter case; and so we have divided these needs into those which we might so attend to, and those which have less claim on us, nay, some which we even ought to ignore. (Those namely which mean our doing things which with our eye on ourselves we ought not to do.) And this of course robs them *all* of their power. What we have to see is that all the needs of others have this value for the spiritual life. That puts them all into their right relation, makes them all to us inevitably the very voice of God. And then when *all* needs are God's voice to us, then we perceive we need suppose no other voice. (Only there comes another voice, the *Spirit's* guidance, impulse restored to its true nature.)

In truth, are not the needs of others which mean our pleasure those which have really the most power on our spiritual life? For those which mean our pain we may attend to utterly for ourselves; and no voice warn us that it is after all for self. But the needs that mean our pleasure, how deep they go. How deep Nature has insisted on their going. How absolutely she prepares all things to give them their full power. The division of the needs of others into two opposite portions is fatal.

In the fact of God's will meaning human needs, and finding its expression in them, do we not see a reason that man has established that will in his thoughts as his ultimate rule and law? Is not this *why*—even though not knowing—he has said: I owe absolute submission and allegiance of hand and heart to God's will? Saying a truer thing than he knew, namely, that he is thus to his fellows' needs. And then because he did not know, did not perceive, that God's will was but another name for his fellows' needs, how its true meaning has been lost. He has made a shadow, put aside the substance. For, divorced from the needs of our fellows, the will of God is but a name.

How can man be bad, be a being to be angry with, when the worst, meanest, cruellest thing in him is his goodness; when indeed his badness comes through his trying to be good ; and if he would only have obeyed the command not to try to be good he would never have been really bad at all ?

Conscience has been placed by men as paramount and infallible instead of impulse. The thought of right and wrong—the forbidden thing—(for the law is not: You shall think of right and wrong, but: You shall not have need to think of right and wrong), has been put where impulse has the true claim to be. The claim and affirmation of conscience is the image of the true rule of impulse. So we call conscience God's voice in the soul, giving it the name that the true ruler bears. And it has come as the result of absence; inability to obey impulse sets up its false image—the shadow of good things to come—in its place. Being obliged to put impulse aside, we have had to bring in an invented substitute.

How simple it was, putting a being in a fluent, changing world like this, to give him the one direction : Be able to do anything. That is: Do not know good and evil.

Christ put the service of man above the (formal) worship of God. We have to put the service of man above the putting away of pleasure. The service of man put aside for obedience to God meant that God was not obeyed, was in truth the mere result and expression of His not being obeyed. So the service of man put aside for the sake of pleasure being put away is but the result and expression of its being pursued. It is both result and cause; it comes from the pursuit of pleasure and gives it a still more fatal rule. For it puts away the very power —the absolute claim of service to rule—that is the limit to pursuit of pleasure. So what remains to prevent pleasure from ruling and being pursued? It will not avail to put serving God instead; that will lead (evidently it must, and we see it does) some into the utmost austerities, and as evidently (as also it is in fact) others will think: " Why does God want us to forego pleasure? Is it not His will we should pursue it?" We cannot put serving God instead of serving man as the means of keeping pleasure from being pursued. The service of man may make pleasure perfectly free, even sought for and incumbent; but it will not be *ruling*. But the service of God, while it makes pleasure not free, still leaves it ruling. This is our choice: pleasure ruling but not free; or pleasure free but not ruling.

And in this again we ought to see how service to man is the true basis and means of worship and obedience to God; it must have the same relation to this as it has to the not ruling of pleasure. And to affirm the traceable needs of man to be the law is identical with saying they are God's revealed will. Here are two laws proposed by men: God's will; man's traceable good: both imperfectly seen until they are seen as one. Except by seeing it as the true command of God, it is impossible really to affirm the traceable needs of man as the law. (That is, because they so forbid our thought of goodness—which we attach God's name to—in restraint from pleasure.) So is not this recognition of man's needs as the law, as much the means of sustaining the true worship of God as it is of keeping off from us the *rule* of pleasure? It is the means of liberty, of God's rule—Nature's instead of self's. And we see that none of those who ignore God ever think of affirming simply that the traceable needs of men are the law of right; they all—and surely inevitably—insist on some rules, some laws of things, which at the bottom mean restraint from pleasure; that is, which mean the thought on pleasure, on self. To affirm the absolute law of *God* as revealed in human needs is the only deliverance from this.

Is it not clear that the idea of a *place* to worship God arose partly from that of taking trouble to do it? (The feeling still exists. ———— said, "God likes us to take trouble to worship Him.") How inevitable that those who let the needs of men pass without calling for their trouble, should be looking out for something to "take trouble" about. How strange that we cannot let Nature determine the amount and kind of our trouble for us. And "serving God" will not do for it. Lacking the reality it ought to have, wanting a "revelation," and so being left to fancy, it may be so conveniently little (as with us), or go to such extremes; it will, in a word, be anything but doing what is wanted.

What Christ saw was the relativity of law; there were conflicting laws. "Our fathers said . . . and you . . ." And the answer, how simple: "It does not matter; only serve God in spirit." So if it were said now: "Our fathers said: 'Kill such and such of your children,' and you say: 'Keep all of them alive,'" the answer would be equally simple: It does not matter; only love and seek the good of all. Is not this the true meaning of all opposing laws, and indeed the only real solution? The law of worshipping at Jerusalem came because men did not worship God in spirit; it never would have come but for that. But there are still many people who do not, and cannot be brought to, worship God in spirit; yet does any one propose they should have to go to Jerusalem to worship, or think it would do any shadow of good? Yet do we not insist on such very things, as if there were some good in having, on those who cannot be right within, the laws that come from being wrong? Surely if it were seen that those laws were only for those who would keep being wrong within, it would be seen also that they were not needed at all. When once the sight has come that there *is* a truer right, then the other laws have completed their work and are needed no more at all.

Christ's new commandment is *art;* doing without doing, making to live by leaving out. He leaves out loving God. It shows the instincts, the true apprehensions of the man throughout. And the things to leave out are those which put aside other claims; Nature must guide to them. The true missing is having them *in* the other things. Now, it might be asked: "But may not man be served in serving God as well as God served in serving man? In sacrificing the traceable good of man for the sake of serving God are we not truly serving them, missing that service only for the sake of serving God, and not at all self-wise and arbitrarily? Why is not this the right way of uniting the claims? Has not God the first and chief claim, to which all others are rightly subordinated, in that most truly obeyed?" Now, respecting this, may it not be truly said that it has probably been man's thought always, and that we ought to apply it in judging of the cruelties of ancient superstitions? When men killed other men in sacrifice, no doubt they felt that way, and fully believed they were only making the right subordination. We see that that was a mistake, and that the traceable good of men should have determined the form of the service of God there, and did rightly determine it, inverting that other order. It was a misinterpretation of the fact that God has the first and greatest claim. It was quite misread when it was read as meaning that men should be killed in His honour. What it really means is that God has the first claim to be served as a Spirit; that His service is a power and a life, not an outside thing.

Christ's "born of the water and the wind" is so closely parallel to "the wind of God moved on the face of the waters." Now, see how the false (or not-regard) law is overthrown into chaos; false form and true service are alike put aside and mere disorder comes. Here is the parallel: on this chaos comes the being "born of water and the wind." The chaos, or breaking down of the imperfect law, prepares the way for the fulfilling of the condition for indulging passion or obeying impulse. It exactly describes the correction of the premiss. And the chaos must come first and prepare for it; that breaking down is the necessary condition. So that is what Christ said to the chaos—the failing, imperfect law—of His time; it is what He says now to the same chaos of our time. Here is chaos; we experience it. It is as definite and perfect an order as any other.

The true God is the Nature-God. And so do we not better see polytheism? Was it not a true instinct, insisting that God was the Nature-God, but needing to be suppressed for perfecting? And so how simple it is to see the problem worked out in so many centuries. God felt to be one with Nature, but then Nature not known; the mere phenomenon felt to be Nature; and so what was open but to make Him like all corruptible things? Then, after how long a time, comes science, teaching us that the physical is but phenomenal; that the fact is something other than that; and then the conditions for God being to us as a Nature-God are fulfilled.

Is it not interesting to note as existing in India, for instance, the belief in the physical as illusion with polytheism (that is, God as the Nature-God)? This surely is not mere accident. Did those who affirmed God as the Nature-God then really connect this with the affirmation of the physical as but phenomenal? And so is the polytheism a degradation of their thought?

Christianity must not be taken as more permanent in form than any other good; it has in it no power to guard itself from decay. It has a power most divine, can save, and to the uttermost; can lay hold of the lowest and carry them from hell to heaven; it can save others, but it cannot save itself; cannot prevent itself from sinking into a mockery. That which was true of Christ is true of Christianity—*and ought to be*. To enter into life it ought to die. "Ought not Christianity to have suffered these things and entered into its glory?" To be present in departing; to live in dying. To have been trodden under foot and made a scorn and mocking. "We thought it had been *it* that should have restored" his glory unto man. And even as foolishly do we not regret? "Into their glory" all things enter by making it possible for themselves no more to be. That it cannot save itself is its praise, not its condemnation. This is the glory of every institution: it saves others; itself it cannot save. In saving it dies.

Look at that sad book the Roman Catholics put into the hands even of children: "Hell opened to Christians." As I was showing it to a friend I thought: See to what extremes man's conscience has gone, into what quite false extravagances of self-condemnation. Now why is it? What do these false self-condemnations mean, making him call any cruelty of injustice right and just if only it is directed against himself? What has brought it? Can we trace it in any way? (Can one find the secret of it in the absence of response to facts? But then see his way of "escaping;" still keeping that, only turning it to his own "goodness.") But, whatever its source, is it not full of significance as a fact? Here has been a false feeling of evil and ill-desert, a perverted self-condemnation. Now, is all man's self-condemnation truly the same? Has there been truly *any* evil in his life? Has all his feeling of his ill-desert been an untrue feeling like this? And in fact has not human life been perfect in beauty and good, intensely rich with a pathetic beauty of which the very self-condemnation is but one part?

Seeing evils as forces ending in results is seeing them good; this also is the expression of the use of the moral reason. And it is visibly one with regarding the human relations; for so evils *are* powers. In truth, recognise as the end a change in the moral life—a spiritual change of truer apprehension or completer response—and what can the powers to bring it be but evils? What but the *feelings* which that term expresses could be the agents?

Human life must be what it is (as all things are) by virtue of its relations; it is that which is around it which makes it what it is; and its whole course and character have reference to that. Now, will not a clear recognition of this, and perchance understanding what those relations are, make man's religion new for him?

It must be an inversion to say: Love to God, and love to man founded on love to God. It was the very opposite that Christ proclaimed. Yet He, most of all, was full of the love of God and lived in and by it. He went to Him through the true way. And so do Christians also when they truly go, namely, through Christ. They do but conceal the fact from themselves by doctrines. Man is the "way." And in our trying to put the love in that inverted order this thought comes: "that God's providence will overrule the strange miscellaneous powers and principalities of this world, and subdue them in time to the divine purpose." Such thoughts as that come from trying to go to God some other way than through man, to reach Him through vacuum. Of course that must come. And so it looks to us like mere "strange miscellaneous powers;" this is the name we give to God's very presence among us, turning our back on it and gazing into vacancy to find Him. And then we say of the dim image we conjure up: He will *in time* subdue all that to His purpose. But in looking at man's life and seeing the perfect work there carried on—then indeed and there we see God. It is no more "strange miscellaneous powers;" it is God visible. How wise was He who said the way to God is through man. For in looking away from man to see Him we also make to ourselves a false vision of human life.

Is not Paul's true instruction to us simply to be in an attitude of readiness to see and receive the new life, casting off the old forms? "All things are ours,"—all the fresh things God sends, however antagonistic they may seem, death itself, the dying of our dearest convictions, our most loved and trusted laws, death is ours. And is it not this that he meant Christ had taught us: this perception of a life (and readiness to receive it) that could be in any forms, or without any; a life that could let all *things* freely change, all ordinances live in their effect, the revelation of a law in man's life, a new feeling within coming in with the falling off even of the best and most divine institutions? Is not this what Paul meant by the life and light that Christ gave, the state within that made all ceasing and passing of institutions, and falling off of laws of things, simply the coming of a new power into the soul? That enabled him at once to say, on the one hand: "How make the members of Christ members of a harlot?" how let mere pleasure rule recklessly in such a relation? and, on the other hand, to put "fornication" with eating blood and things offered to idols; making it a question simply of good, nothing in itself. This is the very same thought on its other side.

This is Paul's Gospel: You are free *for ever*, and in all forms, from all laws of things: law is on the heart. This is the foundation Christ has laid, nor can any man lay another. It was a method He introduced, not a result; not a different law of things, but how to have none.

Christ had seen that to be as a power, a life, a thing must die; that losing life was saving it to life *eternal*. Surely He felt, too, that He could not make man understand this; that He spoke in vain to that time; that they would not see truly what He meant. But then did He also see beforehand and recognise that He had assuredly given *science* to man; had brought him to Nature:

and that through that—through the teaching of the Holy Spirit—the things He had said should be known and understood and brought to man's remembrance? (What we read in the Acts of the Holy Spirit was a physical misapprehension. It is the universal mistake, turning spiritual things to physical, and so putting an empty material invention for the eternal fact.)

We make the New Testament exclusive, as if it was of one event alone, and not a key and interpretation of man's whole life. Whenever there comes a new law within to man the New Testament will be his book. It will be the explanation and revelation of that new coming of life. For it is of that change it is written; not of those particular events or things. *Any* thing will do.

The great crime in men's eyes is to *hope*, to believe that better may be. How many hold, and do not scruple to say secretly, that our laws are false and bad. That is no wrong in men's eyes; the wrong is to think they can be made better, to hope, to speak openly—in a word, to trust in God. This is the great crime in society's eyes, and that was Christ's great crime. And of course it is the greatest of all. It means freedom, openness, the fading of dead laws, *the putting away of safeguards*. That is the point: our safeguards or belief in God—which?

The absence of reference to any other world in the Pentateuch is very striking. May we not see how enormous a benefit it might have been? For ceremonies and religious usages generally tend to fix themselves especially around the future state, and that leads them into any extravagance, betrays them into a cruelty that is limitless. But that restricting the thought to this world and its good and evil—to traceable good—what a limit and protection against their own foolishness it was. If we lay hold of any other thought of goodness than that of our fellows' good, there is no limit to the cruelty into which even the best and wisest may fall. We see it in our own cruelty; it is the same as all. There is no limit.

How plainly Christ's feeling about the absolute authority of traceable good flashes out! "That the law of Moses may not be broken"—the very most emphatic law of God—you circumcise on the Sabbath. But here is a man made every whit whole. What is the law of Moses compared to that? Here by the side of a written statement of the law, however authoritative and revered, is God's very present law itself, not written on tables of stone, but on these fleshly tables of our own hearts. Could any terms of the absolute enthronement of the traceable good of man be more decisive? And so from this we can see how Christ must have insisted so on rightness *within;* as enthroning this revealed will of God, and so demanding the rigid letter-law to cease, He must have demanded the right within that could alone permit its ceasing.

The idea of "serving God" still lets the thought be upon self; it may be simply a projected reason making use of that which comes nearest. The thought of a "God" or "Creator" being inevitably present, the feelings of self-virtue lay hold of it; and of course man's first "goodness"—being still about himself—comes in the form of a theological devotion, a reference to some god or gods.

And indeed is it not the fact that to have the regard true is the last thing (in any given application of force of moral kind) that man will do; that all modes of applying it are tried before that; in a word, that all the other things than this—which is the becoming of his life—are simply the effects of the force that is to bring the true regard, operating in various other directions until it can do that? All the other results mean simply that that is not done.

And now yet again may we, by the parallel of this force which thus works the life of man, see the working of the force in the organic life? Do we see the same process there, in the various effects of the force before it produces its last effect of bringing the living or organic state? Does that come in the same way as the ceasing of a tension (or *reductio ad absurdum*)? The force first has various external operations, as it were, before it makes the internal one, which answers to the true regard, that is, the living state. As if this "becoming living" were the special difficulty. But of course this means only that it comes in its turn, when, and as soon as, it becomes the direction of least resistance.

But thus—because in it there may still remain the regard first on self—we see how the early stage of man's aim at right will be one with emphatic reference to God. Yet this also surely is an anticipation, and though it has to be put aside is suppressed only for perfecting a true position. Our relation to God—our deepest, paramount relation—is introduced through this negative of an untrue regard. And here surely is the key to what it is to become.

It is not that man is so wicked. When he sees how he breaks even his own laws—all laws indeed—and what cruel evil things he does, of course he thinks: How wicked! But he looks at the wrong things. It is his life, which expresses itself in making false laws, that is lacking; of course, because impurity makes false laws. He does not think of saying: I must be a person not making things evils. That would give him a different thought of his evil.

The Decalogue throws such a light on Christ's action. So dead it is—not a word about loving; a long insisting on having only one God, and then a long sermon about the Sabbath—and then a few moral precepts briefly added. (Is it not as like as possible to the Wahabee telling Palgrave that the great sins were polytheism and smoking tobacco, and murder and theft were slight offences, and God was merciful?) Now Christ broke the first two; those put first and most insisted on; and surely those most intensely regarded then by the Jews. They had been *trained* to regard them most. He broke the laws probably most regarded (and broken?) in His day.

And in this is there a light on how far and in what sense He did really claim to be divine? (It is evident we do not know this at present, for persons the best qualified think quite oppositely.) But may we not *know* what it was He did by seeing it as a breaking of the letter of that law and fulfilling of its spirit? Did He not do by that law the very same thing that He did by the Sabbath law? And so by this we may see the other. That He did break the letter of that law may we not be sure? and even see plainly in what way?

Did not Christ really mean the deliverance from *all* laws (of things)? But His thought was not fully seen. It was recognised as delivering from the Jewish law but not how far it reached, how total the regard to others it demanded. And so was it that its force became misspent and went so emphatically into self-torture? Is this a sign of the misapprehension, of the falling short of the application? There was force (this was the meaning) to deliver from all laws of things; but this not being seen, the other result necessarily ensued; the power that had for its true use to turn the regard from self was twisted around self, and so expressed itself inevitably in voluntary pain.

Does not the very fact of this false effect show there was a power there which did not fulfil its true end? And how visibly the meaning of Christ's words was: "Deny yourself; put away all thought of self; fulfil the command to love, and take the liberty it brings; let the regard be absolutely true." But this not being seen, the true self-denial, the true taking up the cross being unknown, there came instead the thought of a self-denial still with the regard on self, and all its fruits; its fruits, however, of how infinite a value to us, and doubtless how absolutely needful.

Is it not pretty to see how Christ's: "Think of your neighbour" changed into: "Put away your own pleasure?" "self-denial" into: "Think all of yourself and how good you can be?"

To us this "believing in Christ," and trusting to His death for pardon, has become merely an ideal thing, identified from the first with duty and goodness, with doing what is right and elevating and aspiring; the power is turned out of it. When felt thus, it comes no more in its true significance, as the call to do a thing of utmost meanness and vileness, if done for self; this aspect of it gets quite hidden and put out of sight. (And so surely hypotheses have been made to supply the void.)

This, its great aspect and power when it came first, and when it comes first to a low and degraded man, is hidden and lost. Its true nature is lost sight of. But how striking it really is, and at first must have been, to those old aspiring heathen. Before, all thought of coming to God, to betterness, had been by getting nobler, rising, putting away all the mean. Now, what a sudden change; to do a thing, which—how could it be done?

When we look at the evil people, so brutal, so given to wrong, apparently so uncaring and inaccessible, we feel as if the right thing must be to hold ourselves separate, to make a broad distinction and seek to cleave to good, and put the badness at least away from *us*. And when yet another step comes, and we go forth to try to help and deliver the bad, it is still the same feeling at the bottom; the distinction, the separating and putting away, is the same; the attempt is to bring some over from one to the other. We are prone altogether to take this stand, instead of looking in and seeing, and seeking if we cannot get to the heart and root of the evil and find a goodness which will change and abolish, and really absorb it altogether. We find a goodness that in some half kind of way seems to do for us, and we expect it to do for every one.

But we might have a different thought, a different aim altogether, that of gathering them up into a new and better life altogether. Now this is how Christ stood. This would be following His steps and taking Him to learn from. He stood *as if sinful*, opening a better way, a truer goodness. (One sees it was purity in heart He taught, for it had for its outward form making things pure, that is, free. So if that teaching ever comes again to us it must have that outward form.) Necessarily He stood as if sinful, if He was showing the path of a deeper purity. It could not be otherwise; for things had falsely been made impure; and He was showing that God had cleansed them.

Being led by Christ is seeking ever a better and better goodness, one that makes more and more things not evil. (With that great saying of His as a beacon and guiding star, showing at how much He aimed and what His thought embraced: "In the regeneration they do not even marry." Even there man has the law that comes with purity.) Ever a better and better goodness, never staying. And the mistake that has befallen us is the universal mistake of puttings *things* for *actions*. We try to hold to what we think were the *things* Christ affirmed, or set up, instead of seeing that it is His *act* that is our guide. We put the thing we think He ordained in place of the act He did, the principle He set before us.

Christ came into conflict with caste law: "*We* were never in bondage to any law; but this people . . ." He put aside this error, and affirmed the true law universal. So there is this great thing in our society, that it will not have different laws for different people. And how probably through this very thing, in part, it comes that the laws are so broken here. The insistence on having *one* renders the false law less able to stand. So the needful change is aided to come.

And in this do we not see again the part Christ took? He refused a different law. He was assailed with the temptation (by the Pharisees), but insisted that the true law was for all. By that Christianity exists. But besides this, may we see a meaning again in the words of Paul: " He humbled Himself and took on Him the form of a servant?" We may (besides all other meanings) find in them this reality: He, though having Nature herself in Him, that is, being genius, the very instrument and presence of Nature, and so subject only to the law of freedom, though so made free from all laws of things, yet did not claim and use that liberty; He descended from that freedom and accepted the false law we had imposed on ourselves, putting aside His own right, sharing our state of bondage, though not truly under it, in order to raise us to His freedom; claiming so the true law for all by making Himself one with them. So that claiming His right He claims it for every one. They are brought under the true law with Him, because He has made their law and His the same. (So in Him there is a guide to genius, and how it should claim its freedom so that all may share it.)

The words of the New Testament seem so large and deep. (So we have put them away from the present realities we live among, and made up theories for them.) But is not the meaning simple? They express the perception of the writers that this world (seeming so little) is really a *phenomenal* world, the phenomenal of the spiritual. When a person sees this, of course his words begin to relate to the spiritual, the fact. It is as a person would speak who had discovered the real heavens in the apparent. His words would become large, too large for the mere appearance. So is it not simply the fact that the New Testament writers had gained that vision of this world as the phenomenon of the spiritual? And so they began of course to speak and write about the spiritual. Was it not simply a sign of that identification, perhaps incomplete, and therefore suppressed for restoring?

And now is not a similar time come? We also have learnt that this world is but phenomenal, that is to say, that it is the phenomenal of the actual; that it is not two worlds, but one. Now, must not like change come over our words and thoughts? Must they not expand and become too large for the phenomenal because meaning the actual?

In respect to Christ's claim to divineness being the raising the law of monotheism from the letter to the spirit, there may be a key in the words: "He that loveth father or mother more than me . . ." Does not this mean "more than man," than human good? And from that may we not even see a light upon His whole meaning and the whole thought of making the monotheistic law a spirit one? Consider how at that time God was served *against* man, and how Christ's great thought was to have it recognised that God was to be served *in* man, and only so. That is the great thought of all the deliverers from human sacrifices; the one thought always bringing deliverance. It is the true turning to God, because the true and only turning away from self. And the turning to self is the only turning away from God, because it is merely turning away from fact, is merely not-regard.

Now if Christ was seeking to bring men to see this, then may we not see how the words came? By the good of man He meant God in them—seeking, serving, following God as shown in man. Then might it not have come that Christ's *me*, meaning God in man and as revealing His will in the facts of men's lives, might have come to seem that in Him alone God was revealed? And so, by exclusiveness, it was robbed of its meaning. There is that tendency always misleading man; and so it may have come that Christ's attempt (which evidently has not been understood) to make it seen that God was to be served in man alone, was applied by an intruding exclusiveness to *His* being divine. And does not the insistance that God was to be seen and served in man, and not apart from him, truly express a raising of the law of monotheism to the spirit-form? For if Christ was saying this, and He was not understood, must not such an idea about Himself, as exclusive, have taken the place of the true one? Some thought instead of that would be wanted, and it must necessarily have been that He said: Not in *man*, and the traceable facts of his life, God's will is revealed, but in me you see Him. (Was it so the other "divine men" came to be thought divine? Were they also saying: "You must see God in man," and men responding: "We see God in *you*," and still shutting their eyes to God in human needs?)

Now is that raising the law of monotheism to the spirit-form? In one sense it seems so; for indeed the spirit-form of every law (that it means revealed human good) *is* taking the monotheistic law in the spirit. It is saying that God is in this man, in these present facts. So that to affirm the other laws are spirit-laws is to take this very attitude towards the monotheistic one, and say of God: He is and speaks in this man, in every man, in man. Nay, is the true meaning of the monotheistic law this: There is one God, and He speaks absolutely in every claim; and there is no superior authority to set it aside? (If there were many Gods, there might be.) It is one and the same supreme authority who is manifested in every fact; neglect none.

So it was applied to prove that all *nations* were brothers; one God made them. And so, considering that one chief wrong of early times was that tribal antipathy, and limiting the regard to their own nation only, may we not see the great significance of the monotheistic law as being an injunction to regard alien nations, a command to put away not-regard? And so the true meaning of the law is most absolutely expressed when it is made to command the putting away of all not-regard. Is not that its true significance; and how Christ treated it? And in making it mean this—God seen in human needs—did He not restore its true meaning, even exactly as He did that of the Sabbath-law? Monotheism was made for man. It meant that man's claims were absolute from the first.

Making a law a spirit-law is so understanding it that it is felt to be fulfilled though its letter is contradicted. We need this, for the thought of "God" otherwise cannot bring the fulfilling in breaking the letter. Now if we look at the law of monotheism there are visible relations in it to this thought. In the first place, may we not see that the law of monotheism was, as the Sabbath-law, "made for man;" that is, introduced for the sake of traceable human good, to bring in amity instead of enmity among the nations? For in early history we see that this enmity to neighbours was the great evil. Savage tribes, many of them, are brothers among themselves, but are in constant war with all around; and this evil of barbarism infested to a modified extent also the classic civilisations; all but Greek or Roman were rightly to be hated. Now this hatred of other nations was intimately connected with the idea of separate gods (or of special possession of God); other gods made other nations; so it would become even a duty to hate them; they would be "sacrificed to God." Now in that state what should a true seer seek to do but above all things to insist that one God made all alike? He would introduce *for man* a law of monotheism.

Now with this thought of the origin of the monotheistic law, and of its value, we can partly see how Christ stood to it in the same attitude as to the Sabbath. This law, made to introduce and enforce love to all men, was used to injure them. (Give to God instead of to your parents, for example.) Now as Christ said in respect to the Sabbath: "Serving God *is* in serving men, and you must see God in them," so He took in respect to monotheism the very same attitude: "Serving God is serving men, and you must see God in them. Monotheism was made for man; and it is fulfilled only in seeing God in men."

Apart from men, serving God cannot deliver us from letter-laws. And it is because, though for Him in the other way we may put away pursuing pleasure even to the utmost, yet *so* we cannot be brought to put away *refusing* pleasure. There is no power in it to break that form of the dominion of self; it is because of this wonderful power on us of having not to put away pleasure that the need and potency of serving God in our fellows come. It is not that we may be trained up to or exercised in, or brought even to find delight in restraining pleasure, and doing toilsome and irksome deeds, and controlling passion; not for anything of that kind is it needed that God's service must be in serving man; all that can be, would be, has been, done to the utmost in the other form of serving Him. The serving Him in man must be to bring the consenting to pleasure, consenting to lay aside restraint and irksomeness. So we see a reason in the order: first ought to have come the false thought of serving God; that brings the training in the painful things, in the putting away of pleasure, in control and restraint; it has no other meaning; it comes to us for that, and by its very falsity gives us those benefits. (Does not every falsity, every lack, give *us* certain fruits we want and ought to have, supplying to us exercise in things needful for the full good of the more perfect thing?)

Then the coming of serving God *in our fellows* is always one thing: it is always the ceasing of the refusal of pleasure. Our fellows are held in reserve because of the power that is stored up in them to make pleasure free, and bid restraints fall off. The thought of God alone means pain and restraint; the thought of Him in our fellows (that is, the thought of our fellows) means joy, freedom, pleasure, restraint being in its effect.

God has made our fellow-men, and their needs mean freedom for joy, and restraints removed. And above all is this the case by no more sacrificing first children, then women. Thinking of God in our fellows means freedom of delight everywhere, but above all here, that is, in the home. The two elements of the home are those in which man's thought turning to his fellows most sets free joy, first children, then woman. But is this a sign of what will be universally? Will every relation to our fellows in its turn be found even as these? In every respect will the turning of our thoughts to our fellows' good be found not less the instrument of a fresh freedom for delight; and these two cases only the first? That is, will it be found truly that in all not-regard is involved really as much restraint from joy (in the form of "self-duty") as existed in the sacrifice for self-duty of children and of women? That is, that all our fellows are really as truly organised and adapted for our joy and rapture as our children are, and that in sacrifice of them we do really feel as great a constraint upon our pleasure, as great a burden on our hearts, as our fathers did upon theirs in sacrificing their children.

Monotheism must be truly a spirit-law; the letter of it is no more a true law than any other letter. Surely our thoughts have been very perverted here, perverted in the very fact of not making monotheism a law " made for man." For when we put it into metaphysical terms as we do (making it a letter-thing), do we not clearly make it false? God is one, doubtless, but He is also many. He is not more one than He is many. To make it an abstract statement: "God is one" is to think falsely. It is a law of human good, not a merely abstract law. The very proposition is not true, but expresses a distinctly false thought; God is not what we conceive when we speak of one. Monotheism is a spirit-law—a law which means human good is to be pursued—and not a letter-law. It is false when we make it so. The insisting on the unity is not a metaphysical correctness; it is insisting on that aspect of God's being which human good then demanded; it was not because it was more " true," but because the other hurt man.

The person who will assail the established things, the things that good has established, our best, the man who will have the instinct for that will be the man who can give them up and yet hold them. He can still keep the good of them, that is, the power, and let it be in another thing; for "things" are useless for power. Christ was one who could let go a thing and keep the good of it.

We think always (our whole plan of life is so): "Men are such creatures; can we expect anything more than this kind of life?" We think such and such a mode of living must be supposed, "while men are what they are." But we must remember that Christ distinctly refused to consent to a thing allowed "because of the hardness of men's heart's." His thought looked to a different method. And He is put aside in every idea of saying: "But it is not human nature to do otherwise than that," &c. (Here the ascetic system was in one way true to Him. Its mistake was in another direction, in its confusion of putting away self with putting away pleasant things.) We adopt the plan of saying that such an order of society is necessary because of the hardness of men's hearts.

We think so exclusively of Christ's *dying*, not regarding His being called "a gluttonous man and winebibber," that is, wicked and self-indulgent. We ignore His free relation to pleasure (from which indeed, at least in part, His death arose). Is not this free relation to pleasant things really quite as much as, and indeed in some sense more than, even His death? For He chose it, insisted on it as His action, while His death He did not choose, but accepted. If the call to lay down His bodily life came He consented, but His self-goodness was the life He laid down. We look at one side only, and not the chief.

Seeing how the Pharisees refused to consider health, and sacrificed others' lives to self-virtue, does there not come a new meaning into His healing? He healed, as others could not, by refusing to submit to the self-righteous *restraint from healing*. He gave health by refusing the "piety" that forbade giving it. Was that what so struck the people around and made them call it the power of God? So might we see the answer sent to John. We might imagine him doubting: Can this seeming disregard of the law, this departure from external piety and restraint, be true? Is Jesus our true deliverer, or must we still look for another? (As much as to say: We thought it had been He; ... but see, He fought so unwisely; He is not only wounded but dead; lost His life in it.)

And so Christ's reply: Tell him how the blind see, the lame walk. . . . The conditions for serving physical health are fulfilled; there is no more duty which means succumbing to disease, no longer any forbidding good. Is not that that which should come? Is there not a light on miracles in this? It is not "power" but "liberty," freedom to use all that is for good, which is the finger of God.

Then how complete is the answer to John: This "license" is fulfilling the conditions of giving health to those who need it. And then, of course, the good news to the poor was of the same kind with the sight and power of walking; not the one physical and the other spiritual. The blind see and the poor hear of a new life and a new right that must mean the ceasing of their distress. (And we see how in losing one we have lost both.)

So again there is a new meaning in the Jews' charge: He casts out devils by Beelzebub, that is, *by wickedness*. And Christ's reply: The kingdom of God—*God's true law*—is come to you. This new state of the heart, this new direction of the regard that gives liberty for good, this is the kingdom of God. (And is not this always the truth with genius? Its miracles—which men call divine and ascribe to power—are *freedom*, the not having restrictions.)

Oh, the hard task imposed on so many, wishing to see their lives and the lives around them *better*, and compelled to strike at their *goodness*, their own as well as others', from Abraham downwards. And all one compulsion, one change. It is a goodness that kills; it hurts others; that is, it is thinking about self.

How plainly Christ's attitude was this: the law that supposes a true regard must be for all; the law that supposes a false regard must not be any more consented to. He saw the time had come for making that change then, at least so far. Now what were the signs of it? Special goodness? Apparent special readiness? (How plainly He said: Let this order be reversed; let the law that is on those with their eye on service be put as *the* law. That reversal is so plain.)

We do not rightly see Christ's life in thinking of it as is usual in respect to its higher goodness. He did not urge and reinforce restraints, but insisted above all on their falling off. His life was an instance of Paul's saying, "to the pure all things are pure." The good He was an example of, which He taught, reinforced, and urged, is that of having the thought true.

This is what Christ said: Not the things you so insist on, but having the heart right. Now we should say: "Yes, the heart right, but the things too." But what did the apostles find but that keeping the things too was absolute hindrance to the other? Their experience is of true use and meaning for us. But, as Christ said, men could not bear that then, not even His own friends. And we see they could not. If He came now, would He not say the very same again: "Not these things you so insist on, but having the heart right?"

"Following . . . *whithersoever He goeth.*" We had not thought it might mean, *to us* also, anything else than where our best thoughts and most cherished aims had taken us. . . . But it is *whithersoever.* And is it really any wonder that there should come the call yet again for going beyond these? And indeed must it not go on being thus —always; again and again? Is not that the nature of our advance?

## PART II.

In Nelson's face how plain is the character: the quietness, the mere receptiveness and yielding, the utter passiveness before Nature; with, latent all the while, ready and ever on the watch, the spring, as of a cat or tiger, the instant action too quick to trace. That latent *spring*, what intentness of eagerness it is! Every emotion kept so still, it does not need restraining; and yet it is a passion of desire at its utmost stretch.

Looking at a portrait of Beethoven, it was evident that his face had in it the face of an animal; it was plainly the face of an animal combined with that of a man. And this reveals genius again. Genius is a cross between animal and man; both are in it; it is an animal combined with a man; its face tells the tale. And is not what it derives from the animal its absence of self-consciousness? In this is a law already known: Nature returns on herself in her advance, and embodies again what has been before.

Does not this join with the articulate and mollusc being both in the vertebrate? And, by the bye, how prettily that raising of the articulate animal to be the nervous system of the mammal is parallel to man's own action. It is the sculptor's part. Nature first makes a clay model of the nervous system, and then reproduces it in her "marble." She makes a model (as it were in clay) and puts into it the instincts, the adaptations; a kind of "working model" it is. These "instincts" of the articulate, are they not the very qualities, the very tendencies or capacities of the human brain? Is not the character of man's "consciousness," its tendencies and capacities and modes of working, to be studied in the insect's "instincts?" And then how this indicates man's perfectness in being one with Nature; here is genius in going closer to her again. It is less different and apart from her than other men.

———— remarks on the large mouth and jaw of a person of marked genius. I think it is true; the gift of genius is simply that it cannot keep Nature—the sensuous element of Nature—out. And that form of the mouth, &c., marks this character more than anything else. Now how pretty it is (if this be so) to see Nature turning our thoughts into a joke. Think what we have imagined about genius; how it has stood as the name of all that is most grand, spiritual, intellectual, elevated, as a quite super-sensuous inspiration, and how we have regarded these things as indicated, and looked for the signs of them in the face; what nobleness of brow, spirituality of form, &c.; and that it should be found in the big mouth and jaw! That is pretty.

F. W. Newman is typical of the absence of genius. To take the good side of him first, how he can't see what is against his sensibilities. In all that pamphlet of his on the great social evil there is not one recognition of any badness in woman, not an idea that the corruption of the world has one atom of its root in her depravity. Of courtesans he speaks as "those simple creatures."

Now this has a certain loveliness. . . . But—if any

danger could be fearful—how fearful it would be for such a hand to be laid on prostitution. What dreadful mischief might ensue. One must not think simplicity like that too beautiful. It is more weakness than goodness.

Then that "purity" which covers with so thick a coating that pamphlet, is it not even loathsome? Here is a remedy for the world's unchastity—to put it into women's heads that to have sexual disorders treated by male physicians is indecent! To commit to unmarried women, merely, all the bleeding heart of whoredom—to that which in all humanity can *sympathise* least with it, can know it least; not to see that the closest, tenderest thing to that, that which could most profoundly and with least violence to its remaining delicacy be its friend, because known by itself to share its own strength and weakness, must be pitiful, married manhood.

Then to have its hope always in repression; evidently not to see that a chastity maintained by fear is as unchaste as harlotry.

And, in fine, that pervading feeling—of which this is but one expression—of a kind of *anatomical* chastity; a feeling as if some physical relations of things were in themselves pure and others impure, which seems to me the most intense and profound of all possible impurities. It is as if his whole feeling were not at all of conditions of the soul, but of the physical problem how to prevent certain relations of certain tangible things—a lowest depth of sensual feeling, than which no lower could be imagined. It is only *loathing* that can express one's feeling for it. It seems as if the only proper answer to it would be deliberately to make a girl, whose purity is something not bodily, a prostitute, and say: See, chastity is a thing of the soul; the bodily act is indifferent—which indeed is, as we see, Nature's and God's reply.

Newman's pamphlet makes one feel glad that prostitution does exist; for it reveals to one that there might be something worse in its place.

And then, besides, he does not see that his proposed remedy is but a giving up: he does not know that what it expresses is not hope, but despair. And, above all, that if his methods all succeeded perfectly, the result would be but impurity crystallised and turned to stone, the last current even of its feeble and perverted life frozen in its veins, and so its last chance of cure for ever lost. The *physical* current might be dammed up, but it would be all there, and the chance of its true removal infinitely far off.

And what a sight were a world so poised between impure desire and fear. When we had it what could we wish done with it but that, as soon as possible, it should cease, and no longer uselessly defile the face of Nature?

This makes me feel afresh that purity must come, not from any thought, or effort, or anything we can do about the sexual passion itself, but from banishing it from thought, letting it sink down into a mere instrument, as it is, of human life; not thinking of *it* at all, but only of its uses. That is the true purity, and it must come.

Is it not a blessing that the false purity does not and cannot exist alone; that with it there is—and must go on to be—mere unrestrained lust and bestiality? If it were otherwise we might be enslaved by it for ever, and never know that it meant foulness.

How beautifully, too, this shows the profound truth of the Christian doctrine: "You can't get good by trying." No; neither can you get pure. We can only be good or pure by *life* coming into us—a true enthusiasm not about ourselves at all. Life is the only thing that purifies.

I get very strongly the impression that Huxley is a man of genius (decidedly of genius) who is not giving himself to the work to which the true bent of his genius would carry him. And therefore (since he grudges his sacrifices) his work has not the true mark of his genius upon it. Surely the true bent of his genius is to metaphysics. (A strong metaphysical element is surely inseparable from genius.) See how he reads it, is evidently fascinated by it, although repudiating it. In giving himself to science does he not give himself to a subject which has less primary interest for him? And so he truly sacrifices his genius; for has his scientific work that stamp of genius it ought to have? I do not see it. If this be true, here is one man of genius sacrificed to the negative doctrine. He cuts himself off from it because he thinks he ought. But genius when it does geniuswork never does that—only because it can't help itself.

Not only is intolerance common to science with theology, but the very same characters seem to show themselves in individuals. We can trace surely the very mental elements which impressed special characters on the forms of the old thought. See Morley, for example, what a stern, rigid Puritan, what tendency to an iron and repressive sway. In his hands into what a hard formula life would have been coerced. He is a Calvin and more. In truth, can we not know the past through the present persons as we never could without? It *was* as our compeers would have made it.

The very same tendencies which we see in different persons operating (tyrannously or otherwise hurtfully) in the old ecclesiastical forms are really visible under science; and are (now at least) even more dangerous, because under the new forms less known, and so less watched against and apprehended as dangerous. The very same evils may come unsuspected in new forms. (Here is a use of history.)

The seeming heartlessness and disbelief in good in some parts of George Eliot affect me with an intense pain; but I think I see the true meaning of it. It is really intellectual and not moral. What irks me is that, well or even perfectly as the individual characters are drawn, there is no unity, no *necessity*, through the whole. The persons stand in a merely arbitrary collocation. It is, in a word, like a "self-rights" picture, and my art-sense is dissatisfied. This mere collocation of people with no visible necessity or reason is not possible to be the truth; it is at most only an observation-true; we want here— the human mind demands it in human life to the full as much as in anything else—a fact that shall make all the " phenomena " to be seen as necessary.

This truth below the mere individual appearances is what we demand. Most likely the very excellence of her delineation makes us feel the want; because she is so true she makes us feel we want another truth. Inferior work, doubtless, obscures this; does not make us feel so strongly that it cannot be the real truth; a false seeming of reason is suffered to come into it, and hides the necessity of a true reason. Now this is but feeling again in a special instance what I have felt so long; that the true work of the dramatist is with *man*—to show men, all men and all their lives, as necessary " phenomena " of the fact of human life. To find the unity which gives that many; the fact which causes all these appearances to appear. This juxtaposition of individuals must be raised out of the region of mere accident, and shown necessary, before the novel can be "true to Nature." Not enough is it to say this man is so and that so; it is even *false*—the falser for its being true to the appearance. The portrayer of human life must say: "Thus this man must have been, and thus the other, and thus they must have been related, and these are the things that must have happened," and this down to the very bottom.

But is there also another reason for this absence of unity and necessity—that is, of meaning—in her presentations of people; namely, that George Eliot does not see *women?* For surely she does not see their complex nature, the opposites united in them. The world in which her women exist is not the world in which we live. Every woman has (at least) two sets of passions, tendencies, sensibilities, impulses; is, in truth, at once a heroine *and* a woman of the world; is at once sensitive to moral, heroic emotions, has a passion for tenderness, devotion, self-disregard to the utmost; and, *with it*, sensitiveness to sensuous prettiness, pleasures, self-centered comforts, splendour, grandeur of material things, a sensitiveness to the delight of unscrupulousness, of unthwarted possession, of absorption of the mind in whatever is her special care, however petty. In every woman are (at least) both these. Whichever rules, the other is there also. Under the most worldly breast lies the heroine; within the most heroic, the worldly thrill. The untemptable Dorothea, for example, does not exist; nor the merely empty Celia. In the true Dorothea a Celia lies hid; and in the true Celia there is shut up the germ of a Dorothea. George Eliot does not see women; she paints them white and black; sweeps up women's qualities into two heaps; all of one set here, all of the other there. It is not the world. Women may practically divide themselves so; choose, or very often have chosen for them, which opposite within them shall rule their life; but it is the novelist's precise business to show us more than this, to make us see the thing that is latent as well as the thing expressed; which last indeed is such as it is because the other is latent.

For by virtue of this very union of opposites within them it is that the actions of women are so marked. The element within them which has the rule given to it rules by that very containing of its opposite with the deeper and fuller dominion. In this again is not woman like genius, the vigour, the absoluteness, coming from the balance? Now if this were fully seen would there begin to dawn more light on the significance of human life? May it be indeed that its darkness *prevents* the seeing, compels the thought to be of some women at least wholly " good," and so clouds all? Till we see the meaning of what we call " badness " how can we put it into our best?

But may it be that women do not know women? It is the man who draws out the hidden things in them; his hand—alone perfectly—unlocks the secret springs within her. Perhaps women never fully see them, and so do not know the oppositeness within each other. Then is this the basis of what truth there is in the saying that women never love each other; are not " friends; " —that they do not truly know each other?

Is it not curious how George Eliot does not see the opposites in women? Is not Maggie Tulliver the only real woman she has ever drawn; and for the very reason that the opposites are in her? And was not she taken from herself? Then does it mean that she does not see looking from without; that her eye, as it were, resolves the complex thing into a part only? Or is this true art, a *revealing* by means of leaving out?

What Nature cannot have for her work is a man who must ever say: "Now I must be good;" who can go with her to a certain point but then must stop and say: "But here goodness forbids." She must have a man to whom that is never necessary. Nor is it difficult; it does not need a wonderful man at all, least of all a good one; only a man with a passion ruling and using all within him, and that is not for himself. Of course this must be so. What she has to teach him is her right and wrong, her good and evil, to teach him a new right. *The* necessity, therefore, is that he should not put up his own. Genius means learning to see a truer right; the demand, therefore, must be that its own feelings of right and wrong, of good and evil, must be wholly put aside, that is, that it must refuse no evil. "He that will lose his life shall save it."

I am sure this feeling is deeply visible in Christ. Not only in His words about losing life, but in this, for instance: "I am not come to call the righteous, but sinners to repentance." Here it stands: "You good people obeying the law, doing your duty, helping society, maintaining order, relieving the distressed, you have your place and work. I do not interfere with you, nor do I propose to make you better. As my nature belongs to another class, so my work is with them. I want them to understand themselves better, to know better their own desires and their meaning. I have a *new law* for them, my own law—Nature's, the only law possible for them or for me. I come to call them to a new thought, a new perception, a new passion. I have good news for them, news that this law (which they cannot obey) they need not, never did need to obey; that *God's* law, for which their very sins have been protests, is quite another." No man, I am sure, ever found himself in possession of a new law who did not turn from the keepers to the breakers of the old one, and find his kinship with them. How should he be ashamed to call them brothers who only do, fearfully, blindly, confusedly, without guide or compass, what he with clear intent and a resolution more reckless than their own, is set to do? They are flesh of his flesh and bone of his bone.

Genius has liberty to obey its impulse; that is the price it has paid. Others can do what it does afterwards, the result and meaning being made clear; it has to do not knowing what will come, not foreseeing, only compelled, driven even to recklessness. So here is a reason that its work remains for ever the greatest and unmatched, namely, because never again in the same thing, is there or can there be the same demand for passion. Others afterwards can do in cool blood; it first, only with passion driven to its utmost, and against a pressure the most intense. Never again *can* there be in that thing the same united passion and pressure, for they depend upon the ignorance, the result being unforeseen. So that first work is the greatest as well as first; not because there is more power in the doer, but because in him *must* be the wilder, intenser passion, and only on him the pressure. So it is the passion only, and not a greater power, makes the greater work;—the passion impossible again in that thing, raised to equal height, because the *pressure* cannot be again.

(Is there any light here on the rising of new grades of organic life? Do they come as genius comes, by the passion and the *pressure* joined?)

Genius is nothing but saying: "You need not abstain from this pleasant thing; it is for service."

In this is given the sign that it is to be; namely, that it does not pursue ease and pleasure. Must not this be the mark of its "early" work—a kind of instinctive abstinence from taking the *allowed* easy and pleasant things (not a putting them formally aside on a theory, or for reasons, or as if for virtue's sake, like "pre-Raphaelitism" seems to be), but a kind of instinctive turning away from them, as from things not desired, a kind of "instinctive asceticism," before the discovery that forbidden ease and pleasure, being for service, may be?

And this gives another suggestion as to the relation of the work of genius. Is there not before it comes (or perhaps can come in any efficient form) a state of license, an accepted ease and pleasure which is *not* for service (as now in our moral life) united with abstinences which are against service? Is there not always a license as well as a restriction against service? Is not that universally characteristic of the condition into which genius-work comes? So the ease and pleasure which genius instinctively rejects is essentially *license;* a pleasure for pleasure's sake and not for service. And so in its work, when most it affirms that this pleasant thing may be, this hard thing and restriction be thrown aside, it always affirms an opposite with it, that this *license* may *not* be; all this pleasure and ease, which has not been taken for service, may not continue. And is not its repudiation of the latter the condition of its freedom for the former?

Now is there not here a key alike to the past and to other things than morals? Has not the interpretation ever set aside easy things taken for pleasure, as well as opened easy ways for service? In thought and in art also, genius with its new freedom also puts aside a license.

Can we see it in Copernicus and in Turner? And is not the history in all cases the same; a restraint first adopted, and, that falling off, a license taking its place;

and by it in part the evils coming whereby the true basis is compelled?

But apart from this, does it not seem as if what distinguished genius is a mere and total absorption in its work that banishes alike pleasure and pain?

For is it not thus: That when pleasure and pain are not perceived, there can be no law; the *law* cannot be perceived; its basis is gone? A man cannot be called on to fulfil a law he does not know and is not conscious of. The law falls off him; and its having fallen off him *is* its falling off the race, off humanity.

And so what a promise this is of infinite good for humanity; it means man's rising wholly above right and wrong, out of the region of the "moral;" his falling into which was his "fall;" and his rising out of which is his only true good.

So is it not wonderful how perfect an echo Christ's words are to those of Genesis? The writer of Genesis says that man's evil is that he came to "know good and evil;" that is, to be subject to questions of right and wrong; and how beautifully Christ repeats and interprets the thought: "To enter into the kingdom of heaven you must become as a little child;" you must escape from having to ask questions of right and wrong; the law must fall off you again.

Is it not simple? First, the knowledge of good and evil is negatively denied; then it comes in the self-form; then it is positively denied.* It is simply the universal law; and so there exist—now as ever in the "theory" stage—the opposites, each with a negative, the self-

* The subject of positive and negative denial is well explained in a paper by Miss Caroline Haddon, called "A Law of Development." J. Haddon, 3 Bouverie Street.—ED.

passion and the self-virtue; and the true good grows up unperceived amid them, ready and destined to absorb into itself the true position of both. We see it already in its germs—the goodness that is one with passion.

To see genius truly, the importance, the absolute bindingness upon all men *then*, of the law it breaks must be seen. If that be lightly thought of—because genius has shown it was no true law—it is mis-seen wholly. Especially is it robbed of its true thanks. For that is its one and only claim to thanks; it does not withhold its *goodness* from the sacrifice; it gives its life. If in that losing it finds it, that is exactly because it gave it utterly, and no thought of finding it again was in its heart. That is its one claim to thanks; it lays itself utterly and wholly down before Nature, and says: Ride over me wholly; be a Juggernaut if thou wilt; here is my neck beneath thy car; ride on. *All* thy billows shall go over me; cast me as a wreck, a corpse, upon the shore; it matters not. Must I die to look upon thy face? Behold, I am as a dead man before thee.

But not to see how terrible that breaking law is which genius does for men, is to rob it of its one claim to thanks. Take that away and nothing remains; for it is not great, it is not good; it has not done much, has not had power to do much; what it seems to do it does by others' power, not its own; it reaps where other men have sown; it owes thanks, not deserves them. But one thing it does for man—and tears and silence should commemorate the gift, not praise, for it could not help it —it gives its life. That is all it does; it says: "Let me be numbered among the transgressors." It is not much; only enough to make men *silent* when they think of it.

How like the earliest ages must have been to the rest! That story of Prometheus is exactly genius. It gives *fire* to man—knowledge and passion—and it *steals* it; it *breaks law* for it. And then—(is it not exact? How plain the groan comes down through all the ages and makes the very words the heart longs for now)—then it is chained to a rock, and a vulture gnaws its heart.

It is all one story: how can there be an exception ever? How can a "solar myth" end but in sunset—sunset and darkness? Oh me, what pathos it is! What made you write that story, O friend of mine, of old? What rock was it to which you were chained down, what vulture gnawed you?

Was it the same whose talons are in me, yet undiscovered through so many centuries? Did you think failure had come, failure for ever, not having the light of all the days since yours to confirm your victory? I wonder what you had seen; of what "art" you gave man the laws. And what laws did you break to do it? And did you know some man would hear your own voice, saying: Pity me, beneath that story, in days more distant than you dreamed of, and would answer back and say: I too have stolen fire for man, and I know the chain, the gnawing? Did you feel sure of this? Was it for his fellowship's sake you said it? Were you weak, too, and full of trembling, and could you not refrain from groans and self-reproach; not knowing rightly which was joy and which was sorrow in your heart? Not knowing, and coming even not to care, which was evil and which was good?

It is because a false right has to be broken that there must be the utter extremity of passion that puts away all rule, all calmness. It is not an action, an effort, but a spasm, a convulsion, of the soul. Nothing less will do; at less price the boon cannot be purchased. It is no use to look back and regret; waste and needless it may seem, but less would not have done; only passion that would not hear, nor see, nor care. All other things might be done with calmness, with tempered energy, with considerate will, with saving of things too precious to be lightly shattered—but not that.

Plain is the story of the Sleeping Beauty; till the time is come she sleeps (Man sleeps; the beloved of God; the bride prepared for her husband); and the bones of lovers who have perished whiten the ground around; and when she is to wake it only happens that another comes, and does not care about the bones; will be another one to die. If he were frightened at the bones he would not be the man; that is all. The question is not whether other men have perished; only whether she is prepared to wake.

So Christ said: "The time cometh, and *now is*, when they that are in the grave shall hear." He did not care for the bones; the time had come for man to hear.

The false law from which genius delivers is always one: You must not do this useful thing, because it is pleasurable. Does it not want delivering from? Or rather does it? Is it not deliverance enough to say it? Can any one say it twice? And that is its freedom and its power to announce to the world its freedom (for it only announces a fact that is), that it desires alike pleasure or pain if it is for its work. That is the secret; that pleasure is free which would be done equally if it were pain. (That is saying it is not for self.)

So genius ever preaches deliverance for the captives, breaking of their chain to them that are bound. It says:

This pleasure you have been selfishly pursuing or self-righteously refusing, this is the true use of things; act for use.

Is not this beautiful and true to Nature, nay, exquisitely like her (who is a woman to her inmost soul), that the secret of the liberty of genius for pleasure is that it is willing to bear pain?

Thus is not genius at once ascetic and indulgent? It foregoes everything not for use; it takes everything that is for use, and cannot care whether it is "sin" or not; it must be willing—and ready though unwilling—even to sin; or it cannot do its work. That is its pain. It must be ready to break the laws it loves (just as to grieve the people that it loves). Its goodness is not in its own hands, but in Nature's; its safety lies simply in the certainty (and only if it be certain) that Nature will not let its desire go beyond the use. It can feel that it is safe, only in so far as it can say: Nature will take me to all that is for my work, and stop me when that ends.

Is not this the incommunicable thing in genius—this putting its goodness out of its own hands, and yet holding to it; this readiness to be bad and yet not being so; this not only *doing* what the bad do in outward form, but being as the bad are in the letting go of goodness; in pursuing something else and letting it take its chance? Yet what is it but having a passion absolutely ruling for something that is not for self? Why should not that be for all? Nay, is not the power of passion that is in the hands of woman pledge of it? Has not love that very character? But is it not wonderful that the character of genius should be in this losing hold on goodness? Is not this that unlikeness to others which fascinates those who are capable of feeling it?

Is this especially its power to move and take captive women? For are they not made to be moved above all by this power of doing rightly what is, in another view, wrong? Is not this emphatically what love and marriage is to them? Is not this above all the thing that has power over their souls—this freedom, true freedom and right, in what also is wrong? Genius is to them as love, another version, as it were, of the same thing. It is like love, only raised to a higher and fuller revelation. It is love itself going into a new region, enlarging life, showing new possibilities; making the future new; darkness and limitation radiant with the glory of the one brightest, surest thing.

And in this do I not see a glimpse into the soul of woman, how it comes to be the intense, tremulous, passion-laden thing it is? To her love is almost what genius is to a man. It is a right that is in the giving up of right; it is the highest and utmost exercise of emotion; it is that grasping of opposites together which makes a thing to be—most intensely be—in its own absence. So one feels how to obtain this capacity in woman. Nature must have sacrificed in her the qualities she possessed in man; they must have been given up for this; and worthily indeed are they given and well repaid. They are all there, still, and more. It is no wonder woman is so keen-eyed, yet so ready for the true breaking of the law whensoever it comes, so delicately poised to the light touch of Nature, so readily responsive (even all the violence to her nature that our life involves cannot utterly banish that); she has that deepest of all experiences of the right that is in giving up the right; the highest law fulfilled in breaking law. That gives her her truth to Nature, her deeper, profounder soul. That is *all* that genius has.

Genius not only can say: My passion does not want restraining; it is bound to go on and say also: And I will not restrain it. How can it abstain from pleasures when they are for good? That is its very gospel: Pleasure is free; passion need not be restrained. It would be false to the *world* if it restrained it.

Is one reason why genius has seemed so hard to be married aright to be found in that utter inversion that takes place in its life? Is it that in its youth it is *ascetic* —truly and sincerely ascetic—and so prefers a mate whose goodness is of that kind; then it turns wholly round and insists on an indulgence unheard of before (for ages at least); and how is the mate (who is by no means bound to make any such change) to understand, or be prepared?

See how women are attracted by genius, are fascinated and absolutely ruled by it. It is the breaking of law, the power to break it, that commands their souls. Even against themselves and what they have counted dearest, how that new liberty compels their whole nature to itself. And surely this reveals them. Is not woman in her own nature the law-breaker? In spite of all her proneness to rigid conventionality and strict adherence to the forms of morals when she is "good," is not the law-breaking deepest in her? In truth, is not that conventionality and strictness of hers a result and sign of this nature, the especial strictness coming exactly because the tendency is so decided to the contrary? (Does it not indeed palpably go with her intellectual constitution as the "guesser," that is, the defier of appearances? Even in the intellectual she is the law-breaker.) And are not the indications of it in her life visible enough? What wantonness of wrong comes up continually among women; and when a man is ready to break a law is there not always a woman ready to help him?

Is there not, then, a wonderful wisdom in that representation of the woman as the first breaker of the law? And is it true in this that it is strictly the desire to be wise that prompts her? Is she not exactly this—the breaker of the law not for self? So is she not closely akin to genius, which is the breaker of law, not for self but emphatically " to be wise "—to *know*?

Is not that history of woman's part in the Fall the very history of genius? And then the consequences, have not they a truth also? From that eating of the forbidden fruit by genius for the sake of knowledge—that man may be as God—there comes continually, not at first the higher life, but evil upon the human race. Man *falls* through it.

What a thought is here! Do I not see it all through history? Is it a destiny upon genius ever from that first breaking of law for knowledge sake in Eden onwards? And is it yet to be—yet, even to the end? But even if it is, it still must come. In no other way can man's life come to him.

How should genius be afraid of evil, or evil beings? How afraid of hell or devils being one of them—the breaker of the law? As the girl with rattlesnake blood in her was not afraid of rattlesnakes, nor could be hurt by them, their blood being in her, so is not the blood of the " bad " in genius, and it cannot be hurt by them? That story is good for genius; genius is as a birth from man " bitten " by Nature.

Would that make a better tale? Genius made as coming from human parents, with an intrusion of the natural powers, and this in the end reclaiming the youth; working in his blood all along, and disordering all his relations; and at length bringing into human life—Nature herself—the force we call inanimate? That is what genius has always done; bringing into human life ever more and more fragments of Nature; bridging the gulf over, till at last the reunion is complete. Genius is the reuniter of man and Nature, and so itself partaker of both natures.

So all in man that feels itself raised up above Nature refuses it and calls it evil; says: "You lower me; it is degradation." It clings to its false rights against it. (And can it be that the thought of Christ's two natures and its reasons is not one with this?)

Then is this incapability of genius being hurt by the "bad" the source of the tales of men whom no passion could hurt? And is there a reference to it in Christ's promise to His disciples that "no deadly thing should harm them?" Was He not speaking of the spiritual in them, the new vision of good and evil? He had given them a new relation to all "crime;" had shown them how to break law, and do all the "bad" did.

Is it not striking that if a painter try ever so much, and have the utmost skill, by no means can his painting ever be exact?

This, by-the-bye, must be one of the things that emancipate genius and enable it even not to think whether it is doing its duty or not, when it yields to Nature's call. Genius does not reason, but must it not feel: "This exactness might perhaps be of value, and necessary to be preserved at every loss, *if it were;* if there could be true real exactness, one might seek absolutely to hold it; but why hold, against Nature's urgent demand, a thing which cannot even be? What is the real good of a thing like this that always has been imperfect, evidently always will be? Why should this be held? What goodness is given up in giving up this?" And how evidently now this is the case in life. What sort of "goodness" is it that would be given up in giving up ours? What likelihood of perfectness, or any decent pretence of it, in that? What good in holding a thing that is not; holding it for something that is not in it, nay, never will be, nor can? In truth, we may see plainly that this is one of the things that determine when the genius-work is done; that it comes at the time when, among other conditions, it has become quite clear, felt, even accepted—however reluctantly and with refusal to accept it—that the goodness aimed at (in this case the restraint-goodness) is, and must be, utterly imperfect, fails and must fail; and the feeling could not be suppressed that it has been valued at a false worth, and being what it is, can hardly be worth the keeping. This is always a mark of the time when the genius-work is done; it is one of the things that enable it to let its goodness go. Secretly, in its heart, it knows it is not goodness, and if it were remonstrated with, and asked, "Will you do that badness?" would it not reply with a bitter smile: "Heaven knows I am bad enough already; that cannot make much difference; at any rate *this* can be done—my badness may be turned to some use." Can one look at Turner's intermediate pictures without seeing that he must have been sick with the palpable failure of his exactness, with its total falling short of being what, to be what he wanted, it should have been? The better it got the more he must have become discontented, and have felt that it did not matter much whether he painted *so* or not; yet all the while trying and aiming, as his work proves.

Is it not a pathetic sight? O Lady Godiva, doubtless you too had felt that the modesty around you, and even your own—most modest though of women—was not *much* worth preserving, nor would ever be. As indeed have not the ages proved, for see what that modesty has consented to? That was a true foreseeing in your eyes which saw that what you gave up was not much to lose, nor ever could be.

I see that by no means could any painter's painting be exact; his trying would be but prolonged failure; his best work need, not praise, but pardon. But when he puts it all aside, and his exactness is implicit, when he no more has to do it, but, *doing it in his heart*, does with his hand something else, then it is, as it were, perfect; all his failure is blotted out. It is just as if his hand was skilful enough, his zeal and toil absolute enough, to do an altogether perfect thing; nay, as if that perfect thing were done. If it had been done, if that power had been in his heart and hand, it would have been just the same; they would still have been put aside, still done only in heart. They are all as if they were there; all is as good, as perfect, as if they were. He is just as if he had gained that power of drawing that he would have given his life for, and knew he never could gain. He is what he never could have made himself, perfect in righteousness. He prays to God: "O God, make my drawing perfect." And God says: "Yes, I will; leave off that and do this." Plainly is not "righteousness imputed to him?" It is all well that the painter cannot do that right which is not the true one; Nature wants the weakness of his hand as well as its strength. Nay, does she not want that very tendency or "natural passion" whereby part of the weakness and imperfection comes, in order to guide her friend and instrument to truth to her?

In all this imperfection of our goodness there is necessity and right; but in the true right it is as if it were perfect; there is no falling short, no failing purpose. What does it mean? Desire the good, have passion for man; that is, surely, to be one with Christ. This is the *faith* He commands—one sympathy, one passion, with Him. Have this "faith," and is not righteousness, perfect righteousness, "imputed?"

How is this a mystery? Could story be written larger or in characters more legible than this imputed righteousness, without works, through faith, is written wheresoever art has placed her brush? These are the plain and simple matters of fact of our life. And indeed if they had not been, should we have cared about them, even as we do now? Would they not have been forgotten, as silly fables, long ago, if they had truly been the things we thought them? Imagination was never more utterly thrown away than that expended in making up another region, and another bearing, for these things. But we regain our possession of them as we learn to see. It is a mistaken thought that because man rushes into vague speculations about things far away, he has had such a tendency towards theology, and clings so strongly to it still. It is because these things are here and now, and never referred to any other things at all, save the fact of these, that man so clings to them. He makes mistakes about them, but the instinct tells that they are the important things. It has only to go to the fact instead of the mere appearance.

I think I see more clearly—even clearly enough, I hope, to make it seen by others—what the difficulty is to genius being understood. Surely it is just this: that every true attaining must come in the form of a losing;

that no *better* can be except in the giving up of the felt good (no fact except in the passing away of a phenomenon); or, in other words, that the true form of being is "being in absence." This must make the difficulty; because genius sees and feels the coming of the new and better, but those to whom it speaks feel that same thing as the wresting away of good; as the contradiction of all that is true and beautiful and sacred. This is its pain. But could not the eye, by a little remembering, be placed on this line? So that it would be always felt or at least understood, that this overthrowing of what is true, or good, or delightful, or refined, is *to it* the coming of a better and completer. So that, though with a certain effort of remembering, it might always be thus recognised and received; always felt that this putting aside was the affirmation of a better; of a good not indeed of that effortful kind, but of one without the self. A better must always come in that form.

So what Nature wants is a breaker of the law. It is written all beforehand. One sees how no kind of goodness, of power, of wish for right, of sensibility to a power of beauty, can do her work save as carrying out the process of unreason to its end, as helping to make the intolerableness of the yoke complete. All these things added on to that false structure, built on that false basis, cannot avail; be they as exquisite, as perfect, as mighty, as magnificent as they may—they are all away from the point. Nay, the best things lead to the worst results; as does the truest logic on false premiss. What Nature must have is a deliverer from the law. That is the universal demand. So how our hearts beat in sympathy with that burst of triumph: " Christ has delivered us from the yoke of the law." It is the voice of universal man in all ages, in every sphere.

Thus, because *seeing*, genius is the rightful breaker of the law. It destroys but fulfils. And (this is the wonder) what it alone at first can rightly do it is sure that all can rightly do also—*and they can* when it has shown them the way.

But, indeed, what a hard task it is that is laid upon genius—to introduce again the doing as we like as the law; and this with its sensibility to right, with necessity of right so laid upon it. Does it not seem hard and cruel? And not only has he to do that, made so hard by the opposite necessity in him, but also he has to do it in spite of the righteous condemnation of the world (and his own surely still more intense repugnance) against that very thing as it has been wrongly done. How little Nature seems to care (but indeed she cares) for the crushing and bruising of that soft body of his against those hard rocks. She forces him against them, surely as she forces a fungus against a paving-stone, knowing that that little life can raise it, and resolving that it shall. But is it not a terrible force alone that can make him do it? Only all Nature surging through him—as it surges through the fungus.

Might not this necessity alone suffice to account for all his weak and wayward impulses?

"Tempted in all points even as we are." It is an attraction, a charm in Him. He knew how the thief, the murderer, the seducer feels; was tempted even as they. So what an easy goodness He brings to them! It is not necessary for them to be different; their passions need not be put away. He does not want them not to be such people. He knows they cannot balance themselves on such a tottering pinnacle of virtue. He knows the thirst, and that it must be quenched. *All* these passions may be; every one dwells in the perfect life; they need not be put away, nor those in whom they are feel any shame for them. All these worst and lowest are welcome, honoured; there is place for them. There is only one call, one duty—the same for all: to have a passion for the good of men. They may keep all that makes them tempted and need not blush; only this is bidden them; only this desire.

It is hard, very hard often, to love persons, persons who are unlovely, repulsive, or merely instinctively repellant to us; that is true. But it is not hard to love *God*, that is, to love humanity. All history proves this easy, man's most natural passion; whatever stands to him for man, that he loves; the clan, the tribe, the nation, the country. Man—God—it never was hard for man to love, and with all the heart and soul and strength, too, it is easy thus to love God; all absorption in any work and labour that does not turn on self is this: it is not hard. Will not the world be different when this is seen as it is? Now this and its fruit are held sin and checked.

Genius seems to have such special instincts; but it is not so at all. It has simply the power of obeying its impulses. Supposing all men but one were gluttonous; either greedily indulging, or equally greedily restraining and regulating; and that one had his thought off his pleasure and ate naturally. He would seem to have a wonderful and unmatched "instinct" for eating; knowing by a kind of special divine endowment exactly what was best. Yet he would simply have the common universal power of man, that which all animals have indeed. (And this bears on the whole moral life also. Man in his true life will possess what all the animals have. And think of genius being so akin to the animals; and of the same appearance in women. Do we not see, as it were, the animals "raised again in glory?") When a man is not a glutton—as soon as he has escaped from having his thought on his pleasure—the "Holy Spirit" comes to him, and "guides him into all truth." Nature acts in him.

It is simply letting the pressure, as it were, have its full effect freely *in all directions*, like the pressure of water, not having a stoppage at one point. Why should there be one there? Why should the force of Nature not have its due, equal effect within as well as without? How plain it is! If there be this stoppage, the very adding of the new matter may be—must be—itself an evil, for it means distortion.

Why should it be difficult when it is understood? It is difficult at first, because it is against the conscience. For the sense of right is one of the things that make that refusal to let the force of Nature operate within as well as without. (So in looking at Nature we see no conscience. And that is true; there is no *self*-conscience. There is life, the free working of Nature all through, with no part that refuses her operation.) But see how the refusal to let what is within move and transform itself mars and distorts everything; how it makes people refuse to see, puts such arbitrary limits on what they can permit themselves to perceive, as well as such arbitrary ways of arranging what they cannot help seeing. That is *the* intellectual distress and unreason.

And what it means is simply that men will not let

themselves *grow*. " No," they say to Nature, " hang on about me what you must and will, and I will' sustain it as best I may, and will believe, in spite of all, that there is a truth and goodness at the bottom deeper than I can see. But put no more within; do not make me grow; keep *life* out of my bosom, life which changes ever, and will let nothing rest. Art thou come to torment me before my time ?"

Is not that eating of the fruit in Eden—the forbidden fruit taken for knowledge sake (why, it is the very history of genius)—the type of all genius-work and of the consequences that come from it ? Does it not ever usher in a fall ? Can human history indeed be interpreted another step by this ? Is man now what he is through such an act as that of genius ? Is that what ever brings the loss of the " anticipation " life of innocence, the " death ?"

See in history what fruit has come of genius-work. We will not speak of the sword Christ brought, and knew He would bring, into the world. But see it all through. See how the drama died with Shakespeare; how the "differential" followed Newton; how art perished, as it were, when it attained its true power; how (as some think) Turner has destroyed English landscape art. Is it true ? Does the next step to the work of genius ever lie through loss and ruin ? And is the meaning of it—best seen perhaps in mathematics, but well, surely, in art also—that what genius does, *with the conditions fulfilled*, the world follows, trying to do, without fulfilling them ?

(But will this be for ever ? When the law is known will it not be different ? May not the genius-work be truly entered into by all ?)

Is not this plain in the calculus ? And in painting I have seen it; seen how when genius is untrue to things because *using* them merely, and so is truest to them, others through it still serve them, but yet are untruthful; losing the one and not attaining the other; neither truly serving nor truly using. Now must this ever be? Or cannot also this result of genius-work in man be had in its effect, and be *so* no more? If it is known that the very thing consists in fulfilling the conditions, will not that bring with it the true receiving of the work of genius, instead of the mere imitating the outside?

So is here the special significance and condition of the solving of the problem of life. Does that demand especially the recognition of this element—the *fulfilling conditions* as the basis of the non-restraint of passion? The ceasing of the restraint is only possible on that condition. And so does it not cast a light upon all the other problems?

The tree of knowledge of good and evil and its eating, might it not be the lament of a savage tribe over its lost innocence? It would answer exactly to what comes, through the missionaries, to such tribes now; in every particular it is the same. The missionary is the serpent: it answers exactly. He teaches them to know good and evil; and by the promise to make them "wise," has things good for food and wisdom to give them; and that fatal gift lies hidden in it. The knowledge of good and evil comes through him. And the women ever receive him first; they are the persons attracted to the missionary ever; and the first sign of the new fatal knowledge is that they become ashamed of nakedness and make themselves clothes, in a fresh sense and with new feelings.

It is clear, the missionaries try to do, and do, for such races the very thing the serpent is described as doing: they give them the feeling of some things as evil and others as good; they teach them a right apart from service, that is, they do introduce acting for themselves. They introduce that which has been a curse among us. May not the future Tahitans, for instance, have precisely such a tradition, and some poet weave it into such a story, and imply a prediction, absolutely true, of the restored Paradise when *service* shall be the absolute law, and knowledge of good and evil be no more, nor nakedness make ashamed?

But then there is a light, too, upon the serpent. We can well understand the South Sea poet looking back and calling the missionary a serpent; he would seem so to him; but we see missionaries are the bearers of a higher knowledge and a better life; and the purest zeal took them forth. May it have been so with that serpent too?

Now this story is evidently the expression of the absolute spiritual truth; it tells the tale of the coming of every truer perception, of every truer life. And yet was it not, so far as man's consciousness extended, the lament of some poet looking back to simpler days, and throwing them into that pathetic story?

The correction of the premiss means an *easier*, as well as a better, way; in the moral life it is the presence of a passion instead of its absence. So, evidently, this was Luther's thought, an easier goodness—a passion. (And it is always called "immoral.") But in the case of the Reformation was it not imperfect? And so we see it never fully triumphing, and now put aside again. What, then, was its imperfection?

Our thoughts of a better are of a harder also, of greater effort, more strength, and subduing of opposing things; we have not had clearly before us the perception that there is a better that is easier too; and yet as we see in the evangelical theology (and in other instances also) it has ever been flashing before man's eyes, and he has been thrilled and overpowered by it, and has consented to almost any theories for the sake of holding it. Shall he not have it perfect? Does everything he is to gain thus come first on him in flashes that he cannot hold? Seen, but lost again, yet leaving an ineffaceable longing in his heart; nay, a conviction that no doubt can obliterate nor thought of duty really overthrow.

The special relation of Christ to the Sabbath is very striking; and yet how evident it is! The Sabbath was the point above all in which service was set aside for "right," that, taken in the letter, expressly and deliberately, as it were, put aside even the question of good to others; that might not even be asked. Now with us the relation to woman stands in the very same special relation. It is as if each had been made for that very purpose. In this sense, more full and complete, how each was made for man, made for the glory of God—His true will, His nature and law—to be revealed. The blind man was blind for that; the trampled-on and destroyed humanity, destroyed now for that.

The Sabbath was expressly adapted to take in self-virtuous people; and even so our feeling respecting fleshly "purity;" it sets a person, who is thinking about *his* being right, against service. And whatsoever sets itself against service ties a noose around its neck, and Nature instantly proceeds to tighten it.

"The sensuous is that which reveals the evil—then the body is the light." Now can we gain a truer glimpse of Christ's real attitude? Look how He put the needs of the body as the expression of God's law, how His eye was upon Nature, and also how theology could not endure Him.

Was His real attitude this of having His eye and

thought always on Nature (that is, on that which we perceive as physical?) That is, was He the man of science of His day and race? Was He the person who accepted the physical, saw in it the light, the guide, the maker-manifest? Was it in defence of that, and of regarding it and accepting God's guidance *in* it, that He said : "Whatever makes manifest"—as this bodily is the thing that does—"is light."* "You mistake when you think there is evil in that because it makes manifest so much evil ; that is its very power and glory ; that is its being light."

So was He a man who had His eye upon the physical, and read God's will in that? And do we see it in the history of Christianity, it alone possessing science? True, Mahometans gained it first, but it perished with them, and is lost. Now Christianity has it, and will it not retain it permanently?

Was Christ looking on the physical as light? Observe, we find in it light for the intellect ; but it is light for the soul also. And must there not come the full recognition that the sensuous is light for the soul—making it manifest by whether it needs to put it away or not—even as the sensible "made manifest" the want in the old Greek thought : there we see it acting as light. Is not this simply a parallel to science, the other half of it, as it were? Light in its two functions makes manifest, and then shows the path.

Surely the "light" must be the things which, if we come to them, bring to consciousness the inward state ; which make manifest whether we are evil or not. (Are not such things now the sight of woman's beauty, and giving needed affection?) Have there not always been *some* things in this relation, visibly and especially so?

---

* The reader may notice that Paul's words are here attributed to Christ. The misquotation scarcely affects the argument.—ED.

Truly *every* thing is a light; for everything that can be done is evil, if done (for self) with the evil within; but some are, as it were, specially singled out by the evil within having made them forbidden; so that they are special revealers. So there were special things of this kind in Christ's time, and of these He spoke. How dared they refuse to come to facts? what could make them but their showing *evil* within? what gives us light but facts? Is not this what we have found in science? So is that coming to the light anything else than the very same thing in life that science is in thought?

"Christ shall give thee light,"—the man who came to facts, who erected them into powers to guide, and so to judge, who bade us refuse to put them aside. So is there not a new light and a new hope? *Coming to facts* is the power in morals. Surely it always has been all through history. May it be traced how morals has been made so (and thus at once a harmony between it and science, the oneness not in the things or results but in the *act*)? The struggle has been ever that men have been excluding or turning from facts, and so making a goodness or right on a different basis. That is, without basis, a goodness which set itself therefore against fact, being necessarily against pleasure, having no other form to take; that being the expression of its emptiness, but this being also the introduction of the power. If we have not seen the real force, can we have the natural hope? Is not life kept evil only by these things being kept away? Men say of the light: "Let it be away and there is no evil." No; none to their feeling.

This is the meaning of theology: it is a reflection of our life for man to judge himself in, and see that he hates it. That is the doctrine of being happier in heaven because of hell; it is the reflection as in a glass of what we *do*, and we see that it is hideous. Man is his own Nathan; and he comes and tells himself his parable, and says: "In heaven it will be so and so." He says what he has done and is doing.

So shall we not find a key here to theology? Does not every age tell its own story to itself, as it were? As these thoughts reflect *our* life, so do the theologic thoughts of every age reflect theirs. And can each—social life and theology—be read by each? It is evident man's thought of God must be a reflection of his own life, as he accepts it and thinks it right.

God speaks in "dreams and visions of the night." The ideas of theology are dreams, fictions merely supposed by man "in the night," but they express the truths of our real experience. They are a fictitious stage, a dream-world, in which the things, feelings, relations which are really in this world are held up as in a vision before us. What has no meaning as expressed in these ideas, because no foundation, is the very key to our life when expressed in terms of reality; read in this very actual world. (It is like another *art* to teach us; so that our life may have light cast on it in every way; every "imagination," false and cruel ones even, are brought into this service.) In dreams and visions, prompted by darkness and possible only in the very sleep of the soul, still God speaks to us; puts before us the very image of our life, and extorts from our own lips a prophecy. *Here* are the heaven and hell: it is a fact, not a fancy, a present fact, not a fancied future, we are speaking of. The dream does its work.

Why that dream of heaven and hell? Open your eyes; the dream has lasted long enough; its purpose is revealed.

The assumption that man is the highest thing in Nature comes so insidiously and unsuspected into our minds. The course of science has rendered it inevitable. It is not that the emotions and powers of man's soul, his aspirations, responses, deeds, experiences, are not exquisitely lovely; but it is the false position they are put in, the false exaltation given them, the exclusiveness—nay, the compulsion to take the negative parts of them as if they were parts of the good. Their false position spoils them; exalting itself it comes to be abased. The beauty and the glory are spoilt by being put on that pedestal of a dead Nature.

What is it when Wesley exclaims: "Let us find our full salvation perfectly complete in Thee," what but: "O Nature, complete our life in being one with you; not any more of our self-doing, but you in us."

So any one who will try the thought of Nature being above man, and man to be filled by her, will find that it gives him the evangelical expressions and thoughts again, all full and complete as the expression of the facts of human life, as the terms science wants to express herself in. And surely that would be a real gladness and feeling of gain to every man, whether he had retained or abandoned his hold of them before. How could it be nothing to reunite thus our own past with man's past; to restore our disunited lives; to have such lustre cast on that which had seemed mere mistake; to reopen an abandoned mine and find it full of a truer wealth than ever had been sought there!

How significantly divided thought is now, how definitely grouped around some insoluble centre! There are four thoughts especially: theism, anti-theism, the disclaiming of any opinion, and the Christian thought—more or less complicated solutions. Does it not mean just one central error, the exaltation of man over Nature as the living? It needs just that touch.

Is it not as a solution, on the verge of crystallising, is full of such tensions?

And looking at our theology—the old theology in which the demands of man's nature expressed themselves —what a spendid thing, how magnificent, it appears! What a rich nature the being must have who expressed it so! Think of it. Its God—to be *its* God—must be a being who comes down from heaven. (It is that very story of Yudhisthira. The Christian theology is this story seriously affirmed; as if when it was thus once expressed the human soul had leapt to it and said: Yes; that is the truth about God.) He comes down from heaven and takes our nature, our sin, our helplessness, and dies for us. This is the God man's nature demands. And surely the loss of all things were less loss than the loss of this. And this thought of God is the key to the universe. Save by it nothing can be seen.

Was it not a loss indeed to change this God for that mere Father who is so well content?

Man can do with one fiction-geometry, but he wants several fiction-theologies.

Is not the position of Christianity now like that of Judaism in the time of Christ? Was that *pressed upon* by the Roman power—the power of fact, of rigid and unbending order, a clear look at this world—even as Christianity is now under the force of science? And did this pressure and hostility produce an effect upon Judaism parallel to that produced upon Christianity now by science?

And in each does it prepare for a newness? (And see what suggestion there is in the very word "pressure." It means *development*. And even through killing, through the very force of destructive influence.)

Can we not understand how the claims to divinity or divine authority have come; that they were never direct and spontaneous claims, things said in and for themselves, but always service-acts? It always came in this way: "If it is true that in order to have a right to do or say these things I must have divine authority, then I have it. I must accept that condition; for these things must be said and done." Is it not always a response to the question: "By what authority doest thou these things?" Thus always it was a practical service-claim, not a theory; never a metaphysical proposition, but an assurance: "God does speak in me, does give me authority to say these things." Monotheism used to mean: "God is one; there are no divine men." And Christ's reply was: "Yes, there are, men in whom you see and hear God."

Is there not seen now a clear vision of the close of this period of strife? Look thus, and is not the destined unity already in view? For there must come reconstruction, positive affirmation in place of that which is to be put aside; and when that comes in such a way as to be a reconstruction in which all the parties that seek to destroy can join, will it not be the very thing which those who seek to maintain have been really seeking to hold—no contradiction, but a mutual confirmation taking in the same elements? For so long as the destruction is merely negative it is impotent; no real force can come of that, no real overthrow; when the reconstruction comes, it must be one in which all who destroy must agree. At present the only distinct reconstruction is the Positivist, but in that so few agree. What is wanted is agreement; not, perhaps, a single opinion, but complementary opinions, the practical presentment of that which man's nature demands.

We want, then, a union of the destructive parties in a reconstruction; that will be their union with—absorption of, if they like—the preserving parties. Till then they are essentially impotent, or beyond a very narrow sphere only impotent for evil—spreading an unearnest scepticism for a time, to be followed in due course by a wave of superstitious earnestness. And it is to this they should direct their efforts, to attain a reconstruction in which they can unite; their work is now among themselves. Christianity is killed as much as it can be killed; it is all corpses or ghosts, killed or unkillable.

Looking at theology as forms prepared and empty, how interesting it is to note that matter and force, the generalisations made up on the scientific side, are also empty; are an algebra expressing relations, but not anything existing. So then we have two sets of empty formulas. It is curious: Science also finds herself, as soon as she begins to try and express universals, compelled to go, even as theology was before her, into unrealities and use mere symbols. And granted she sooner finds it out, yet this is not much, for it is so plain her symbols won't do for the facts. No one could long go on believing in a real matter and force as the substance and power; the ideas of theology gave much more excuse.

But we have now in our possession (thanks to theology and science respectively) two sets of empty formulas. (And we see theology and science thus as parallel, or as of like kinds; as we see sight and touch both as appearance-perceptions; or intellect and emotion both as objectively valid.) One set starts from sensation; the other surely from emotion, and each gives its own set of symbols, expressing relations, but not answering to existence. Here they stand over against each other; the relations given by examining sensation, the relations given by examining emotion. Now, what is to be done with these two sets of symbols thus ranged side by side? Let them be made one, and we have the united relations given by sensation and given by emotion. Here these two stand ready: nothing but relations affirmed on either side.

It is needless, wasteful, to fight again the battle of Christianity; what is wanted is for the non-Christian sects to unite in some positive thing, not an opinion—these as various as we like—but some positive emotional thing which shall be in the place of Christianity; and then all will be done. For that will surely be Christianity itself, that is, the children on each side will find they are one. The one side will say : "That is what we mean," and the other: "We are grateful to you for keeping hold of these things for us."

For this is what has been : Christianity has kept hold of these demands of man's nature, but under such a weight of ignorance. And the anti-Christians come and remove that ignorance; they fulfil the conditions for bringing the fiction-theology to facts. They give it liberty to sacrifice itself. (For this is the universal liberty, the one gospel: You *may* sacrifice yourself; you need not hold your (self) right, your (self) virtue, your perfection that comes by being alone.) They "preach the Gospel" to theology, deliverance to that which is bound.

And this is so interesting : the extreme form of anti-Christianity, that is, atheism, is the form which is of all closest and most akin to it. For atheism, *if it is religious at all*, is emphatically Christian. Its two great affirmations are, and must be, the Christian affirmations, namely: (1.) Look at man for God; (2.) The world is spiritual. So it is these extreme forms that are nearest; they manifestly teach and mean the same—when atheism becomes a religion at all. And it is still more striking if we look more minutely; for it is with the extreme form of Christianity itself that atheism is so closely in contact, namely, with Roman Catholicism. It is the extreme right and the extreme left that touch. (Like the beginning of a new octave: atheism is like the " si " that wants but a step to be the old " do " again; and indeed is but the same, only more intense and twofold; two in one. Is man making now the scales of his life-gamut? It is a discordant process, but it *means* music.) For Roman Catholicism, above all other forms of Christianity, affirms that God is in man, that they are one. Not only in the Incarnation, but in the Pope on earth, and the present inspiration of every priest. And it also affirms that Nature is spiritual. For this is the true meaning of the sacraments; that the physical is spiritual; this is what transubstantiation means: nay, it must be the accepted feeling it expresses (see Newman); it is no contradiction to say a thing is at once physical and the highest spiritual —the very things atheo-religion says. So these two extremes are the points that above all are near.

So that not only should the object be to unite all the anti-Christian sects in a positive religion to substitute for Christianity, but even more definitely should it be to perfect and carry out these extremes—Roman Catholicism on the one hand, atheism on the other, so as to let them unite. Each leaves out something,—cannot each receive?

Might one not almost say (even as Christianity is union

of monotheism and polytheism) that Christianity is a union of theism and atheism? Quite truly it appears so. "He that hath seen *me* (a man) hath seen the Father." As if first there were in Christianity a picture, a kind of symbol, a vision of the whole, but the conditions of its reality not yet fulfilled. Then this symbol becomes divided into two complementary parts—theism and atheism. (And observe: this is simply saying there has been the fluxion process; each element has been bidden to stand aside.) Then if this is so here, and Christianity has been a kind of vision or model of the whole, and then has divided thus into halves, surely this is a universal process in man's experience.

I said that if the anti-Christian sects could agree upon a positive religion it would be one with Christianity, and in a generation all would be joined. But there is another possibility. There might be only more and more antagonism and putting aside, so that Christianity would be swept from the earth and forgotten, and men might go on for centuries trying to understand human life without considering its relations—relations which must be emotional, how to have power to make loss gain and sacrifice a good. And then after long ages it may come that some man would say: Had not the ancients a better way? And he would look and see the Christian way and say: This old method, which our fathers could not grasp completely enough, this is the plan, and we can use it and possess it for ever.

I cannot help thinking this as among other contingencies. See how, just when a new religion—of what promise—was spreading over Europe, and when perchance if the old culture and advancement had remained, it might have grown up more perfect and made a true union, just then the old civilisation was swept away, and new, untamed, untaught, undeveloped hordes came over the whole land, and the religion perished utterly, save what—perhaps mostly evil, at least for it—the new embodied. And so the union was deferred, and long ages passed ere the old Greek culture—which might have made Christianity different from the first—was regained. See that, and then think whether it be not like the same thing now. True, Europe then was overrun by hordes from without, and they are not here now; but there are hordes within as numerous, as untrained, as ignorant, as much untouched by the civilising influences of the time. And observe also, it was a decaying of the old religion, and with it the old enthusiasm and reality of life, that gave the external barbarian hordes the power. And does not the same thing give the internal barbarian hordes the power now? Is there, as the old religion perishes, another overthrow destined to come on Europe, a people sweeping over it to whom its old life will be strange, so that Christianity shall truly pass away even as paganism did, and have a long period ere it be again recalled? Would it not be *just?* Ought this "new religion" of atheism also to come in the self-form first, or may we be wiser for the past and need less delay? (Look at mathematics. Does it not show that the false course *must* be taken?)

The Roman Catholics claim that their religion bids and supports a certain kind of virtue (called by its opponents the ascetic); and that this is the true one. And when we come to consider, is not this strange phenomenon of the uniting together goodness with serving and pleasing self expressly and exclusively a fruit of what is called Protestantism? Does it not in a sense, and as regards what is essentially distinctive of it, consist even in this? So those are really right who refuse to regard it as truly a religion at all. In what it has apart from Catholicism, is it not a *not-religion*?

(But how wonderful that this should have come from Luther's work! Is it not a wonderful instance how genius breaks law, and there comes—*death?* Is the penalty inexorable? From breaking law does there and must there come, even though it be rightly broken, and a false law—death? Is it ever written: "In the day that thou eatest thou shalt die?" Is *death* so precious?)

This is very strange about Protestantism, and worth thinking of. Evidently it is now a negative, not a positive, denial of the ascetic virtue. And in respect to this ascetic Catholic goodness, do we not see in it the legitimate superstructure upon the basis of man's self-being, the truthful issue of the thought that he cannot cast out the self? Very well; let that be considered so; the position of the self in him is fixed, and his morals must be adjusted accordingly; then his goodness must be of that type—the ascetic. The Romanist is completely right; there is no escaping it. So that all Protestantism, all the real moral force in it, is truly (though it is not seen) proof that the self can and will be cast out, that there will no longer be a demand for man's goodness to be ascetic, for virtue to be opposed to use.

So is not this beautiful? This is what Protestantism on its moral side truly means; this is its argument; one which itself repudiates, but in vain. It says that pleasure is free. How can it avoid implying that the conditions for that *can* be fulfilled?

Then there is another thing which is beautiful also—which I have always felt, but in this see still more distinctly: this thought of the casting out of the self and the freedom of pleasure is not opposed to Catholicism, but is truly one with it. It does not (as Protestantism) set itself against it, and put aside the ascetic virtue. It admits it, embodies it to the full, *is* it. In truth it embodies both: "With this basis of life virtue must be ascetic:" "Pleasure is rightly free to man." What contradiction here? It means that that basis of life is destined to pass away.

Both Catholicism and Protestantism aid to maintain that thought; each is one necessary constituent of it. The one says that with the self-basis pleasure is forbidden; the other that pleasure is not forbidden. What more is wanted? The Protestant falsely affirms that, on the basis he allows, so much pleasure as he allows may be. The Romanist denies this; it is not free, and the vitality of his thought proves it. And then if the basis be altered, the lines the Protestant draws also have no basis. The very existence and power of Protestantism prove that the basis can be altered. So that evidently Protestantism is, in this relation, arbitrary; its right is not any right at all: neither on the self-basis, for then it is too free; nor on the not-self basis, for then it is too restricted. There are two rights, and Protestantism misses both.

Any attempt to arrest the progress of disbelief by dogmatic teaching that cannot be demonstrated, and by unanimous consent, must be absolutely mischievous on the one hand, and on the other entirely needless for any desirable purpose.

For (1.) the condition of absolute scepticism has been proved to be one in itself not dangerous to any good; to be perfectly compatible with an exquisite moral life. And (2.) the attempt to teach a non-demonstrable dogmatic religion as a present doctrine must tend to make the scepticism it could not largely avert infinitely more mischievous. For it may easily be felt by all that the failure of the particular forms in which the religious emotions embodied themselves in the remote past, in undeveloped stages of the intellectual life, may have been erroneous, and unable to stand, and yet the sentiment itself and its essential demands be perfectly truthful; but if the best religion which the intellect can even now propose be baseless, it would almost justify—at least it could hardly fail to produce—a sort of absolute and scornful scepticism of the most deadening kind.

And then it seemed to me that the right course to pursue was plain, and promising and good enough entirely to content us; that there is really no danger threatening that need in the least degree alarm us. The absolute sweeping away of all religious doctrine threatens no danger to *religion*, if it be met truthfully and without panic.

Let us accept it freely and fully: no specific statement that has been called religious can stand against the evidence of modern knowledge. What is the meaning of this? Exactly the meaning of that decaying of a seed which makes the life; exactly the meaning of the false astronomy which introduced the perfect. This last surely Eastern races would feel easily. They would see that Europe with its clumsy hand could not help crushing the truth in the very process of completing it. And yet the hand was not clumsy, for it was Nature's; nor does Nature ever touch anything except so; never gives her perfect life to anything save on condition of its first giving it up. All of the seed decays except the plumule, and into that goes the life that was in all the rest, and with it infinitely more. So into that plumule which is the ineradicable religious heart of man goes all the life that was in those cotyledons, the doctrines, the unliving bound up with the living, that by their death more life, a true living union with Nature, may come. The decay furnishes the force that shall institute the new growth. Is it not the manifest fact as well as the inevitable dynamic law? What else can become of the life, the force that was—and is shut up still—in these decaying doctrines, bound close to a reverent and loving heart, but this?

And then this must be true of every case; the "decay" that constitutes the suppression of every anticipation must be in this vital relation to the anticipation; there must be a plumule, as it were, which is all the while drinking up the force of the falling structures.

So the same thing is seen in the development of the moth. When its higher life is coming, what comes first is a great process of decay, a casting-off of that which was part of its very substance, and which no knife could have dissected out without leaving it a shapeless ruin. It casts off part of its very substance and sinks into apparent death. And so it is universally. Every case of anticipation and suppression (that is, everything) teaches the same lesson.

Thus, surely, by fully and happily, because understandingly, facing the fact of the decaying of religious dogma before the forces of Nature—the dying in the kindly ground of science—by fully accepting and loving it (as indeed it should be loved by all who love religion) this very process itself might be made to cherish and strengthen the religion of the heart; to result not in any scepticism, but in the most earnest and faithful, but at the same time rigidly truthful, expectation of, and seeking for, the new forms in which the re-informed and life-swollen sentiment of reverence and faith should manifest itself. We must see that these facts respecting religion prove it instead of casting doubt upon it; that they show it to be exactly in a line with all the other things that are ineradicably based. Whatever thing holds Nature by the hand, or rather dwells in her heart, is fearless of death, and this religion now has proved itself to be.

First comes a living skin; then it dies. The creature could never have put on a dead skin directly; but it forms for itself a skin that is destined to become a dead one. Then the power is exercised upon it; it has gained the condition for its own development. It gains the dying that bears fruit. Thus comes the pressure which raises the life. (Is it that the contracting skin causes that dying of part whereby the higher life of the rest ensues? and may we apply this to the organic sequence? The higher are so often also less.) And in respect to the chrysalis condition, the way it comes is this: the caterpillar forms and finds one skin after another die and throws them off. At last there comes a skin that dies and is not thrown off; the caterpillar goes on wearing it dead.

Now man has formed many religions and found them die, and has thrown them off. But now he has one which, though it is dead, he cannot throw off, but goes on wearing still. (And is not the constraint of its dead contraction strong upon him?) At last he has come to a religion which even when it is dead he cannot but go on wearing. And the reason too is manifest. Formerly when one religion was dead there always came another; probably another ever stood ready; now there is none. We go on wearing our dead Christianity because there comes no new religion. (See the attempts: are there not parallels in the chrysalis, abortive attempts at the formation of a new skin?)

And is not the reason in each case that that form or

mode of life has come to an end ? The force in that form is exhausted, and the thing that is to come is a different life. But that the dead skin cannot be cast off is not so much that another cannot be carried farther in that direction; that mode of life has reached its limits, there is to be no more extension; intension, a more vital life, is to take its place. A different process comes; the mere growth has reached its limit; for the caterpillar *falls* into the butterfly.

Christianity must have been different from ours when it utterly absorbed Stoicism: true. But by its very degradation can we not estimate the work it has done? Granted it has lost its force, its life, what then ? It has imparted it. By what it has *lost* we measure what it has achieved.

And so must we not think also of every religion ? Is not this why every one so decays and tends to be degraded? Is not this its doing its work? Each one comes with a certain power expressed in thought or idea. Then in its work this is lost. But the people are made different and the future begins on a new level.

Buddha looked at human life and saw its misery; *all* misery almost it seemed to him; and he gave a remedy, too; Nirvana—absence of self-desire. It is the remedy now: human life is still misery; still one thought of cure, and only one: absence of self-desire. But what is the difference; what is it three thousand years have done for us? This: that then this absence of self-desire was sought negatively; by putting away, shutting out regard. Have not the long centuries brought us this—enough, an ample fruit—that it must come by a regard made perfect; by a sensibility to all; nothing left less heeded ? (It is simply a passing from the negative to the positive denial of self-desire. And this is the law: Every self-thing is to be positively denied.) Buddha sought to help man, not by aiding individual distress, but by trying to discover how the whole evil state might be remedied; by striving for *knowledge*. He felt that this condition of experience is by a negation; opposite to the present Western notion. So what large *waves* human thought goes in! The whole Western thought is but one element, one phase, with a relation to that. If the thought that this whole condition of ours is by a *minus* (not as we have felt about it as a "creation," a *plus*) comes again, will it not be a union of Asia and Europe?

This also is striking in Buddha: he could not endure the beautiful and delightful things; was repelled by them, found them intolerable. That was the force; he could not enjoy them in the presence of the world; they were hateful.

Then also can we see further about Christianity? Was it not as a germ of the East to fertilise the West; the condition assumed by that great Eastern thought in order to pass over into the West (as it were passing *through* the Semitic race to come back to another branch of the Aryan?), so that it might receive from the West what it had to bestow (being "suppressed" also) in order that it might be brought back perfected?

For it is evident how Christianity in its formal doctrine and ideas that are "above Nature" is the very same as those older and more Eastern thoughts; it is they, yet with a change; and by that change they become able to enter into the West. None of the other forms of the Eastern thought have been able to do so. So we may say that Christ gave to the Eastern thought a form which enabled it to enter into the West.

Buddhism recognises the problem of escaping from the phenomenal condition as a spiritual one. We have lost this (not the New Testament, indeed, which is still Eastern), but the unthinking West has dropped this, with its fancy of getting into the spiritual world by a mere phenomenal change.

(But Buddha did not recognise the unity of man, and that this was a question of *man's* life. And so he had to refer it to the individual alone; and what a task it was! This recognition of *man* is a gain of ours. And do we not see it already in the Old Testament? It is already in our relation to Adam; we see the condition of all resolved into that of the one. So does not Christianity retain this as one of its chief possessions?)

Buddha never thought once of mere dying (a little chemical change, though he did not understand that) as taking one out of the phenomenal. Our feeling of entering the spiritual by "dying" is mere paralysis of reason, contradiction of thought. (Is the idea of a "soul in the body" one whit less absurd than that of angels on pins' points?) In this aspect our reason has been crushed and paralysed till it cannot lift its finger. Here it is striking to see the complementary relation: we are to the spiritual as the ancients were to the physical; unable to give authority to reason. The relation has shifted; they succumbed impotently to unreason when presented to sense, and had no idea it was their place to say to every such unreason: "You cannot *be;* you are irrational;" but they could put aside unreason in the spiritual; as we thus see Buddha did. Now we are exactly in the opposite position: as unable to challenge unreason where they escaped it, as they were to challenge unreason where we escape it. Then here what a basis for union!

In another respect, too, there are opposites prepared for

union: our thought is not of how to escape the phenomenal, but (thinking that must come soon) how to make better—" good "—the life *in* it; this is very marked in this last time; Bacon truly expressed it when he avowed this as the true end of man's labour. Buddha, on the other hand, sought *only* about escaping, not about making it good. Now is there not to be union there of the thought of escaping, and that of making life good also? Is not that the very thought that has been with me? We must have a different consciousness, and yet how good this world; how good to live in it again, and yet again, nay, *as phenomenal*, to lose it never.

Most striking is this contrast between East and West, that the East *assumes* that we cannot get out of the physical by dying; the West *assumes* that of course we do. For it is to be observed that neither argues it at all; each takes it as self-evident. Surely it might be possible to decide which is truest here. And on this does not the whole attitude, the whole spirit, of the thought in great measure depend? And truly seen on which side is the New Testament? May it be that the reason there is such an extreme divergence between its spirit and our life now, is that it is really Eastern and we are Western; that we succumbed to it, so far as even yet to retain its name, but that the oppositeness was never really overcome as, indeed, can it be, except by the union of the Western elements with the Eastern? Christianity had to *incorporate* the West before it could truly rule the human race.

Genius gives up its anticipation first, and then its accuracy of detail; but the first it gives up in tears and sadness, the last in joy. The first is letting pass from sight, the last is emphatically seeing, and the only true seeing. Surely this is sowing in tears and reaping in joy. Is not the seed the strict parallel of the anticipation? Is not the sowing, the burying in the ground, exactly giving up, passing out of sight, becoming the "unconscious constant?" The buried seed is the very type of it. So it becomes the mould into which the forces of Nature are cast; they all assume its form, and reappear with its stamp upon them. Surely this growth and multiplication of the seed is the very fact, seen with the body's eyes, of conscious life in every form.

The seed gives up; it yields before the forces of Nature; they enter into it, just as into the anticipation-work of genius the phenomena of Nature enter, and take possession of it, and seem to put it altogether aside; but the end is, that they reappear *as it*. The seed " comes again in glory," in the harvest. It comes altruistically; made one with Nature, embracing her; truly *it* comes, because no more itself, but other. And in the mind of genius the anticipation has this character—which the seed has —that though it gives up, lets Nature come in and take possession of it wholly, it still holds on; it keeps its life; it grows. Nature does not subvert it and turn it wholly her own way. Almost all gives way and yields, but one little secret part holds on its life, and all the yielding of the rest, and all that is received by yielding, becomes its life. Genius then, like the fruitful seed, has in it that which at once yields and resists. Here, again, its twofoldness appears. And in this it is as the flower again. In the flower there is decomposition and growth, the upward tendency and the downward. In the corolla is the tendency to decay, in the ovary the tendency to growth; the more tendency from being less carried out. The colours of the corolla are really a premature autumn.

The flower unites autumn and spring; it is Nature's hothouse; the decaying corolla produces the warmth which is like a new spring, and forms the seed. The hothouse truly is but a flower of man's making. These two, the yielding and the not-yielding, are also in the seed; it incorporates Nature so; and that is how genius does it too. It casts Nature into its own mould, yielding and resisting at once, but makes her therein the truest to herself.

It is not that the seed (or genius) compels Nature. Nature assumes the form; assumes it because it is her own. To become another, to be altruistic, is ever "natural" to her. It is but a direction of less resistance presented.

Genius gives up its anticipation, its insight, and yet holds fast to it; it has a secret consciousness it must be true, a conviction of it so firm, indeed, that it does not prevent its looking. It sees that its idea won't stand looking, and yet holds to it while it looks. It is so strong in its conviction that it cannot be afraid. Is not this twofold attitude perfectly seen in Newton's reply to the observations which negatived gravity, "that nothing could stand against facts?" There is the immediate giving up, recognising that it did not fit; yet, surely, not less visible, though hidden, the holding fast too. Genius can see that its thought will not do, that the phenomena are opposed to it; but does not feel either that it is false on the one hand, nor indisposed to look his very best at the phenomena on the other; he sees it won't apply, but does not feel that it is therefore false. He looks and looks, more and more; takes Nature's force more and more into him, until it moulds itself at last into that form it seemed to oppose.

But even thus have we arrived really at the bottom of genius? Take genius in intellect proper, in thought.

Does it depend ultimately on *intellectual* qualities at all? Is it not rather on its *personal* constitution; as, for example, on its absolute yielding to its intellectual vision, on the fact that this controls it absolutely, and meets with nothing to oppose it? This is rather a personal than an intellectual characteristic, and may well be by a minus. And surely some personal quality of such a kind is essential to genius. Is it not possible that this is ever a minus? Others cannot yield thus absolutely to the intellectual vision, because they feel other things, and things at least as important, too much. And surely there must be a moral element too, for does it not labour so intensely *before* it sees?

Is it not beautiful thus—seeing genius as the seed—to see how human life has, as it were, its *years:* the stream of living force poured through it with the spring, until in its due course it fails with the declining sun, and sinks into the autumn, " the autumn of our discontent; " then by this very failure the two poles are united, a new spring bound up in winter's bosom, and the harvest is made sure. For the development, the rise to a higher grade, is the very same thing as the multiplication by the seed. So genius also is Nature's hothouse, part of the achieved life sacrificed, as in the decaying elements of the flower, to make more. They make a way for Nature to come in afresh, a new channel for the infinite. Yes, truly, in being as a seed genius is strictly a channel. It is most suggestive that man begins with a negative, ignorance, which has this most striking relation to the truth: simply by virtue of its ignorance it makes that affirmation of the unity of Nature which is the last affirmation of science. Surely this ignorance must be knowledge; knowledge, but not ours; only recognised by us as ignorance giving the false feeling of knowing. This ignorance, which seems a mere absence, has definite relations to knowledge.

Must not our sin, our badness, be the same? It is not the thing it seems to us—though as truly bad and needful to be destroyed, as the sole condition of any good, as ignorance is—but something having definite relations to good, some altruistic good.

That ignorance which makes the truest affirmations is not truly ignorance; and in this must I not come to see how every negative is a true plus? This is the same as that the child's broken line in drawing is not a mere negation of drawing, but has a definite relation to the broken line of the perfect art. The skilled hand must repeat the utterly untrained. Here we ought to see what anticipation is, and what childhood is also. Childhood preceding manhood is not a mere physical necessity as it seems,—of course it cannot be, but here we may see positively a glimpse of the true necessity which causes it. The absence of the powers of manhood has a definite relation to these powers, *is* they in altruistic form. They are powers which are impotencies to us, as the true joy is in pain. May we say that that which is our ignorance and impotence is the true knowing, the true power, just as we say our pain is the true joy? Yes, knowing with ignorance in it is altruistic knowing; joy with pain in it is altruistic joy. The passive necessity is the same; it seems a negative, but it is the positive in some altruistic way. We feel it on the negative side. It is truly the active necessity.

*Man*, too, sows in tears; humanity has the characters of genius, and each may be read by each. Man holds his anticipations while he gives them up. This is the meaning of all that endless fight between the men of progress and the resisters, all the wide and all the narrow men. All that fight is what goes on in genius. It is all there magnified.

Could a summing up of the law be more perfect than this of Beethoven's: "I have had the temerity to introduce a dissonant interval here and there, sometimes leaving it abruptly, sometimes striking it without preparation. I hope this is no high treason, and that the *judices doctissimi*, if ever I meet them in the Elysian fields, will not shake their periwigs at me. I did this to preserve the melody intact, and will be responsible for it before any tribunal of common sense and good taste. Passages that are easy to sing and are not far fetched or difficult to hit cannot be faulty. These severe laws were only imposed upon us to hinder us from writing what the human voice cannot execute; he who takes care not to do this need not fear to shake off such fetters, or at least to make them less galling."

Of course the world shall have its genius-period. That will be the age of the integrated Greek. The Greek, how plainly, was the child; the opposing elements lay unopposing side by side in his mind. So he had that free and sportive life, and enormous because uncramped energy. But it was but the life of the child; and we see the differentiation begin: Plato and Aristotle mark the epoch, and Greek life under the most favourable circumstances could have been the true Greek life no more.

Then came the dark ages, and Christianity swept over the world with its thought of sin and deliverance, and feeling of tremendous moral problems blackening into despair. Just so the youth whose life is not perverted, or heart incapable, grows into a dark and earnest strife with moral questions.

I say the world must have its genius-period—must have; for differentiation exists but for the sake of integration; and that beautiful unconscious life could not have been suppressed except for perfecting.

Man is genius, and his life is the genius-life; he accomplishes ends unforeseen, and does by instinct what he could not do by trying. The method, the conditions, to restore that envied life are plain. It is written in genius.

# THE COMING OF THE LAW.

# `PREFACE.

*I have thought these thoughts in the order and almost in the very words that are here: I cannot alter them; it were a sort of sacrilege to me.*

*People must think of them, and of me, just what they like. My thoughts are these.*

# THE COMING OF THE LAW.

THIS is the fact, that no external thing is or can be right or wrong, but only the action. It is to this that children have to be trained; it is the educator's task. He has to make that "license" safe. That is to be fixed in the human heart; any *thing* may be done; but if I act in any way but one, I am a bad wicked man. I must not do it.

How can this be harder than the other; or why? As we have seen, all things teach it and re-echo it; it has such a perfect basis of reason and unity; it is not subject—as all rightness that is in external things must be—to the sudden question: *Why* is it wrong? often so unanswerable; and so fatal in its asking.

Man making his right to be in *things* instead of action condemns himself absolutely to disorder and to failure. These results are written and embodied in his constitution, taking duty so. The stars in their courses fight against him: his own goodness, his best impulses, that might be fruitfullest of good, determine him to ruin. It is true that if the goodness be recognised in the *action* and not the external thing, men must cease to judge. And surely this holds them as much as anything, or most of all, to that fatal error: that if they give it up the attempt to control men by rewards and punishments must cease, in its present form. Is not this what frightens them, so paralyses them, that in dread of it they cannot see that they passively succumb to, or vainly strive to put down, evils and wrongs boundlessly surpassing what they dread?

But why should this right—in action, not in things—be harder to teach or to enforce upon the conscience than the other? Even take the mere ground of pleasure, and see what motives it has; what reasons to enforce it. It is simply that we are to act not for self, or for the sake of pleasure, but for good and use. Now see the obvious reasons by which this is urged upon us.

First observing two things; namely (1.) that by acting not for pleasure does not mean, not under the stimulus or prompting of pleasure; when the true right is chosen, pleasure becomes the fit and proper prompting and motive-power; it is made free to become so; it means only that the pleasure is not to be the object sought. It is the right motive-power, the wrong *end*. And (2.) that when there is pleasure open to us, and no apparent motive of *use* either for taking or abstaining, then the taking it *is* use; it enriches human life. There is always *right* in taking pleasure—right in form of *use*—if no use forbids.

I say, on the mere ground of pleasure, what reasons there are for adopting that right of action and not of things. It is not that Nature wishes us not to have pleasure, but in order that we may, that she insists on that as our law. See how she has united pleasure and use; making the seeking of use to be, inevitably and in all its main current, the accepting of pleasure too. She has provided for our pleasures. She has not left that for us to do; as if knowing that our very having to do it would be to prevent it. To pursue use *means* pleasure coming. And see what alone can come of not doing it:—these two things; both simply the banishing of pleasure. First, that in pursuing pleasure against use we introduce disorder, prevent pleasure from being, and bring in pain instead; pleasure pursued against use must be its making less. And secondly, by acting for self, we make all pleasures wrong that may not be taken self-wise; we make the best pleasures *forbidden*; we bring down upon us the conscience, which says continually: " For self not that;" we make our own flaming sword, *turning every way*, to cut us off from Paradise. Turn which way we will, we put it with our own hands before our selves; that conscience, armed with the law the self imposes, says: "Not that, not that, not that: that is not right." But if we pursue *use*, see how full Nature fills her lap with pleasures for us. We are like children once again in a garden. Even if Nature had been niggard to us and made the use-bearing pleasures scanty, we could not have mended it by neglecting use for self; we should have incurred the same evils, simply made the little less. But when she has been so bountiful and so joined pleasure to all use, what reason have we, what temptation for setting ourselves against her? Why should we wantonly refuse and spoil?

So wonderful it seems to me, this freedom, this fulness of delight, this boundlessness of pleasure, that is for man when once he opens his eyes to see what Nature calls him to, and on what simple condition—itself the chief joy of all—of regarding use and not himself, of casting off what never was aught but a shackle. Is it not amazing, bewildering with delight? And this is what men have thought of as that impossible thing—the casting out of self. Was ever error more pathetic, more totally mistaken? Did ever a poor child more pitifully delude itself unto despair? And all the while they were saying it could not be,

Nature was showing them that very thing in every man of genius that she made.

*On the Moral Life of Man.*—How complete a new apprehension is wanted; but we can reach only some fragments. The foundation of all is that the only good is in acting not for self; and that the end and meaning of human life is the bringing this to be. So asceticism is the worked out *reductio ad absurdum;* and what has followed is the interpretation. When that was attained there was force enough; the next thing was to apply it to the new beginning, which must have different results, cannot co-exist with the same.

The conservation of force—the equal opposite processes—is the key also to the moral life; especially in the practical aspect; the ceasing of force, that is, of an attained result, being the means of attaining another one. And this, in the moral and intellectual, is essentially correction of the premiss. Should one not begin there? First showing the conservation universal, and then its form in the conscious life. But the correction of the premiss is but one form of it.

Deliverance from thinking of self can come only in the form of giving up restraints from pleasure as pleasure; because these mean thinking of self; and goodness, *in self-serving,* can come only in the form of restraints. So not-regarding self must come in this way. For on self-serving in the pleasure-form the true not-regarding self cannot come at all; only that "goodness" which acting for self makes, namely, the restraint from pleasure, *can* come then; so for not-regarding self we must have these two steps: first, the restraint from pleasure *as plea-*

*sure* (that is, apart from whether it be serviceable or not), and then the giving up of that. Truly it comes, rather, in the form of simply not seeing whether there be pleasure or not; going straight up to the service, however it may come; and only finding out afterwards that it *was* pleasure.

It must be in the giving up restraint from pleasure, because goodness cannot come in any other way while taking pleasure means taking it for self. And yet that restraint means thinking of self. Here is the dilemma—which admits of but one issue.

Art speaks morals so inevitably because it shows Nature demanding, as a condition of the more, the leaving off also, the not doing—the giving up of a thing necessary and right to do, and not to be left off except for the sake of the more. Now this relation shows a *dynamic* process; wherever that is, there is a relation of force; it is force stored up and used. And conversely, wherever there is a dynamic process it will have this character of a more being in, and by a leaving off, force prepared and used. That is what a correcting of the premiss is always.

We may say that wherever *power* is to be used it must be collected first. This is a law we must absolutely recognise; we fancy we can have the effect of power without having stored it, but we cannot. It is a process of moral education, of understanding, that we need. A foolish childish ignorance wants casting out of us; it expects to have power without having first gone through the attaining it. And it expresses itself in the feeling we have (we being as individuals related to *man's* life), that the stored-up power is not to be used, but kept as it is; and then the other thing (which men knew and understood they wanted, and indeed aimed at; and stored up the power for effecting it) this other thing, we find, cannot be done without that stored-up power, and thinking that must be kept as it is, we come to the opinion that it cannot be done at all. It is plain how that thought comes, plain how this special doctrine of ours that man must act for self arises. We are so fascinated by the "nutrition" that we object to the "function." Does it not naturally come from our relation, as individuals, to the life of man? And how plainly is it to be seen in the intellectual life, and by it read in the moral.

Whether acting not for self—that is, doing simply what most wants doing—can be substituted for acting for self in man's life? It can, if he has been so constituted that something is "natural" to him, which his moral nature will forbid his doing if he is acting for himself. If it has not been destined to be, it is not because there was difficulty; it might have been effected in any one of innumerable ways. Only make this relation; that his moral or emotional nature should come to forbid his doing, while acting for self, anything that his physical nature (or any other element of his nature) implied or was constituted for. That would inevitably bring acting not for self. It is clear that it might be so; that this simple adjustment, in any one of a multitude of ways, would bring it. (Truly the argument is much stronger: if we see what acting for self is, it is evident that man's nature *must* imply what his moral nature, while he acts for self, must refuse: that is matter of necessity.)

And then more things are obvious also: the *way* in which the substitution must come. How, in a word, acting for self will lead to asceticism; how the giving up of asceticism will *demand* this very substitution; but that will not come at first; only after a time. At first there will be the attempt to mix the two, to keep the acting for self without the asceticism, and draw lines of what we may and may not do in acting for self. But the only possible end must be the substitution. Now what is there that would mean this? It must come as a correction of the premiss always comes: by a change of the right. The method of it implies that: something our nature tends to, which our moral emotions forbid while we are acting for self, has to be established; so that the acting for self may be put away. The *kind* of change it must be is evident. Now are we thinking as we should, and looking out for this? If we understood the case truly, would the problem seem so hopeless? Consider: acting not for self is a change of the *premiss*, and must have the characters of that: have we thought of this?

And then what would it be? Is it true to think of it as demanding heroic virtue, as too much to be? What has Nature made acting for service to be? What are the relations of service? Taking service as our end *makes* service of all pleasures that do not hurt; that is, that prudence could take. It banishes all question of pleasure, all restraint from it. Then also how God has used human folly to give us the feeling that service, and therefore goodness, is in pain when its natural relations are not so, that we may loose our grasp from pleasure which is the only means of making it free to come.

Then see the "being in effect," especially in its moral forms; the girl's shrinking in the wife's freedom; the youth's hatred of being paid in the man's insistance on his due reward, &c. So man's feeling that goodness is in pain; there will be the effect of that in his life for ever.

Here is the fact now well known (the taking note of this is one of the chief advances of man's thought), that our own pleasure wisely secured, and our doing good or serving, are in the main identical. Now how should this fact be read practically? Which is reading it in its true order, and which backwards: These two are one, therefore pursue your own interests wisely; or: Pursue service; there is no need to act for self? According as we read them one way or the other there exist two wholly opposite rights. We have to choose between them. If we say: Act for self, then we make goodness mean opposing pleasure, and our right necessarily formulates itself in *things*, which will not yield to any call, and must refuse any good. If we say: Act not for self, but for service wholly (which comes to the same as the wisest following of pleasure), then our goodness has no relation to pleasure, no possible opposition to it. Our right is as Nature's, wholly apart from things, and can adapt itself to every call.

If man ceased to make disorder, service and pleasure would correspond. Till then what is wanted for pursuing service is heroism, itself a pleasure (and one that surely would be especially pleasurable now to us, stifled as we are for want of it, it seeming so forbidden, so useless), and a thing that history shows has never been wanting when it has been called for.

Nature's goodness is *living*; it is flexible, adapting itself infinitely to every demand; ours is dead, in so far as it is bound to things. We want a living goodness instead of a dead one. Nature's is an unseen goodness, and so man has thought she had none. We want her goodness; ours raised to the unseen, to be eternal or living.

This is the order of the thoughts: they began practically, with finding that a thing that would be useful was refused on the ground that it would be wrong; and wrong because, though useful, it would be "indulgence of passion," that is, pleasure: and that was because of man's devotion to self. Then from that came the perception: first of how acting for self banishes goodness from all that part of life in which it can find pleasure; and secondly, how it prevents good itself by turning it away from its true grounds into a question of our self-pleasure. But it started from that practical refusal of service because it meant pleasure.

We are at a stage, now, at which, for our *practical* advance in moral respects, a truer understanding is eminently necessary. For it is clear that the understanding as well as the feelings, or will, has a part in man's practical moral condition: this is evident in the case of the individual also; a truer understanding will often serve to deliver from conditions of embarrassment and even of practical though not intentional wrongness, from which there could be no other escape. It is quite possible to happen that even any intenser or more resolute *moral* activity would only make the false action more intense, because what is wanted is a different thought. In the condition of the world a position of this kind has now arrived.

The question is: What shall we aim at? for on that depends what we shall put as wrong, that is, what laws we shall insist on. To alter an aim is to alter a *thought*, not a moral condition: it is a question of seeking, not of attaining: man has practised well, now he needs to aim aright.

Moreover, man's hand *has* relaxed on the aim that he had before him; which indeed is no wonder, for it was not his choice but that of others; of others who lived ages ago, and under conditions very different from ours.

The evils we suffer from are out of proportion to our moral state, or our desire.

The plan of acting for self might do very well perhaps; it is quite true that it does do much good, and brings wonderful results; there is much evidence in favour of its being the plan for man's life, and it is a very natural supposition to us, but we have not noticed one thing—its effect upon right, or goodness.

This result simply proves it unnatural; it is absolute and final: that which does this cannot be man's nature. Acting for self, however it may *look*, is evidently ascetic. Plainly it accounts for all the forms in which asceticism has existed: the fault in them was not the seeking to be good; it was that which made that seeking mean refusing pleasure; the fault and error were not even in the false ideas about this world and another; there is no reason the best way of preparing for another world should be spoiling this; rather every reason against it, as is often urged now. It was not false ideas of that sort made life ascetic, but simply the setting goodness against pleasure: that was the source of the other false ideas which turned men against "this world," as is easy to see. (So, indeed, these false ideas of another world and so on are thoughts projected by a false practice in order to sustain itself; and are revealers of the acting for self. They come out of the goodness put against pleasure.) So if we look into our life and find anything felt right, apart from its direct good, we see an effect of the acting for oneself; an ascetic result. It is absolutely ascetic; it leaves no option but putting away pleasure or goodness; crushing one or the other of our strongest passions: the form of asceticism in the past and now. And it is curious: is it not as if man had been compelled in each period to be ascetic against passion in direct proportion to its strength? Has not the passion against which we are now compelled to be ascetic been distinctly growing in power—namely, the passion for goodness? So that it is against our strongest passion *we* are now made to be ascetic. And in former times was it the converse? were men compelled to be ascetic against pleasure when —and even because—the passion for pleasure was the stronger? Has a change come here; and the asceticism altered its form accordingly? Is it not evident that it is in the very nature of asceticism to choose the strongest passion most to crush? So now are we not ascetic against goodness precisely because that passion is so much the strongest in us? What mistake could have been more superficial than, in the ages ascetic against pleasure, to say that man did not care about pleasure? Yet to say now that men do not care about goodness would be the very same.

Asceticism is putting goodness, needlessly, against pleasure; but man does this without intending it, without even knowing that he does it, thinking he is simply making sure of pleasure. And then when once that step is made he is bound hand and foot till he bethinks himself of retracing it. He cannot help the results: his goodness *is* against his pleasure; he has made it so; he alone can unmake it. And then also: since it is by this effect on goodness that acting for self is proved unnatural, it is evident also that this is the means by which it must be escaped: through this effect on goodness we must find, must seek, our deliverance. And also, it is clear that till then every attempt at making better must be a making worse: life is upside down.

This is *the crime* of man: to think that man cannot

be truly good until another world; for that is accepting and consenting to evil and calling it good; it is not even fighting it, although succumbing; it is joining hands with it.

And to do this is his temptation; for it is Satan coming in the form of an angel of light; the temptation comes in the shape of restriction and restraints of passion; which make us feel as if we were good.

And from this there is one deliverance; the deliverance which alone delivers; and it comes in the form of putting away restrictions; restoring passion unrestrained; with its conditions fulfilled.

Is not a false thought apt to come here: namely, that restraint from pleasure is valuable, and needed, more or less often, in order to gain "strength?" Is not this always a mistake? With acting for self, strength itself is turned to evil; without it nothing, not even weakness, is evil. It cannot be, for we see in genius what weakness without acting for self means. Weakness without acting for self is the true weakness, it is weakness with strength in it; the only true strength also. So there is a false thought in the idea that restraint of passion is ever good for the sake of "strength." Absence of acting for self— true absence, not mere change of its form—is always strength.

In respect to the meaning of excess, as a seeming more pleasure which is less, have we not a key to our senses as instruments of pleasure or pain? For this feeling of what is truly less pleasure as more seems a character of them. The sensation is pleasant, apart from whether it is excess or not.

It seems to be the character of true pleasure that all

the elements in the man are used together and in due relation, sense, reason, emotion. Now, is not this the very same as the character of true knowledge: sense, reason, emotion, all used together? So one is to be known by the other. But in knowledge sense is not crushed or put aside, though *used*, and not ruling. It is most exercised, most abundantly satisfied, filled with its own delights, its powers and tendencies carried out to the utmost; even much more developed and constantly exercised than otherwise it could be. And so in the true goodness with sense as instrument of pleasure: though used and subordinated, will it not be more filled with even its own delights, more exercised, even made more capable of pleasure, than otherwise it could have been? Are, perhaps, pleasure and pain to the senses parallel to truth and error by them? At first there seems to be in both cases more of pain from them and more of error. But in the true use of the senses, the very error is made means of truth; of more truth by far than their own mere truth can give. So in a true life will it not be with their pain? They will be the means of pleasure, more pleasure by far than their direct pleasures. So that in thinking of pain through our senses as evil in any way, we are as if we were thinking of the false perception by them as an evil. Is not the pain simply the preparation for a worthy delight, as the false perceiving is for a worthy truth?

Also we shall see surely how acting for self *makes* pleasure mere excess. For excess is derived by a minus from perfect pleasure.

The right is to do what is wanted; and if there is anything in a person which is a reason he should not do it, that is a wrong in him and he ought to turn it out.

(Then how turn it out? What is the way? Is it not by *doing*—by doing what is wanted because it is wanted? That *is* there not being in him any reason for not doing it.) But, further, it is plain what this wrong is: namely, that it is regarding himself: for only that makes any reason for not doing anything (that is service): only that can make pleasure be against goodness. So again, it is evident how the doing the thing because it is wanted, is the cure: for that is—and that alone—the not regarding self. Not doing it although it is wanted *is* regarding self.

We might go on with self first if it did not affect right: but since it does that we cannot, we must not; for doing that shuts up the kingdom of heaven from half the human race. It keeps others bad: keeps from them even the possibility of being good; for they cannot be good that way. We have no right to forbid them goodness; it is the greatest of crimes; we might break that command of God ourselves and, as it were, "make it up" in some other way; but we must not "teach men so," because it damns them. Those who could only be good with a goodness from which that self first with all its effects—especially its effects of imposing restraint of passion—was cast out must not be forbidden it. If we do forbid it we are accursed, whatever else we do, and Christ will drive us from *His* presence.

The law of service may rule absolutely if it rules alone. I propose therefore a new society on that basis: on the recognition of the fact that service consists (overwhelmingly) in doing pleasant things; that if it be made the law all pleasant things are free; that it is the bringer of pleasant things; that without it in its absolute completeness goodness must be ascetic; and that as a passion for goodness cannot, nor ought to, cease, life cannot otherwise be purged from asceticism; and that for us this is especially important, because, since asceticism cannot be complete, and self-indulgence has established itself, what we have is both self-indulgence and asceticism as well; the two opposite evils combined, and therefore with the worst effects of both; a distorted self-indulgence, and a distorted asceticism, pressing where it should not press.

What remedy is really ever thought of now except the cat-o'-nine-tails? That seems to be the one hope of men. (And they don't see the action there: they don't take account of the rage it makes, the cunning scheming, unsleeping and passionate, it generates in bosoms like mine. They do not take account of the unseen enemies who lie in wait for them.) And if there are any other remedies thought of, how *hard* they are, how intensely difficult; for example, having no more children than a very few; training women so that marriage shall be indifferent, &c. Now why turn to these hard things? Is there not one simple thing that would do the work of them all, teaching children that the right—and only right—was not to act for self? And so introducing, too, a new right; making right mean a different thing.

Here is an *easy* thing which would do altogether instead of all these difficult ones. For why should it be hard to teach that to children? Simply we have not thought of it. If one wants motives, see them here: one or the other we must have; either this, or those other things: which were wisest to try? It is not even necessary to change ourselves: *we* can go on as before; but why hard to teach children, why hard for them to learn? And what too would it mean for us? The difficulty and painfulness of retracing false steps is inevitable; but even so what would it mean, what life would it issue in? And that is attainable, for it is teachable to children.

Man has tried abstaining from indulgence, and it fails: now is there anything else to try? Have we fairly exhausted what might be done? Is going on in the same path the true call of wisdom? Evidently there is fulfilling the conditions of indulgence instead of abstaining: a wholly different task. (But never such changes except by acceptance by a new generation; why do we not seek to bring that?)

It makes the question quite new. And clearly it is simply loving; abstaining from indulgence is not loving; a falsity in our very thoughts is shown here.

And then at once we see why there has been the failure in the other; from a mystery it is turned into perfect reason, order, and good. It was a wrong task; man was never meant to put away indulgence, only to give it a certain form. His failure in trying to do the other is perfectly right and good—even his consenting to it again without the conditions. For this is what our life is: our fathers tried to put away indulgence; we take it without fulfilling the conditions.

Amid all efforts for good, all sacrifices, this one fact stands out, and hides, and ought to hide, everything else: that it is accepted, counted right, as a providence of God, that we should have our life of satisfactions even though others are crushed. This great wrong makes wrong all rightness even, and robs it of its virtue; the regard for others—the maker alive—becomes the destroyer.

But how simple the solution! It wants but a touch; and in the life of the intellect how perfect a guide is given. By overlooking the beginning we make our own problems; and strive vainly in impossible labours when a simple, easy thing solicits us which would put them all away. Instead of all these hard, external motions becoming more irrational with every fresh exercise of reason on them, this little task—seeming so great, so unnatural even, but only try it and see how simple—of accepting our own motion, of putting reason first and letting it determine the very beginning of our thought. So, instead of all these desperate problems, growing more cruel even with each new exercise of love—for the love is compelled to be cruel, since good is made to be restraint—there wants that little one—if it seem great, or hard to Nature, try it and see how simple—of letting regard to others come in from the first, and determine the very beginning of our thought; putting it, as reason is put, where it does not come unless an act of our own make it replace its contrary.

All use of reason (on a false basis) brings more unreason. So in our life all regard to others brings more cruelty. This is because that regard must include also their moral life. This is what necessitates, even to love, the cruelty; and makes it so that we cannot see it is cruel, only it seems so unhappy: even as the unreason could not seem irrational, only that the world was so strangely made. The unreason answers to the cruelty. This simple thing, in each case, is one that we should say could not be, that would seem impossible, until it occurred to try, until things came to such a condition as to make us think: might we not try that?

The greed of our life is worse than that of a schoolboy; it is a thing the schoolboy does not yield to. Therefore it is not "natural." Something must have subjected us to it, some force must have acted on us to produce it. Now what is it?

We seek changes, remedies, improvements, which do not involve any very great change within (as indeed we should be sure to do), but is not a great change what is needed? Then what if there should be some things which involved a great change in us; would not they be likely to be the right things? Two such things there are: all men made able to marry, and marriage not a lottery to women: these would involve service ruling in pleasure; a change how great; absolutely equal to the demand; and yet how simple, even how little; nothing but consenting to what is already our desire, our nature, and yet a whole new life. Here is a true remedy, and a sufficient one, and yet is there any single merely superficial remedy that is not harder?

Why, when one thing is evidently the thing wanted, should we let ourselves remain in the opinion (even though we must have formed it) that that is not to be, and insist on turning our expectation and aim to others. And looking at men and women, is any "goodness" which means that they should go without pleasure likely to prevail? Look at them: is it? Indeed this is the very reason people say the law of service cannot rule, and acting for self be put away. But it is the very reason it can; for that is the only goodness that does not mean putting pleasure away: the other thought is a manifest mistake. Look at them: can there be hope for any goodness that means restraint of passion, foregoing pleasure? Then this goodness that is the freedom of pleasure, the call to indulgence, this is the only goodness that has a chance. Did God make people wrongly; or bid us keep on with a goodness not adapted to them?

But in this seeking of remedies that involve but little change there is a rightness, an instinct that is true. For in fact it is useless to seek things that imply power which does not exist; it is no good to want more than there is for us. The error is in not seeing how much is available; in not seeing that Nature's law is change of form; that things may *cease* and so be in their effect. It is not understanding what the present is; what force it has in it locked up for use. We are as a housekeeper who, having all sorts of provisions hung up, should try to make a dinner with nothing, looking on them as needful adornments of his home; or as a miser who should try to add another farthing to his store, while he might *buy* things that would multiply it tenfold. We do not see the store of force that our life is, that every life must be in every single thing that is restraint and effort.

Even yet it is a new thing, a thing that would change life to say: "The right thing to do is the thing that wants doing." We have thought: "But then people are not able; if they are wrong they cannot do this." And so has come the mistake; we have put up another right that is not right. For the only true right is to become able. That is the thing that is to be sought, and there is no other. So in seeking other things we have sought what we could not get; we have made laws that could not be obeyed, nor ought. For we have consented to *the wrong* (and the only wrong); consented to men being such that they could not do the thing that wants doing. It is this *consenting* to wrong that is the sin; here the crime comes in; and it is indeed the one crime. Being what we are, being as God makes us, as birth determines, there is no "wrong" of ours but consenting to let evil remain and not even take the true right as our right, and make it our law, and count ourselves evil if we did not fulfil it, consenting to leave that law ("Be able to do what wants doing") unobeyed, and yet not counting ourselves wicked: this is the sin. So the good thing in the world is that these false laws have not been obeyed; those who would not keep them have been the deliverers—the people hated, despised, and killed. How differently the "wicked" people, the breakers of the laws, appear at once when we see that the laws ought to have been broken; how humanity expands to take them in. They have a part they seem not to have; our hearts are enlarged at once, and human life is seen more fully in its richness and its promise. The thieves as well as Christ were our deliverers: was Christ indeed ever more truly in His place than when He hung between them?

The things that Nature (or God) demands—and especially in relation to woman—are things that demand acting not for self; that have this as their condition, and cannot be without it. We try instead to put aside those things, and keep the acting for self. That is the fight we are engaged in—God in His servant Nature fighting against our acting for self. It will cease when we choose. And of course it is to be decided "here," it is here especially that the things that demand the decision exist; this world especially is spoilt and rendered intolerable by its refusal.

In two ways we put aside these things that God, in Nature, demands: our virtue and our vice alike are putting them aside; they are two forms of this one thing; putting them aside for indulgence, or self-indulgence; putting them aside for right, or self-righteousness. Here we see well the meaning of the "self;" it is putting aside the things good demands, that service means, refusing God's bidding and Nature's call.

And it is most important to recognise that self-indulgence and self-virtue *are* two forms of the same thing; two forms holding to acting for self (even as mere speculation and the mere observation-true are two forms of ignorance); two forms of putting aside service, they agree infinitely more than they differ; the difference is of form merely, whether pleasure pursued or put away is of no matter; they are two forms of the one act of refusing service. Our feeling them as so different is but part of our slavery to self, which makes pleasure the determiner.

And here how there comes a new meaning into the thought of Nature being "an infinite mystery with nothing in it." In order to be an *infinite* mystery there must also be nothing in it. How this is true of pleasure; it is an infinite mystery, of wonder, of delight, of power; but for it to be so there must be nothing in it. It must be nothing to our action; have no power to determine it. And how especially true of man's relation to woman; to be the infinite mystery it truly is, it must also be nothing. It must have nothing in it, be absolutely unimportant; have no power to prevent service; be any way that good bids. Then what an infinite mystery of joy it may be.

One confusion, easily accounted for, is apt to arise: as if not acting *for* pleasure meant never yielding to impulse, or being moved and guided by delight. At the bottom is the confusion of acting for self with doing pleasant things. When being guided by impulse, and letting pleasure prompt and guide, is the thing that is serviceable to do; the law of service of course means that. We can just as much follow pleasure for service sake as do anything else for it; and why should not service demand that? it might be even always. Shall it not be so in truth when man has fulfilled the conditions of obeying his impulses?

Law is not even against crime; it only demands of it to change its form. Crime can as easily crystallise around law as around anything else, and use it for its purpose. Of course; for it does not say: You must not *hate*; only: You must express your hate in such and such ways. So for the sake of that outside control which we gain by laws how much we sacrifice.

Life is an art with two rights, the right of acting for self, and the right of acting not for self (or the right that turns on pleasure, and the right that turns on need); these are the universal two rights.

And, like all arts, it is created, made to be what it is in its own nature; it gains consciousness of its true law by trying to attain and to keep the first right, doing its utmost for that and having to give it up.

Art has two rights; and genius is simply the bringer in of the second right, the true one. So Christ brought in, not "righteousness," but a "new and better righteousness." This is universal.

The bringing in of a new and better righteousness is the true end; but this is, of course, the putting away of the former. So we see the affinity of this (which is genius) with crime. Crime is one part of it; it is the refusing the former right. It, though failing, though also lacking, has that truer goodness in its keeping. And so is it not plain what folly there is in our thought of crime, and treatment of it? And how fatal it would be if we could prevent or crush it.

The motives for ceasing to make our lives revolve around our own "success," instead of good, are, among others, these:—

(1.) That we need not have any more a pleasure-standard of right.

(2.) That the bodily relation between man and woman would be no more "sensual;" so that there would be no ground for its avoidance, any more than for avoiding fresh air, or flowers.

(3.) That every good thing, such as health of body or mind, might, in every case, be freely followed, and every ill be freely put away.

If good is made to be in control of passion, that is, in pleasure put away, then all pleasure—all that is of force, of Nature's power, in it—is arrayed against goodness, and its prevalence makes goodness less. (It is said: Goodness is in this very struggle and fighting. Is it not the truth, rather, that the thought of goodness being in and through fighting has been imposed on us through that which made goodness mean to us the control of passion?) Thus we see that the power that is in pleasure, and in Nature, so far as pleasure expresses Nature, has fought against goodness, and overthrown it. We see how it overthrew the old enthusiastic goodness; and for ours, how it laughs it to scorn and leaves it as a mocking; like a fungus on a decaying tree. We see how, if we make goodness restraint of pleasure, pleasure fights against it, and how fatally. But if goodness is not in controlling pleasure, but in being able to do all that is wanted, then the power of pleasure is turned the opposite way; not only is its force against goodness gone, but its power goes to aid it; the more pleasure demanded, the more absolute the putting away of the rule of self. Pleasure is become identical with goodness.

Then in respect to life there comes the feeling also that the different starting-point—the *desire* not for self—must be so hard; indeed, impossible. (Of course whether it will be found hard or not—in any sense—will depend really on what it means; if it does not mean more putting away of pleasant things, or more restraint of passion than other rights, of course it will not be harder than they in any sense at all.) But this feeling involves a mistake as to what changing the starting-point really means; it confuses *accepting* a law with *obeying* it—two different things. The change of the starting-point would be the *adoption* of the law of not putting self first; and it would be done in that adoption, apart from all question of how perfectly it was obeyed. The question is of the aim, not of the success. Suppose any amount of failure, still our law is the true law. So changing the starting-point must be easy; it is only a question of aim. Is man, indeed, *ever* to keep the law perfectly? Nay, is there any reason he should? And so of Nature; what we see in her is that she is not under the law we make by regarding self; she is not subject to that law. But is there any evidence there is no "sin" in her, no falling short? May it not well be—and indeed be a key to some things—that there is sin, absence of perfect fulfilment in Nature? But she is under the true law.

The ascetics gratified their souls, but crushed their bodies: now we gratify our bodies but crush our souls. *Life* is to gratify both soul and body; that is, for there to be no reason for the soul to restrain the body, but to be able to let Nature's demand lead us wholly. And so each more perfectly gratified; for neither is truly gratified without the other; it is but a baulking, pretended, half-accomplished thing. Did the ascetics truly gratify their souls? And how far do we truly attain our sense-gratifications? Much as is sacrificed in each case, is the thing sought truly gained? What man has not either firmly to control his impulses, or to reap fruits of chagrin and emptiness in license?

How it simplifies life to have no question to ask but of what is wanted! One question instead of at least two: at once of what is wanted and of what *we* may do; demanding such a balancing of contradictions, that it is no wonder it resolves itself into fixed and rigid rules which are embodied mischief and cruelty—alike in the obeying and in the breaking.

It is not that we regard others too little, or above all that we take too little trouble for them. May it well be indeed that in a true life there will be much less trouble for others, less by far than is taken now? For assuredly, so far as we can see, it would be much better for the "others" that less should be needed. When we reflect, indeed, is not a very great absence of "trouble for others" essential to their welfare being much secured? What is needed is having others first—the desire on the good. How then should the things that make the "trouble" come?

Is there, or is there not, in men now, the readiness absolutely to enter on a new life, the latent force ready to break into flame? We cannot know by looking; it must be judged. Is it not certain, by what has preceded, that it must be?

See the movement in India for social reform: as ever, it is against sensuous indulgences; restrict sense-pleasures, it says, rise above them; now this carried to the utmost we have seen and perceived is not Nature's path: how then should a little bit, if it be so—a little bit not even satisfying the very impulse which calls it into being? Is there not a beautiful thought here, a parallel most clear in the intellectual life? See how there comes, in one stage, a distinct action against sense; it means that the *relation* to sense has been wrong; that is all; not that sense is to have less part, to be less valued, to be put aside, or even permanently reduced and kept under. Not at all that, but intensely the contrary: it is only for the condition to be fulfilled, and sense is to be more than ever; to play a larger part, to be more free, to be constantly called in; nothing that does not agree with it and stand its test is to be accepted. It is not yielded to, but insisted on; it is more, its use, freedom, enjoyment more. The putting it away was means, not end; nor was there any real good until it was wholly and more than wholly restored. Its first presence was an evil; its restoration was the sign of the evil being past. (For the intellect has had to deal with the senses as well as the moral nature: it has had the same problem, and we see how it has dealt with it. How plain the parallel of the perceptive "impression" in the mental life, and the sensuous "pleasure" in the moral.) We will have all those pleasures back that ever were—that were not themselves *less* pleasure—and not steal to them furtively, and with shame and reproach; but insist upon them, even for the sake of rightness. Be slaves to pleasure and you must put it away: know how to use it and it is absolutely free.

This is the proclamation: Good has nothing to do with putting away pleasure. Come in therefore, you pleasure-led people, and claim goodness as your possession. If there is any reason in a man for his putting away pleasure in order to be good, that means evil in him: let him repent. Let him repent and become a new creature.

So it is not that regard to self alone first is any *wrong*, any more than accepting sense-impressions alone first is any wrong; still less that the care of self should be put aside or counted a thing in any way better not to be; it is only that—as sense—by being alone it is itself falsified, and made to be contrary to its own nature. In science it is not good for sense-impressions to be alone; in life it is not good for care of self to be alone. The care of self —the utmost enjoyment of pleasures and energy in securing them—is not acting for self, except by absence of the regard for others. (Even as sense is not illusion, except by absence of the operation of the intellect.) That absence makes the care of self and pleasure to be, against its nature, for self. So what we have to do is to take note of this; to see that we are altering it and making it an evil by this omission; and that that is all. And if it be imagined that it cannot be changed, there is the falsifying of sense by absence of the intellect, alike to show us that it must have been, and that it not only may, but must, cease, and how.

And in the problem of astronomy the moral process is beautifully imaged. There was the sense alone in the absolute assumption of the earth's rest; there the intellect worked on this assumption with immense labour and vast success. And then the question was forced on men: Ought not the intellect to come in *at the beginning*, to have a part in determining our thought respecting the earth's rest? Then these other laborious and most unsatisfactory exercises of it are not necessary.

This is what sets the soul on fire—the union of goodness and pleasure. It is a new possibility, a hope we never saw before, a means whereby all may be brought into goodness. For what is it now that makes the " bad "—those commonly accounted bad, and made to be so—but the hold on them of pleasure? And this is necessarily so while goodness is bound up with notpleasure. But if it be not, then clearly there is no reason for the hold of pleasure to even tend to badness. It is what genius shows: goodness separated from notpleasure, coming down to dwell upon the earth, taking up her abode with pleasure, and with those whose life is in her.

To degrade pleasure is to degrade woman. That is, her nature claims self not first; and her will will come to claim it too. So that, while by her nature always she has been the embodied opposition to the rule of self, by her will, too, she should choose and say: " Let pleasure no more be made worse than pain; for *I* am pleasure. Let self be no more first; that I may no more have to blush because my name is Joy." She was made one with pleasure that she might rescue it. Nothing less than this can she claim when once she sees why pleasure is accounted lower than pain, and what it means to her. It cannot fall short in the end, for she is pleasure, and with pleasure her life is bound up. She must raise pleasure to the perfect height of good, or sink with it. She must say to man: Find how not to have to put away pleasure, or put away me with it. And she carries the secret in her soul; in her body the demand; in her heart the fulfilment. She need not go into far-off regions to find the art; no need to ascend into heaven to bring it down to earth; it is written in her own bosom. The kingdom of heaven—the secret open from the first—is within her.

There is a new goodness: not having reason to put away pleasure. It is but the expression of man's feeling now; his practical deed taking words. It is but saying: Let us have our morals according to our action, and be what we are. Let us see what we are saying by our actions, and come forth and claim our place also in the world; let us have our share in it; not utter the words of other men, which our acts wholly disown; and which therefore while in them they were sublime, in us are merely absurd. Let us, too, have our share in the world, and make it bear the impress also of our life. One can see the reason of our inconsistency, and how it came: but why should it continue?

Man is now *acting* that there is no reason in him for putting away pleasure, but inconsistently, weakly, every way, because his thoughts do not correspond. But they must, and will; one or other must be; either his thoughts will come to correspond with his actions, or his actions will go back to correspond with his thoughts. One or other will certainly be. Either the putting away of pleasure will return, or he will see consciously, and mould all his life accordingly: there must be no reason in me for pleasure being put away.

There is one command: Do not make pleasure worse

than pain; come under God's law, and within possibility of heaven, where all is pleasure. What a splendid thought of man's heaven was: "The time is coming when pleasure shall not be worse to me than pain; when all being better in its absence shall be gone." It is only spoilt by his taking the death of the body to bring it.

In truth the law of man's action is given of course in the becoming instinctive of things first done with effort, this ceasing of the moral is but recognising that law in another region; it could not fail to be there. So now that we consciously carry out a process we have recognised only in physiology before must it not give us a new knowledge?

It is being "automatically" moral. Now do not the automatic processes come by a taking off, or rather a falling off, of the attention from the action, and its fixing wholly on the object? The mechanism having, as it were, been made complete, there comes a restoration of the original (the truly "natural") way of action, without regard or attention except to the object. (This surely is the law of service.) And the time is come when the impulse to recall that first natural mode of action comes; that marks the completion of the process. And here we see a meaning in the law that attention directed to a part or its action modifies it; through this the "completion of the mechanism" is achieved. That is the same as, in the moral, the development of the power by restraint.

Now in the moral it comes thus: we do for others, but first only the not pleasurable thing; this enables us to act for others wholly, not regarding whether pleasure or not. Is there a parallel to this in the organic? Must not the attention directed to the action, in the very fact of it, have an effect equivalent to this, insisting, as it were, on *effort?* This seems quite visible indeed, only that which is effort is perceivable by attention; so "attending" to a bodily action will necessarily have this effect of *keeping in it too much effort*. It is surely perfectly parallel to the moral attending to our actions which keeps them to refusing pleasure. One sees how *effort* is kept in the action by attention directed to it; self-virtue demands to be effortful, and so is disadjusted to the object. And nothing but taking the attention off the action, and letting it fall wholly to the object, can make the effort fall out.

So by attention, causing effort to be (attention answering to the desire for goodness)—that is, restraint—the structure, the life is altered; and then the first natural action is restored. It is simply a correction of the premiss. And here we see again a true "instinct," operating without its conditions being fulfilled; and suppressed to be restored. For the effort stage, the attention is simply the suppression; its characters are given in that.

Now in morals we wish to stay in this effort-stage; we shrink from the becoming automatic, not seeing what it is for, not seeing the new activities which Nature has for us, and for which this is a condition. And, as we see by this reluctance, the very effort itself fails, and the stage of suppression is prolonged till it is utterly undermined, but also made more perfect. But this is what genius is—it is automatically moral. Its attention is taken off its action and fixed on the object, and so the natural impulse is restored. In it we see a thing done with effort become automatic, and how it shows again *man* as "one body." How should the individual elements of a body, if they were conscious, have any direct consciousness of forming one? They could only learn it by witnessing its evidence in the parts they played. It is automatically moral, and that is its power. Then see the promise to man:

a new power, the very power of genius, stands waiting for him. His preparation is achieved; let him but no more make pleasure worse than pain, and all this which has absorbed his power shall be automatic straightway, and the genius-work of man shall be seen.

It is not good for anything to be alone—not even for God Himself. This is what Christ did for men in His day. God stood alone to them (and standing alone is standing in antagonism); He showed them how to have Him no more alone. So we look at the individual alone, and cannot see. The individual relations are of utmost value—they cannot be over-estimated—but to have them alone is not to have them truly. Looking at them alone we cannot understand.

And so, will it not be well when every vestige of the feeling of love being for one *alone* is absorbed and made implicit in a truer feeling? This is the universal error we are prone to. Our having the feeling, so far from proving it true, shows that in this we tend to the same falsity, as in all else—losing the very thing we seek by making it alone. (But it is the necessary suppression, it is the character of the stage when the thought is upon the action). This is visible in art too: the self-rights painting is having things alone. That which we put alone we fail to have. And so does painting show us true thinking also.

And is not the scientific interpretation of nature based on the fact that in her nothing is alone? Always with everything, every law, every force, are present others; nothing is alone, and her life depends on it. Take any force alone—it is death.

And, by the by, does this suggest the difference to us of the organic and inorganic? In the inorganic are forces or processes seemingly alone? But is it not that in the organic we perceive more partially, and see things alone by not perceiving the things that are with them? Is the non-living by a non-perceiving?

Who, looking at the days of decaying Rome, would have thought man capable of such a life as was about to come; of such restraint accepted? Does it seem really one bit more unlikely that he should now be capable of a life that means no restraint of passion?
Then may it not have been the case that at one time the surroundings were such that celibacy was truly the good thing? (Paul seems to imply as much in his judgment.) So that this good meant more restraint of passion. Then did it come to mean less, the surroundings altering so that celibacy was no more good but evil? And so a right with less restraint of passion came: man one step nearer to Nature. And now, by altering of the surroundings yet again, is still less restraint made the good, and man called to be truer to his nature still? Is it a continuous process?

Keep the right order: the change in the woman's relation is the *power;* not the thing aimed at, but the means. The aim is the change in the life, in the very seeing of right and wrong, in the whole choice of good.

The true way to study men—or "character"—the true thought of them, is not, as is supposed and attempted, as of so many positive things co-existing, but inversely to this. It is to study *man*, man as the only existence, as one, and to see the individuals as negations; as forms or modes or presentations of that unity marked by negation, or limits: the "individual" as the *absence.* So to see all as manifestations of humanity, as instruments of it, showing us nothing of themselves, but revealing by their apparent activities the true activity and life of man. I cannot say this as it should be; but I feel it will be done; and then, and not before, there will be some true knowledge and understanding of men.

And here the idea of free-will as a negative belongs again; whatever surely is presented as an "action" of the individual is but appearance: it is not that. That is negation and cannot truly act; the fact is still some act of man's; seen by us as if it were an act of the individual.

To the monks was given the task of working out the problem: "You must not pursue pleasure;" to us the problem: "You must not put pleasure away." How evident it is: this is the problem: "You must neither pursue pleasure, nor put it away; you must deny, not passion, but self." (And self is double-faced.) Of course; pleasure must not determine; what can but what is wanted? Only let pleasure be put aside from determining, and must not service come in and take its place?

Then if man's last task has been to solve the problem: "You must not put pleasure away," how well he has been aided, how adapted the means he has been given. See how exactly suited the culture of science has been, with its inevitable effects, alike upon the intellect and upon the desires. Is there not plain reason that it should have been reserved until this era, an exact adjustment and adaptation in the progress?

Beautiful in this aspect it is to notice how the intellectual and moral progress have been related; the one giving the very conditions for the other. While the conditions for not putting sense away in thought were being fulfilled, the putting away of pleasure was worked out; and when sense was put in its right place then science arose, inevitably, and the moral problem then had changed too and became to learn how not to have to put away pleasure; and science was above all the means: the very instrument had been provided. Has there not been this mutual adaptation all through? Are not the moral relations also those adapted to furnish the conditions for the intellectual process? As visibly the moral dark age gives the very conditions for science.

Then, also, as there has been the perfect adaptation for our moral task, so also was there not for every task before? Were not the very instruments and powers provided also for those who had to put away pursuing pleasure?

Has there not been the very same series of problems for man in his thought-life too? The command on him is here also: You must not follow sense,—you must not (have to) put away sense. (That is, you must receive it freely without being ruled by it. Substitute " pleasure " for " sense," and how plainly the two laws are one.) So the Greeks had the problem: You must not follow "sense;" the "dark ages" the problem: You must not put away sense. And how plainly the last task was the hardest, the cruellest, though leading to the perfect relief; how easy *their* solution when they saw it; how simple their "rule of pleasure and its rightness." Yet how painful to reach it. Their task, as ours, the hardest.

And might we see exact adaptations here also, as in the making ready science for the problem of not putting pleasure away? What helps and instruments and exactly adjusted conditions were there? May we trace these in the corresponding states of moral progress? As, for example, did not the awakening of the religious feelings present the very means by which sense came into the intellectual life, and refused any more to be put away?

Our license of pleasure answers to the ascetics' self-torture. It bears the same relation to the task it has to do. They had to deliver man from following pleasure, and they did it with perverted, mischievous refusal of it; we have to deliver man from the other form of the rule of self, from putting away pleasure, and we also do our part in the like way, in perverted, mischievous pursuit of it. So our license is truly what their asceticism was, the work done but with a negation in it. (They were right to put away pleasures, but they put away the wrong ones with the right; we are right to consent to pleasures, but we consent to the wrong ones with the right. It is one ignorance, one not-seeing, in both; not seeing that the claim of service draws the line; overlooking it and its right to rule, because self was in the eye; that is, because the eye was closed and did not see; because blindness was there.) So our license answers to the old bodily asceticism, is its other side, is a partly false opposition to self-righteousness, as theirs was a partly false opposition to self-indulgence. (And it has been plain before how our license *is* ascetic also; is the very asceticism of our fathers, but carried another step; a soul-asceticism.) Our pleasure-indulgence is as their pleasure-refusal—both are self against others' needs. (And, by the bye, do we not call in Nature as commanding our asceticism, and they called in God as commanding theirs; and both with truth in part; the service part alike of the abstaining and the taking is God's command and Nature's; for these are one.) We have complementary tasks, and these opposites are alike their doing. And so also do not their asceticism and our license have the same history? Both so inconsistent, so constantly breaking down; it is too heavy a tax, too pleasure-destroying and passion-restraining, and the true work is done in its failing.

One can see the parallel farther: the Greeks put away sense (in thought) and followed pleasure; the dark ages succumbed to sense and put away pleasure. The dark ages put away pleasure; this last time succumbs to pleasure. Now the Greek period was short, the dark age long, but may it not be the converse with pleasure; the period of its putting away long, of succumbing to it short? may it not soon end? For it is over when once we see.

And how plain the error too, how natural. There comes a voice from heaven, as it were, to man: "Do not follow sense," and he replies: "No, I will put it infinitely far away." And then the same with pleasure. It did not occur to him to take into account how it affected others. This is the difference of death and life. It seemed to him that of course it must turn on pleasure. That feeling must come from the not-regard to others.

In this course of partial opposites we see how a negation expresses itself. In one sense may we not say that the errors never need have been? Why might not man have had science two thousand years ago? If it had but occurred to him to say: "Why put away sense? why not use it? Our eyes would deceive us if we followed them; but we do not shut them, we find out what truth they mean." Might we not have had science four thousand years ago, if we could but have thought so simply? And so when man found he could not follow pleasure, might he not have said: "Because I cannot *follow* pleasure, why should that mean that I must put it away? Why should we not think of what is good to be, is useful to all, or to others, and do that? Why should our not following pleasure mean our putting it away?

We should follow service." Why should not this have been said when first man found he could not follow pleasure? And so, alike in thought and in life, all the long loss and struggle been escaped? And then again when the body-asceticism fell, and putting away pleasure was banished again, why should not man have thought again of service and made it his guide, instead of throwing himself compassless upon the sea of pleasant things, with no guide to tell him why he must refuse some, and must not refuse others? Why, when life was so fluent, was it let to encase itself in a hard crust again, and still refusing service, refuse it in a double form more intense even than before; so that the law of service, when it comes, must come again with fracture, upheaval, bursting of chains? In the very question is the answer: it is development; this hard crust is the very means of the more perfect life. Man's life needed to become *more* within.

But when we ask why there has been the long progress of loss and strife, instead of man having said respecting pleasure: "Why take such trouble, instead of thinking what is service and doing that?" is not the answer visible? It was done *because it was the trouble;* because man was such that taking trouble must have seemed the good thing to him. That is the fruit of having self first. And here we see the reason of the long and troubled course; of the long wandering in the wilderness even when close to the promised land. It was that having self first that has kept back even man's intellectual progress; things seeming better to him because more troublesome, made to be better by being trouble. So sense was put away instead of used; it was a finer thing for man to rise above it; finer because harder, more laborious. Evidently it was harder, for we see as soon as man relaxed his effort he fell under its power again. And then was shown the evil of having tried putting it away instead of using it; it came in its self-form as a tyrant, degrading, destroying, without the conditions of its coming fulfilled. So that it could come also but partially, and its true use could follow only after struggle, nay, after defeat on man's part, and when the very last strongholds from which he had endeavoured to exclude it could be maintained no more.

Again: the Greeks put away following sense, *and for ever*. Done by them it was done for all—for us. The mere following it could not come back; and though its being forced on man made a dark age, yet mere following it could return no more, and so soon as ever the putting it away was no more possible at all, then the dark age ended, and ended in science. Then there came neither following sense nor putting it aside—that is, using it. The not-following it, done once, was done for ever, and needed no more doing. With the history of Greece before him (and the effect of her intellectual life within too, which doubtless was still more), man *could* not fall again into mere following sense; in the person of his fathers of long ago he had already done that task. And this is even so in respect to pleasure. The ascetics have done for us, in respect to pleasure, what the Greeks did in respect to sense for our fathers. They put away merely following it for ever: no more put away—in spite of all its tyranny in *this* dark age—it is also no more followed; the law of service rules.

Here we see, then, a significance in the revival of classical learning in Europe: did it not bring in the very element wanted, recalling the other "opposite"—the not-following sense? So Copernicus found this very thing in it—sense not followed. And when that was brought back, science came; for *with* it then there was that which it had lacked, sense not put away. So this going back to the ancients was the thing most perfectly adapted for the change that had to come; it united, to sense not put away, sense not followed. And in respect to life is it not visibly the same? The parallel to the revival of the classic literature would be the thought and interest of man returning to the ascetic life. And is it not plainly so? Could any tendency be better marked? And with it goes the interest in the East which has been ascetic from the earliest known times. So here we have the elements; the ancient not-following pleasure coming back with our succumbing to it. The very condition is renewed: our father's work and our own toil and burden together; that is, pleasure not followed *and* not put away; no more ruling and determining our life. What else is possible but service? It means pleasure made servant and used. That is to the soul as science to the thought.

We cannot fight selfishness in that contracted space which is given by putting away pleasure. Attack it and see. It is not even assailed yet; it is consented to, and *because* it means putting away pleasure. That is how it has retained its dominion so long; it has used man's passion for putting away pleasure to shield itself. As if it had said: "What! put away me—put away having the eye on self; it will mean your having more pleasure. How can you do that?"

How intensely the feeling is in us that selfishness means doing what is pleasant is well betrayed by the expressions so constantly used (even in joke sometimes) about selfishness as shown in those whose life is given to what they most like. It is worth considering how this feeling comes; for it is not clear that it always has been so, or was likely to be. Has there been always the confusion in men's minds between selfishness and pleasure that there is now—even in the body-ascetic ages? When there was a distinct *passion* for pain it hardly could have been so. And in Greece before the consciousness had been directed to it, and pleasure simply came naturally, and the eyes were fixed on the relations and uses of things, how could there have been the feeling that pleasure and selfishness went specially together? Shall we not find that truly it is a feeling peculiar to this period? It belongs to the morally dark age, and is one of the powers which make and keep it so; coming with the deliberate taking pleasure for self by the good; making the torture and tension of it; forcing on the human soul the belief that it is condemned to selfishness, which is the black cloud that hangs over modern life. But how it breaks and is gone. Man is *condemned to pleasure;* but that does not mean to selfishness. It means the very contrary: that he must be free. Let him look at those pleasures which are service and take them.

Man in his thought of right in things is left in perpetual wrong. It is a right that refuses claims, and so is at once mischievous and impotent. For that is the character of the false right or law of things—the tradition—always. It is potent to forbid good, impotent to prevent evil; it makes even what were good to be done falsely done, and a thing of mischief. For Nature changes her claims perpetually, and so let man try ever so well, ever so truly, he is still always too late.

And does not this suggest, again, how human life truly seen may be perfect in goodness? Is it not a perpetual attempt to fulfil the law, to obey the claims, and only always too late? But that is no wrong. And the evil and failure, the breaking of the laws, are they not simply the process of the new adaptation? It is still following the claims, only with an interval too long, and with resistance, because man does not know that that *is* the law.

Man cannot fulfil the true claims, for Nature is perpetually changing them, and before he has adjusted his life to any, she has already made them different, so that he is always with his life aiming at a response to a right that was before, the right of fifty or five hundred years ago. And this must be the case so long as he thinks of right in things. He makes particular solutions of his problems, and his problem is ever changing, is another before his solution is gained. What he wants is a universal solution, an *algebra* for the problems of his life; not special solutions, but a universal one. Is not the algebra for life this: Follow claims? An algebra duty, or right (the $x$), means not some special thing, but "claims," a thing with no fixed meaning, to which Nature will affix her own value ever.

The law of traceable service commands away *alike* self-indulgence and self-righteousness: it leaves neither corner for the not-regard to creep into. And by being indifferent to things it lays an absolute command upon the heart; it can be obeyed only in act, in spirit, because no things are available. This power it gets by being not on things; through making them nothing it *is* a spiritual power. If we could have seen beforehand should we not have seen, as evident, that what we needed was to get a law to which things were indifferent; to which, therefore, if any obedience were given, it must be given in act or spirit? We should have seen that our effort to attain things—that is, always certain deeds—was an effort in the wrong direction; one fatal to our own true aim, indeed, our own true wish; that we were *preventing* our law from coming on the soul, keeping away our own deliverance, and that what we needed to bring the power on the act within was exactly the disentangling of the law from things, that it might *demand* some other fulfilling. Is there not in this a light again on " an infinite mystery—or power—with no *thing* in it." By having no *thing* in it any more the law becomes an infinite power.

There is such visible leading of man by Nature, but may there not be a different thought of it? Is it certain that the Being meant by Nature, who leads and trains man, does " know " him, and really foresees what he will do and what is needed for him? Why may it not be that she is as it were inexperienced, and does not wholly understand how he will mistake, how falsely he thinks and feels? May she not be astonished, perhaps, and say: " How could I know that you would be so silly as to cling to a thing when it had become mischievous, simply because, having been service, it had been ' right ' before? How was I to have foreseen you would have fallen into so transparent a mistake as not to know that I *must* change when the need was for change—and that your right had already changed when I had? Did you not know you were to follow me?"

So the command was: " Do not know good and evil; have no rigid rights; in the day you have them you will die." We cannot " know good and evil " in a world that changes; nothing is right, nothing is wrong; all things are right and wrong by turns. (And there is one thing in man's life where the right is rigid and we see that there is nothing comparable to it; we see what comes of it, not only positively but comparatively.) It is when not-regard gets embodied in our sense of *duty*—which is a rigid right turned on self—that it kills.

This is what is amiss with man (and this alone): a not-regard in him, whereby he lays himself under false laws. So things that would be good to be (all of them delights) cannot be. (And he has the feeling that goodness must be against pleasure.) For a chief instance there is that refusal of good—of the sight of beauty—marked so long ago as the very first sign of evil in him. This is what he does: he lays himself under false laws forbidding good to be, at once good and delight; and in this instance too we see its fruits emphatically marked in the intense lustfulness of man's life, due in so great a part to that forbidding; the intense direction of his thoughts to sensuality by means of the very thing he sets up as purity.

This is the one perception that I have gained; that man is not *above* Nature but below her. And it makes all things new. Not that it is a difference of feeling or even of thought in its truest and deepest aspect. It is the same as very many others *would* say, but they are held because they are compelled to think of Nature as if she were truly what she is to our impression; they have not learnt to see clearly, and to feel that the phenomenon is a different thing from the fact. The fact stands there before us, the true relations come, and all is made new. And with it comes a new right, and a new goodness (not only a new earth, but a new heaven too—a new thought of good). Man's goodness, his perfectness, his aim, changes from what it was; the restless struggle sinks to peace; it is no more in being—oh, the hard task, of course only possible to be achieved in "another" world—unlike Nature and above her, but in being simply as she is. The very thought is rest. If any place have been thought of rest, here it is and now.

So one can see that the thought of our goodness being possible only in another world, must have come from our thinking that it must be in being different from Nature. That needs no other source. And thus also it becomes plain what an effect upon man's whole moral life and his religious thought has come from his believing that the phenomenon existed. That has compelled the thought of goodness to be in nonconformity to Nature; that has compelled the thought that it can only really be in "another world." How many other thoughts has not that compelled; how much of our whole moral life and theological opinions have not really their origin in this of the necessity of "another world" before we can be truly good? Might it not have given rise to nearly all? But if our goodness is to be in conformity to Nature, in being according to it, nay, in being simply determined by it, why should it not be here? Here is the very place for it, and why should it be hard?

Not acting for self is nothing but giving due weight to all things; and is it not strange that this should be thought impossible? It is thought possible, held incumbent, that men should do their duty, love God, obey, perform every task of right, but this—a thing so simple, merely duly regarding all—is impossible. When we look, it is evident that what destroys our life (binding on it an accepted rule of self with all it brings; laws that cannot follow good, and which Nature will not enforce), is merely a metaphysical notion; not any moral thing at all, but an idea, a theory about what "self" means, and what acting for it is; the thought that it means some positive power or motive or act, that not doing it would be disregarding something or putting it aside. This *notion* it is that binds us; not desire, not tendency to evil. For even let it be granted there are some, even many, who would not obey the law of service; why should that prevent others from adopting it? The case is the same with the laws we do adopt; many people do not obey them, but break them, and we cannot help it.

It might well be said that among our people there are many of minds so inert and dull they could never be made to understand a law of motive; that the idea of the deed differing with different motives, and there being no right but in that, would be simple confusion to them, and send their moral nature merely to shipwreck. And it might well be that the law of service would demand that while this is so we should all accept a common law, and not some take the better, leaving the others merely in hopeless darkness. This might be perfectly true; but then the true law should be recognised as the true, and aimed at. That would be enough.

Against all these terrible violations of good is there any remedy to be proposed with any real hope of success? I say there is: to restore to service its rightful power by forbidding right or anything in the name of right to trample on it. A limited and maimed authority it cannot even keep: try making it absolute and unbounded. Pronounce it absolute, and clear away all the parasites that have claimed the right to check and limit it. Here is the rightful king; he has been a minor hitherto, and feeble hands have borne the sceptre in his stead. Give him his place and see.

Indulging passion—or obeying impulse—is an art; nay, is it not *the* art? Whenever it exists in an eminent and inborn way it is called genius; that is, the art of indulging passion; of knowing, *or discovering*, impulse. License is not indulgence of passion; it is restraint. That is why it generates its other form—restraint for the sake of goodness. So would not the criminals accept the law of service? It is indulgence of passion. For is it not as certain that *man's* true impulses must answer to human wants, as that the appetite must express the bodily need? But the eye must be off pleasure, as we see in every child. And if it be said: But man is diseased; may it not be said that the having the eye off pleasure is being restored to health?

Let men see that a law of things will not do, and they will see that their task is to be free from the necessity of having one. They will set about that task, to which man has so clear a prompting, but in which he has so often failed, and thinks he has given up. He will discover his powers: he has *grown*. What more constant in a growing man than trying and failing, and finding afterwards that he can do?

Do we not need a sort of adjustment of our thought of man to our thought of the earth? Recognising the enormous sweep of its progressive changes, shall we not learn to have a similar feeling respecting man? We have been much too hasty in our feeling, as if anything like an end had been come to in respect to him. In this respect the feeling given by the thought of his development is a great gain.

It is strange that there should be still on *any* subject a confusion between liking to do a thing and doing it because we like. What comes of it is a law which prevents the most natural of all things from being done—most natural because it gives the freest play to *all* the promptings and impulses of our nature—namely, simply doing the things when they are of good, and leaving them when they are not; going among them, as it were, and gathering the ripe fruits and leaving the rest. In truth, is not the law of service absolutely as this? Men like gathering and eating fruit, but they do not like a sour taste, and they leave the unripe fruit accordingly and take the ripe. Is there "restraint of passion" in eating only ripe fruit? Yet it restrains the passion for gathering fruit and eating it.

Then suppose a law (because men had eaten much unripe fruit and kept on doing it very foolishly) that no fruit should be gathered except on certain days, ripeness not to be considered,—would not a most unnatural eating of unripe fruit be the result? How simply the law of service answers to eating ripe fruit;—*ripe* answering really to all the desires and tendencies. The pleasures that are service are fitted to us in every way. (For how strong man's passion for service is, is visible plainly even now; perhaps even now most plainly.) If man had full liberty to try the contrast, to choose between the pleasures that are service and the pleasures that are not, to look out for that quality as marking fitness, testing and comparing between the two and studying whether its absence did not mean unfitness, would not his choice be certain? But if things that have this quality are forbidden, how can he even know that he ought to make the comparison? (He cannot even ask himself what he likes.)

All this time we have been trying to enforce for ourselves a law Nature *could* not enforce; might we not try the experiment (say only for one century; it is not long) of a law that Nature can enforce, and see if Nature will do it? Can we know till we try? Will not indeed the experimental method—the method of verification—be extended to a larger scale?

This world is a discipline; morals are a training: true. All that can be said of that is accepted. Now the question comes: Is it a discipline and training only for another world; or is it also to have its fruit in this? Is the human race to see and enter into its results *here*, or is it to be only in another state? (This question is almost the same as: Are its results to be only individual, or also to include the race?) Observe that unless the results include the casting out of not-regard, they cannot be of avail for *any* place. While that continues, the work is not done, nor can be; nor can change of place, or condition, avail at all. But if the result be—or include—the casting out of not-regard, then this world is as suitable for it as any can possibly be. Nay, there can be no world not suitable for it, not demanding it; there never can be a world, nor one conceived, in which the casting out of not-regard—becoming true to the fact of it—is not suitable. The fruit of the discipline must be one suitable to be reaped in this world. It may be in another also; but *putting it off* to another is shutting the eyes. And as for the time, and whether it be possible " yet; " observe that it is a correcting of the premiss. Now the time for that is always; seeing it wants doing *is* the time being come. There is no other meaning in the time being come. The whole process that is wanted before it is simply to enable men to see. For only through doing a difficult task can he see;

R

and then the *doing* is bringing in an easier. So when he sees it wants doing all is done. All the labour and toil are for opening the eyes.

Man tries first to have one thing (not-regard indulgence), and he cannot, and then he tries to have a different one (not-regard restraint), and that he cannot also; though he meant the latter for all good, it will not be so. (Indeed, he honestly meant both to be for good.) Thus, for example, in respect to woman: there was the giving so many to that great man, the king, secluding them with such honour in such beautiful palaces, with every sort of delight; what could have seemed more exquisite? Then there was one woman to be strictly to one man; what could have seemed more honourable, beautiful, just, than that? And nothing will do: each is a fresh evil. Whatever *things* he takes all go one course; a course of evil too great to be endured. What does it mean? What but this: that man must have no need to have any *thing;* but be free for all. It means that what that freedom implies must be achieved within him.

There is one thing absolutely universal in man's life: namely, that he has to give up everything that good and right first lead him to. This is his difficulty, ever greater and greater with his growing appreciation of good and right, until it is understood, and then it is over.

In the facts of our life—the needs, the demands of service—Nature provides us with all these things: a *revelation* of God's will; pleasure; and restraint of passion. Through ignoring service (or not regarding facts), man had deprived himself of Nature's provision of these things for him. She has brought them all and spread them out before him, and he, shutting his eyes, has said : " But I must have a revelation ; but I must have pleasure ; but I must restrain my passions." He has had to make up for himself each of them, because refusing them as God placed them before him. Here is service : a call to indulgence of passion, and a restraint on passion, both in one. And man has made up "revelations" which set him against his fellows, and make him think that the value of his revelation is that others have it not ; pursues his own pleasures and cannot trust them to Nature ; insists on a goodness that shall be in restraining passion. This is distrust of Nature. It is *faith* he wants.

Another goodness is at least conceivable ; instead of this " restraint," or doing certain things, to walk straight and simply on with the desire upon service—with a perfect *heart*—so that no question of whether there be pleasure or not need arise. This is conceivable. Why should we not teach it ? How emphatic is the command to teach the children aright!

But here come in two objections ; one that of the Catholics (and those who insist on the ascetic thought of good), that man's nature is corrupt, and needs repression, for the sake of its discipline and internal effect, apart from use ; and the other that of those who say that no enthusiasm of humanity is enough ; that we must be looking to a larger end, and be seeking to serve God and be devoting ourselves to Him, &c.

When man thought of "restraint of passion" as the good, the fault was that he did not go deep enough ; that he said it without seeing the meaning of his own words ; contenting himself with restraint on the *deeds* and leaving the whole true evil unremedied. The evil in our life is that the restraint is not on the *passion*.

Or may it be that the man who first said: Why do not men restrain their passions? did truly mean restraint of passion, and that only afterwards the meaning was lost and restraint on the deeds put instead? When it is said now: Men should restrain their passions, the reply should be: That is the very thing; their *desires* should be right, in order that there may be no restraint upon their deeds.

There are two rights: one that consists in putting away wrongness, the other in using it. We have not seen this in respect to life. There is one right which consists in doing certain things, another which consists in being a certain person. And these two rights do and must exhibit themselves in different deeds; in refusing, and in yielding to, needs. Here our confusion shows itself; we tend to say: Yes, certainly; let us *be* such persons; that is the true right; but still let us do the things. But it cannot be (and here art holds us up); being the person means yielding to the claims. It means having nothing within us that can resist them.

It is not doing certain things, but doing in a certain way. Any "things" can be done in the most different ways; whichever we hold fast to—deeds or way of doing—we necessarily let the other vary. The force being put on the one is not on the other.

Man is trying for a right at once too hard and too poor; too hard for him to attain; too poor for God to give him. A right that need not put away but can *use* wrongness: this is the key to human life also. And the true thought is that the wrongness is *used*, is a power; that it is not merely included, but that its including is the power by which an effect is worked. In the fact of the thing that has to be done being "wrong" (wrong done in one way, and as done before) there is a power exerted on the way of doing. It is wrongness *used*, and made into a power; because, through the demand to include, it demands to be made not wrong. It exerts so a power like a leaven through the whole mass. By the fact of this that has to be included being a wrongness, how everything stands with a fresh relation, a fresh necessity, upon it.

This is the evil: man has directed his efforts at goodness to his deeds and not to his being. So there have been two stages quite plain: an age of effort—the ascetic age; and our age, succeeding it, an age of exhaustion and relaxation. Two stages, both inevitable; both with their advantages as well as with their fundamental wrong; both plainly preparing for a state in which the fundamental wrong shall be escaped; and the latter especially being a visible preparation and approximation to it, especially as it nears its end. And then besides these two stages—showing the effects of the wrong direction of the effort, its mischief, its failure, and the consequent relaxation and inertia—besides these is there not visible also a third state before these; one in which the effort for goodness at all has not in the same way arisen? Then here is a question full of interest: What is the meaning of this effort for goodness, and of its arising? What is there in man that insures its coming? In a word, what *is* it?

Now the effort for goodness being directed to the deeds instead of the being is simply one case of the phenomenal put for the actual. And we see too, how the actual goodness (the goodness of *being*) can only come by regard to others; it cannot be attained by effort. It can only come by a ceasing from effort; as we see in art. And here how plain a light comes on the New Testament writings; on the seeming contradiction, that we are urged so to a true goodness and yet told we cannot attain it by trying; that God must work it within us or it cannot be. Transfer it to the region of art, and how simply it is seen! We should say the very same about every art right. For that is the right to attain to which we are called, which alone is of any true good or of any possible permanence; yet we cannot attain it by effort; it must be " given " us; worked in us without our doing; our attitude must be of receiving. We must be, for it, to Nature, as we are called on to be to God for goodness. There we see "faith;" the saving faith that makes a man a new creature. And what is affirmed is simply that *living* is the universal art, to which all men are called, to which all shall be raised. Here in all art we see the goodness to which men are called, but which also must be given them. Our work is so to ask that we may receive; which is, simply, not to refuse.

There is a falsity in our very thought of selfishness. If we look into it we certainly see that we include in it, in some vague way, the desire for pleasure, the response and reaction of the desire and the powers to that which is the source of pleasure. But this is an intense mistake; this desire and reaction of the feeling towards pleasure is not selfish; it is part of the perfect good, of the true normal power of Nature by which life is. What is needed is that it should be universal. (Again, it is but that the desire for pleasure too comes first in the self-form. It comes as excluding, we want it as not-excluding.) So far from this action towards pleasure being selfishness, selfishness is *its absence;* only the absence of it is selfishness; that is, the want of response or desire for pleasure or for good. The reaction of the feelings to our own pleasure is part of the perfect good; the only evil is in its limit, that is, in its excluding. We want it in a not-excluding form. For, indeed, the whole is this: we need the response of desire for pleasure raised from the form in which it excludes to that in which it does not exclude; simply the universal demand (that which is the fluxion raised from physical to spiritual).

Not-regard is quite a different thing from selfishness; nor is Nature's demand: "Do not be selfish;" but: "Be true to the facts."

My one perception is this, that force must operate according to the nature of force also in the moral world; that the continuous life of man is a dynamic thing.

What I see is simply the dynamic relations in human life. But this is seeing it all as poetry; it *is* poetry. Then is all poetry—that is truly poetry—the same thing essentially, little as it may look like it: the perception, or feeling, rather, of the dynamic relations? (It is this above all that makes diverse things one.) If it were so then it were one with science, which is also the perception of dynamic relations. And science too is one with art; so that all the three thus were one.

The coming of the law of service, how parallel it is to the first introduction of law! The very fact seems to repeat itself. The very same lawlessness exists again, only in another form; the very same open defiance and questioning even of the right of law. The very same chaos has come again, only in a different way. Again the call rises up to heaven for *law;* but for a different law, and one to be established by a different means. Not now by force; or rather by a mightier force than arms.

What a curious circle it is! We find ourselves—having not-regard in us—with a right which means restraint of passion. Then this evidently implies something wrong. (Palpably it is an embodied wrongness; we must have the thought of a truer, better state when right does not mean restraint; and besides, where right means that sin is sure to be; goodness cannot be perfect.) So finding ourselves with this right which visibly implies a wrongness, instead of looking for that which makes the wrongness, and recognising it, and putting it away, seeking a right which does not mean the presence of a wrongness, instead of this, how curiously we say: "*In this world* there is a wrongness; it is inherent in it; it is an evil, inferior world. It is to another world we must look for the true and perfect good." What an inertia of thought it is; and what a worse inertia of the soul it brings, making it consent to rest in wrongness and evil, and look for deliverance from it, not to a new life, to becoming a new creature (with a new *right* therefore), but to a mere passive change, to dying!

Is not here a clear light on morals? If men are not thinking according to the fact there inevitably comes a *reductio ad absurdum,* leading through intellectual and practical mischiefs of every kind, and of utmost degree, to the end that the thought is made true. So if men are feeling falsely—that is, if there is in men an emotional consciousness not corresponding to the fact—there must follow a *reductio ad absurdum*, leading to utmost emotional and practical mischief; and with the end that the feeling is made true. In both cases alike this must be. The false thought or feeling is in individuals, as it were, and the results also, but it is in *man* that the process is worked out. And this is an especial character of it; namely, that there comes a false truth, a false right; truth and right are made to mean what they do not mean. This is an inevitable part of the process; its most distinguishing character; from that indeed come the other characters; at least the evil and hurtful ones. Because having a false truth or right of course brings refusing right; it means a false law, and that means law refused, with all its consequences, every conceivable complexity and extreme of ill. Here then surely we see morals, and all its history: a *reductio ad absurdum* of an emotional state in man not answering to the fact. And as a matter of fact is there not evidence that man does not feel himself the mere individual we have formulated ourselves into? History has something to say on that point. See the feeling which prompted early nations to treat whole bodies or groups as responsible for each member, and to accept it so, to regard it as right. The reason that man breaks laws is that he makes false ones. But is not all done when he knows the true law, that he must always seek a perfect regard? For it is not hard, but joy; no more to make false laws is to obey.

We see how mixing up the idea of pursuing pleasure with that of "selfishness" perplexes us. We say (when, for example, we speak of man's desire for the good of woman, and the oneness of her heart with his): "But man is so selfish." And why? "He is thinking of his own selfish pleasure;" as if these were the same. He may be thinking instead of his own selfish goodness. His selfishness is merely that he is not regarding the welfare of the other. And how does that come? Is he not taught it? Nay, taught it for his goodness? If we ask whence comes this terrible, cruel not-regard, have we far to look? Do we need to take it as a primary thing, capable of no tracing to its cause, and no explaining? In what men have been taught, and led into, is there not a visible reason for its being?

Regard to self first means that certain things must not be done. Now man's plan is to keep regard to self first and put away the things. And Nature comes against it with inexorable demands. It means that he must put away the regard first to self. This is what we see as man's "moral life:" his effort to put regard to self first and put away things; that is, to have a different life from Nature. In the ceasing of this we see simply Nature overcoming man. We want a herald, as it were, from man to Nature; to go out to her with a white flag and bear to her his submission, to tell her that she has conquered, and that the war has ceased. He has tried to poise his life differently from hers—with self first—and to accept its consequences—but he cannot any more. What a pathetic folly is in that distinction he has drawn: Nature! it is mere matter and force, it does not matter what Nature does; but $I$ am a moral being; there are certain things I must never do. "I am a moral being." It means: "I have my eye on myself."

Man's sin is not that he does wicked things; but that he is such that he has to aim at a false right (so that his very aim is kept off the true). And so Nature herself in him works unrighteousness; the natural powers themselves in their action become agents of sin. It is so all through. This is man's crime: that he becomes such, that, having to seek a false right, Nature's very working in him is sin.

So does not this seemingly great and unnatural thing —not having self first—appear in quite a new light? Is not our thought of it itself a twisted or forced one, not the natural idea, but one which is made artificial as it were by our not having seen what it truly is? So that we only get the notion of its being self put aside, or anything to do with self at all, by a curious inverted way of looking at it; that it is simply the feeling of *unity*, almost the strongest and first of all the human instincts or tendencies; that by which, above all others, all science and all art are made; one the baffling and putting aside of which is essentially a state of violence and tension to the feeling of man in all things. So that to think of it as a not having self first— as if it had anything to do with a self, or were the putting aside of a tendency, &c.—is to take the thing up according to an entirely false seeming; the fact being simply that the putting it aside is a thing to which man is always *forced*, and would never do without being forced; that this putting aside of the instinctive feeling of unity and impulse to it *has received the name of acting for self*, being really the putting aside of regard to facts, a closing of the eyes, and checking of an impulse; then this name having been given to the putting aside of the feeling of unity—it having been described by this appearance of a "self" put first—there has come the quite artificial thought as if the simple restoration of that natural feeling, and letting the forced not-regard cease to be, was a great new thing; it has been thought of as a great act of putting self not first; of escaping from the rule of self, &c. It is all a perplexed seeming; there is no "self;" it is simply the feeling of unity that has been put aside returning. And this thought of a banished feeling of unity should take the place in our thoughts altogether of that of self being first; which is merely its appearance to us, and quite a false apprehension.

Man has tried being a "moral being," and we see with what success. To say nothing of anything else, how it divides him into two; sets him against himself, puts strife within his very being, makes him into "good" and "bad," opposing, hating, striving against, each other. (Nay, has taught him to accept it as his very nature to be so; so that he does not even believe any more that he is one at all; a madness has come over him whereby he believes that he is really several quite distinct persons.) Now shall he try instead *not to have to be a moral being?*

So shall he say hereafter: " In the days when I was a moral being this is what it came to: youths of sixteen thought it no shame to use women for lust, and with utter disregard to all besides; and women, even the best, had to rely on that for their purity; and business was a lie; and poor wretches who never had a chance were flogged, and good Christian men drank *souls* in their wine. . . . That was when I tried to be a moral being, and base my life on not-regard; making myself different from Nature, thinking I could poise myself so and not fall. I thought then that I could sustain myself in mid-space and not fall. I did not think that Nature's laws were everywhere. What a strange pitiful sad time it was, when I chose to make my life such that I had to lay on myself laws that did not mean service, and try to do always the same things —but it has borne its fruits."

For observe: To have a life perfectly fulfilling the law of a perfect regard it is not necessary to *know* all things, nor even many things, nor to have the eye at all on all the things that really do need regarding; it is no matter at all of knowledge; it is only necessary to know—or rather to feel—that that *is* the demand, and to obey it in the heart: that is, to be seeking to follow it and ready to respond to every new call that comes into our knowledge. It is only willingness and readiness that are demanded; the obedience is perfect in them.

Pleasure would have been impotent—to any great degree—against human good, if it had not been given it by virtue. See the savage tribes; those still free from superstition. Do we not see how the very thought of one's own pleasure against others' good has not come? It has not *occurred* to them (that is, within their too narrow bounds; for that limit is the negation there). As the man said: "It is not the custom with us to eat when another is hungry." It had not come into his head to do so; the natural relation of the emotions had not been disturbed. (And it is *right* that gives it this disturbance.) Is not this a distinct lesson of savage life?

"Could it be for all?" There is a mistake here: it is the *natural* thing, natural for *all*; just as giving reason rule over sense is natural for all, however it might be impossible for some—even for most—to *begin* it. It is not doing any hard thing; it is simply not having to do hard things; not having right mean labour and restraint; not having unpleasantness made—wantonly and needlessly—to mean being better. (This we see in art: the artist's perception and action is not doing any hard thing; it is simply not having reason for the right being hard things.)

Now when any of us think of pleasure (of recreation) we turn away at once from the thought of useful things. Yet they are pleasure. Now is there not a simple practical thought: would it not be well (to help to save men and women the trouble of finding their own pleasures) to have a list of things that want doing kept and published; so that any one wanting a change might simply have to look over it and see what would please him most to do? Now we cannot find them; but how many there are, and how pleasant to do them. (And might not money easily be raised for supervision or instruction?)

We hear: "The time will come when all will be mutual helpfulness." This is what we must think; a vague hope that, after centuries and centuries, there "will come" mutual helpfulness. It is all we can hope. But instead of this dim far-off dream (unhelpful as it is), we may have it now, if we will insist that *right* shall not put it aside. That is its condition. If we will not let right put mutual helpfulness aside it may come now; so long as right puts it aside it will never come. It will remain a dream until right ceases to bar its coming. Let that cease to withstand and it may be now. We falsely make it a question of time; it is a question of refusing *right* its power to put it aside. We are like the traveller who waited till the river should have flowed past. There will never be any road to mutual help but *across* that river; and we may cross it when we choose. ("The river of death:" how strangely it fits—the river of laying down our goodness. Is not that the true river we must cross to enter Paradise? And here the question comes for us: the river rolls before us and Paradise stands beyond.)

But the thought that the time "will come," instead of seeing what hinders its coming now, is infinitely hurtful to us. It keeps us from seeing the real wrongs, the real banishers of helping, and fixes our eyes on false ones, on merely fancied ones even that do not exist. It is our *good* lives, our beautiful Christian homes, our duties so well fulfilled, that keep the evil, not mean greed and selfishness; these are not the causes. We fight against them fruitlessly. They *are* not, and even if they were, they would not cause the evil. Our efforts are worse than wasted while turned against imaginary evils; we are kept from seeing our true hindrances.

We cannot tell what man "likes" to do by what he does (at any one time); and now he is not doing what he likes. It is not beautiful for some to be finely dressed while others are in rags; it can seem so only by shutting up the eyes of the mind and the soul; and men do not really find it beautiful or like it. Man is a being, whose joy, whose liking, is really determined by his mind, and not by his sense. Is not that what is claimed as his distinction?

It is not that we should not have pleasures, but that we have not fulfilled the conditions of having them. (It is more and more striking to me how constant this demand is for fulfilling conditions in everything.) And so we cannot have them enough; not wide, deep, free, unchecked enough. We can have them in multitudes indeed, but how marred they are and limited; and how spoilt by that painful shutting of the eyes they demand.

Let us fulfil the conditions of having pleasure; those that we can have without are not enough.

We have to recognise the difference between acting *from* impulse, and acting *for* pleasure. To have confused them is very curious; for not only do they most evidently not coincide, but in truth they are mutually exclusive. (And impulse is essentially unreflective; but *for pleasure* is as much reflective as for pain.)

The change is so simple; merely, instead of right being one thing always, that it should be one way of doing all things. ("All things one way," instead of "One thing all ways.")

Why should it disturb or grieve any one to have it proposed that we should make this exchange of putting the way of doing in place of the things? Why pain or grieve any one to think whether these two changes might not come together: a new way of doing all through, and the things the other way made to be forbidden no more put aside; and so the power given us for another and farther use. True, it grieved and angered the Jews, two thousand years ago, even to killing, to have it suggested to them that the true man should be like Nature, a child of the wind, having nothing forbidden to him, and that this was what was for all. It was probable enough that it should so rouse and pain the Jews then. But why us, two thousand years after, and having learnt so much? Why pain any one now that man's life should be restored to being one with Nature, his motive so absolutely assured that his deed would be sure to express love? Or why doubt it? We have not tried. (It might well have roused utmost anger in the Jews— to whom, besides all other reasons, it must have expressed that licentious life of the Gentiles they had been so taught to pride themselves against.)

In the streets of London at night—and not the "degraded" ones—one gets to understand the despair that exists. It is rational enough. And if there were no hope but in the power of what we think of as "good" to fight the evil, it were the only possible conclusion. There would be no real hope. If our only course were to go on trying to add to the good things we have gained, we could not really hope. We must have also the giving them up entirely, and having them in their effect, a new *beginning*. There were no hope if we were compelled to be misers and could not use our coins.

But saying: "Do not do that, because all cannot, and they will falsely imitate," &c., is like saying to a merchant: "Do not buy corn with your money, for other people do not understand, and will throw their money into the streets." They won't.

Art has learnt the method to make what was its wrong its right (that is, to attain a spirit-right instead of a thing-right; right in modes of doing instead of things done; a right that can be in any form): and we call it divine, wonderful; we stand before the artist as a being more than human. But it is not only art that knows this secret; if it were we might say it was the special prerogative of art, its gift whereby it is not as other things are: it is the very same with mathematics, the most strict and exact of all exercises of thought; so that it lies deep in man's nature. Now if life could know the same method, how changed it were! The law not to know good and evil would have come back with its conditions fulfilled. Man would be what we dream of angels. (And the law which has not learnt this method is the one which is not obeyed.) And in art and mathematics we see that when this method is learnt it is the "wrong" thing that is done, that becomes the constant act. It is not only introduced sometimes, while the mass of the action continues of that which was before the right; but that which was the wrong becomes the action all through. Now must it not be so in life?

We do not see: we can be in Eden again as soon as ever we choose. Nay, we are there and do not know it; we only want to see. For it is nothing but to have our regard on others and act accordingly, and we are in Eden, in innocence again. (Nothing all the while has been changed at all; we have made all the change.) It is but to awake up and see what we are, to enter into the fruit of the labours achieved. For now the care and regard of men—of more than the half of men and women here in England—truly are on others, and what is needed is not any more change there, but to act according to the fact; to see what *is*, and let our action correspond. We hang around ourselves fragments of chains that are broken; what wonder that they do not bind us? Their very failure to bind proves that they are broken.

We might say that it is no wonder Adam and Eve "fell;" for there were no others for them to regard; there were not the means (which God has provided for us) for keeping the regard off self. Not having others to think of, what could they do but think of their own goodness? In them do we not see the history of the family, and how fatally it *must* "fall" if it be not subordinated to claims from without?

We have lived so long in the wilderness that its habits cling to us even now when we have returned.

We bring with us the old ways, the old rights; and they suit the restored Eden even worse than the other state. It makes a greater perplexity than ever.

While others have to live as they do, our lives are not pleasant. Nothing but absolute absence of imagination could make them even seem so. And now—it is the gain of the modern time—the imagination in this way does exist and is powerful, and the life of the well-to-do is lived only at an expense of crushing the imagination (and the desires it prompts), that spoils the life and prevents it from being really pleasurable.

Mechanical necessity is a negative merely, non-action; therefore so fit for a universal "form." But now when people say existence is unknown, but our experience is best formulated in terms of matter, of force, may not that be questioned *and put to the test?* Since it is all one—the physical and the conscious—might we not well try if an expression in terms of consciousness would not really suit best? And the more, that if it all *is* one it assuredly all *is* conscious. How can we suppose the same thing conscious here, not conscious there? The *process*—storing up and liberating force—is adapted to be a conscious one; there is no reason in it for its not being so. How then can we suppose it not so? How invent a difference? So to use terms of consciousness is to use truer terms. How can it not be the best? If we want a guide, here is the very same thing in our consciousness.

Sensuous pleasure will be to the moral life of the future as sense-impressions are to the knowledge of the present: and with the same history. It will not be a thing put aside, as evil, or degrading, or misleading; nor merely succumbed to as necessary, or ordained, or irresistible "in this world;" but recognised as the very basis and means of the life, and used absolutely and to the utmost—nay, surely, with enhancements and multiplied powers undreamt of by us.

The claim for a mode of life that will make pleasure free (taking away the need for our asking: "But how much pleasure will that be to me?") is the same as the claim for a mode of thought that shall make sense free. Here is the necessity for insisting on it. See what it is insisting on: a life that shall not make right mean any question of how much pleasure.

May we not say that every evil exists to correct a premiss? So we see the mistake of meeting them by mere direct remedies, mere restraining (save for the tension's sake). By this thought our eye becomes wholly false to human life; man appears a being quite different from that which he truly is. He is not a being with tendencies, and passions, and promptings needing restraint. He is a being simply who needs the premiss, the starting-point, on which his life rests, enlarged and made more and more perfect ever; and as at once the sign of this and means of its attainment, finds that his tendencies, passions, promptings—not evil at all—lead to evil that must be put aside. He is a being needing *more* in the very basis of his life, and so destined (and in perfect good) to make perpetually *tensions*, and bring by his activities intolerable results—alike his passions and his goodness bringing them —by which the basis of his being shall be made more true. How different a thought from that which we have made up. And yet our very ignorance has led us to the right work, though so tedious, and so sad. (By the bye, considering how the baby's work of perception itself is a *reductio ad absurdum,* may we not learn by man's life hitherto to see the baby's? Is there to the child such consciousness of *sin?* Such struggles and such failures, and such distresses? And even indeed may man's thoughts of his own life bear the impress, as it were, of his baby experience?)

So is not that idea we have formed from human life of a being with such evil propensities or passions that need restraint, with positive wrong within him, an impossible one? That is the "phenomenon" of a basis of life that needs enlarging.

Here is the value of pleasure being *indefinite:* the thought on self cannot co-exist with it. And the question for man is whether he will accept the condition for it. (The question is not of amount but of fixity.) And one reason for having it indefinite is the power it gives us; it gives us, *to use,* all the power expended in keeping it definite. And is there not use for it?

And this indefiniteness of pleasure—the absence of fixed limit to restraint—is itself the joy, the very essence of pleasure itself, more than any pleasant things or multiplication of them; this is *the* pleasure. It is this the desire longs for, which in license and excess it vainly seeks; not the *things,* but the absence of limit, is the charm, the temptation. Is it not absolutely true that in all excess, the attraction, the pleasure sought, the thing that deludes and carries away, is the longing for indefiniteness, for freedom from limitation? It is falsely sought, indeed; the true freedom from limitation is in Nature's indefiniteness; present ever, and never needing to be sought. *Sought for,* it is already lost. It has this in common with all pleasure.

Is not the very reason we so pursue pleasant things, indeed, and are so unsatisfied, this, that we have not this indefiniteness—this absence of fixed limit—not having fulfilled its conditions. And so, failing of the true delight, we want so much to compensate us, and try to satisfy ourselves with that which never can—getting at the utmost a false feeling of freedom from fixed limit, not its reality. Lack of the proper *infinitude* (which is man's desire) drives him to license. (Is it not parallel to trying to gain the idea of "infinitude" by extending space, or thinking of more and more "time" for eternity?) In freedom from limit *all* is; that is infinitude of pleasure, be it much or little. It is the having to forbid ourselves the indefiniteness makes the intenseness on the pleasure: for *the joy* is forbidden, and we are left hungering with an appetite we cannot fill, because the things we try to fill it with are not its true food. We want not the pleasant things, but freedom from limit.

Making goodness mean less pleasure cannot prevent the thought from being on pleasure; rather it must tend to intensify it, as we know we tend to think most of things if they are forbidden. But making goodness mean accepting pleasure involves not having reason to put it away, especially if it makes it an indefinite pleasure which man feels, without that condition, he cannot have.

So is not the feeling of a demand for *indefiniteness* of pleasure one emphatically true to Nature—relations determined only by force which is one, not bound into rigid things? Is not this truth to Nature in a man the necessity to feel all things *fluent?* This, and perchance unweariable joy of action. And are not the two one?

The "everlasting hills," said the Jews: the "everlasting motion—the changing hills," says science. That marks *the* change in man's thought, the advance we have made; it is an action put instead of things. This is science: it will be morals; action instead of things.

—— should have said, in repudiating the "Mystery of Pain:" "You say all things should be estimated by their service; but then you mistake in putting pain as the best, for pleasure is *more* service." But how necessary it was to see pain thus as good: without it how could pleasure have been seen so? How could we say: "Indulgence, if it is service, is the most good morally," or: "Service is the most good morally, however much it is indulgence," if we had not first said: "Service is the most good *emotionally*, however much it is pain?" These are correlated; one cannot be without the other; pain, if it is service, must also be the most good emotionally. We don't "feel" so in either case; we *feel* the pain not the most good emotionally, and we feel the indulgence not the most good morally. It is a common error of our feeling, and the cause is the same. The question is not how we feel, but what is the relation to the fact? (How should a limited being, growing into its life, not feel falsely until it has learnt?)

We must be walking arm in arm with our fellows, not nursing them with broken limbs. The powers of good are wanted for other things than that; there is scope enough for them. Yet the nursing is good to have been demanded; it is good for man not to have had the idea of the walking arm in arm, in order for the other to have been wanted of him; it was a needed means to train him. Till he had had that harder thing to do, the easier might not have been enough, because the force that is in the other would not have been.

We must *gain* the force first before it can be used; we need transitory " organs " to give us this force; then we do not want them any more. Now in moral training might not much be seen in this? At once we do not seek enough, and we make things too easy. That is, we put children too soon into easy ways of doing, while they should rather be led *through* harder ones; then the easier would set free force for doing more.

The easier, if it had come first, would not, in its coming, have sent a new force throughout. But though it is true, that the hard nursing was needed for training before the easier walking arm in arm came, yet imagine any one proposing, for the sake of the good of the toil of the nursing, to keep on not walking arm in arm!

Might we not say that the power which is the restraint exists in three forms (and how possibly never really varying in amount): either (1.) the external restraint, or self-virtue, expressed in the laws of things; or (2.) in *tension* in the life, pain, and discontent; this in or before its transference to a new region; and (3.) in the changed starting-point, the thought or feeling raised and made living. So that thus one can trace it simply, and, as it were, from the beginning. The living condition, the true vital (force-containing) starting-point, is the equivalent—the other form—of the very force that is in the restraints or self-virtue, and that (turned against itself) makes the discontent, and bewilderment, and pain of the time when neither the restraints nor the right beginning exist. But then, if this is so, the force that is in the restraints has its nature and source evident, as it is the force which is in that true internal state; so its *having* the other forms, its presence so, is simply the expression of its absence there: it is but another aspect of that absence, and is its inevitable fruit. Do we ask whence this power which is in the restraints? It *is* the power that is absent in the starting-point, the power that should be life in it. It is man's life, but not yet within his soul.

And how simple it is; for how simple and visible a part of Nature man stands, seen with his regard perfect, his eye wholly on good. And without that how evident is his toil, his failure, his painful arbitrary duties that are never performed, his fancies about God. How simply the former is his *living*.

And then when life is thus taught how appropriate science will be for education, and how exactly the aid needed; but must it not have been waited for until this thought of life had come? How could it be really welcome, or really used while morals meant, not being true to fact, but having the question of our pleasure first? For this is what is *taught* as morals; they teach it, enforce it; it is what is made " duty." So how could science—which teaches the very contrary thing, the perfect truth to fact —be really suitable for education till there was another thought of right than that?

So we can understand how there should have been the difficulty about science as a means of education; the seeming unreason in the opposition to it. It wants a condition. But thus we see science may have a parallel place to art in teaching life; it also teaches truth to Nature.

And thus do we not see how the old thought of education as a teaching of *life*, how to be men and women, comes back. Now training the intellect has taken its place, but it is only a suppression. And how many boys will not respond?

The reason men could not get perpetual motion was because they had it; that is, they had the true thing they falsely aimed at. And is not this the very type of man's non-success? He tries for the thing falsely, and needs only to understand and accept the true. Man has tried to attain goodness, but he has truly to understand Nature's and conform to it. It was not perpetual motion that men sought, but to prevent it from changing its form. (Really they were trying to put aside the very condition of its being perpetual.) And so is not man's attempt at goodness the very same non-perception, the very same fixing the eye on a form instead of the reality? He is not seeking goodness, but only to prevent it from changing its form, which is the very condition of its being. They thought there was no motion unless a particular wheel moved; and so now men think there is no goodness unless certain things are done. Now as men left off seeking perpetual motion, so will they not leave off seeking such goodness? And were they the most truly scientific minds—those of the kind that now do the best work—that gave themselves most to the discovery of perpetual motion? And so will it be found that those now most intent on keeping goodness in one form will be those to whom a truer goodness most belongs? Will it not bring in others rather?

Now may we not be able to see how a new apprehension of goodness, and acceptance of Nature's goodness, will come to men by seeing how the thought of making motion perpetual ceased in accepting Nature's? Will not the steps be the same: the failure and the ceasing to try? That is, the conviction that some other and better way must be, the feeling that there must be a perpetual motion to be got, and yet that we shall never get it so.

They were not really trying to attain motion—only to

prevent it from changing its form. And so they were without it, so far as their aim and their feeling went, though it was perfectly perpetual all the same. By thinking of it as only of one form, they lost it, though they had the fruit of it unconsciously. So we, in trying to keep the goodness in things, are not really trying to attain goodness, only to prevent it from changing its form; and so, to our feeling and so far as our aim goes, how it is lost to us; yet it is perfect still; and we really reap the fruits of it.

The dynamic laws prevail in the moral life: to have force to use some force must be set free. What we want is some exertion of force which may cease without loss of goodness.

So to prepare it we want something to which there is a tendency in man, and in which, if done in a certain way, there is no wrong, put aside. That is how a store of force should be given us. Then how beautiful our life can be made. We can gain the store of power and hold it while we go on to learn how we should use it. So what a life of conscious wisdom is made possible to us. We are sent force-laden, or *living*, into the world. And the law of service being less effort, less restraint of passion, there is power ready and enough. It needs only a change and all is done so far.

In a correcting of the premiss there is a thing not without its goodness, which yet might be absent in two ways: either in a worse condition or a better. This is the state in a correcting of the premiss; and is it not certain also, conversely, that whenever there is anything of which this is true it is always the middle term of a *reductio ad absurdum?*

Then, observe, this is the case with every restriction, every rigid law whatever. In fact, its ceasing in a better *is* simply, always, becoming as Nature. Or perhaps this is the question: Is becoming as Nature, in this aspect, a better or a worse? So we see again how "heaven" is Nature.

Thus we may see how the idea of "going to heaven" has come. Man has had before him the vision of the ceasing of these "good" things in a better state; he has felt in his soul the "correcting of the premiss" in which he is engaged, and that these fruits of good were destined to cease in a better; but he has not been able to grasp the real bearing and meaning of his life, and so the thought of going to heaven comes in as a faint shadow of it. Thus we see the thought of "going to heaven" in its relations; it has come from man's imperfect apprehension of the correction of the premiss that his life is.

And can we even trace the causes which made that thought of going to heaven take the place of a recognition of the fact of the correction of the premiss in man's life? For one thing, is it not a result of men not seeing that human life is truly one, a whole; and not a mere set of fragments? But men did not feel this; they did not recognise a moral life that was carried out in all; they thought of the individuals only in that aspect; and this drove them to the thought of a change coming by mere externals; by mere getting rid of the body. And then see how easily it wrought backwards; for having to make the truer and better life depend upon being out of the body, they could not but carry out the inference that the being in the body was the evil, and so have their thoughts set on putting away pleasure for goodness; that is, the thought doubly bound on self, bound for goodness as well as by evil. Here we may trace again how man's thought of goodness in putting away pleasure was bound on him more and more, and how he was made subject to it even unwillingly, and even apart from not-regard to others, how that very not-regard might have been forced upon him. And so one thing worked with another to confirm his wrong. Every thought of mere individual goodness would tend to confirm his idea of "going to heaven," instead of a truer life for *man;* and then this would confirm his thought that *here* he could not escape from the rule of self, or else what would going to heaven be for?

So there is this value besides in the perception of man's life as a correction of the premiss; it compels us to cease to dwell exclusively upon the individual in respect to the moral life; compels us to recognise it as a life of man, of the whole; a life in which we are not many, but one. So what a wall of partition it breaks down; our very aim at goodness, our very aspiration has been dividing us, instead of doing its true work of making us one, which is seen to be its true work as soon as ever we see that our call is to have our regard true to fact. So how this perception at once fulfils the feelings in man which have claimed and sought a universal life.

Man is to be one with Nature; which is simply to take her law. It is all ready. We have misapprehended what being one with Nature is. It does not need any change of our condition. It is a thing now for us to choose. And Nature no sooner has any thing than she begins instantly to fulfil the conditions of its not being. When we think, of course this must be so; or there must be unreason in her; for it is sure to pass, and the conditions for its passing are the things needed. Here man fails: his things pass too; but he does not prepare; the passing comes on him with the conditions unfulfilled, and he falls into strife and evil. His being one with Nature would be in his ever having the conditions fulfilled for everything to pass, when the time for their passing comes, to carry out that act of Nature's *consciously*. As soon as man attains anything (knowing it can come only to pass) he should begin to fulfil the conditions of its passing.

That is Nature's life, her constant moving; ours is to become a moving life too. It is simply accepting Nature's law of constant change: consenting that our life should be what it *is*, a part of a continually moving, changing whole, and acting according to what this implies. We must seek to fulfil the conditions of everything passing instead of trying to keep it rigid. Knowing the thing has to pass, we turn at once to fulfil the conditions for its passing. So we do not deny but affirm the goodness of the things that are to pass. It is only looking to the fact instead of the form. And see the *power* in it over the soul: if we are not to have that *form* (which we find so good, and in which therefore we can rest and be satisfied, though it hides all wrong and badness beneath it), then we must have the goodness, the power. We must insist on that if we are to let the form go. Its time to pass has come when under it can be emptiness or wrong; when it no more necessarily implies and means the living power. And that is surely at once, instantly that it comes: then is its time to begin to pass.

The powers or forces remain; this is the thing to keep the eye upon: The forms vary and must; and the demand is to have *them* expressed, whatever changes come: not to identify the form with the presence of the forces, because, by Nature's very being, the forms will change. And this change is our good; it makes the demand for the force to express itself in new forms. And this has its most evident use; we can see it in every case; the form passing, men gain the power in a new sense. It comes more into his apprehension what it is; what the demand is; it comes on his soul in a deeper way; he sees it more truly. The ceasing of the form has special value for him.

In Nature the preparation is ever made for the passing of each form; man does not prepare; and so the forms pass and find him unprepared; so he has to find the new form amid the decay, with strife and fear. Everything is an instrument, and if not *used*, which is its true "decay" or passing, decays with a mere dead decay.

This also is a key to morals: Man's part is to fulfil the conditions for morals passing away. (This is one with morals being a stage in his learning to obey his impulses. But we do not think, yet, of this: of how man might not need to be moral.) What a change it would be all through life to have the eye fixed on this.

There is such an infinite power in the simple recognition that everything passes; for it means our preparing for its passing. And man's works must pass, for he is also part of Nature. And his works are her works, and obey the laws of hers; although he does not feel himself so, he is so. And that is what he has to learn: to feel that he is so, and to accept his life accordingly. He has to feel the fact of his life—that it is part of Nature, and to make his conscious act in accordance with it. That is his being restored to Nature. And this recognition that all things must pass is simply the law of service; the law on the act, not on the forms.

About the word "altruistic" and the suggestion of "otherish," the real meaning of the difficulty about a word for "regard to others," is that we do not want it. It would mislead us if we had it. The very thought of a true regard being "for others" has in it some of the perverted thought of goodness. It is not a regard for *others* we need, but simply a *true* regard, a regard to the facts, to Nature: it is only a truth to facts in our regard, and its nature is obscured by a reference to "others," as if that were the essential point. It is an accident rather; the truth to Nature is the essential point. Putting it as to "others" as opposed to self, brings in our false thought of *goodness*. It puts the idea of regard to self falsely, as if it were a positive instead of a mere not-regard.

It is not as being for others, but as being *true*, that the regard for others is demanded.

I perceive that one thing I propose to do is to match the "fatherhood of God" with the "motherhood of Nature." And as in a child's earliest years the mother's part is the most important, may it not be that as yet it is so also for man, and that he would have done well to have thought relatively more about his Mother. He has had too much to imagine his Father.

It is felt that the shifting results—the law of service instead of things, use instead of holding—must at least be hard, and always so, like learning to stand on a rolling ball. But it is not so; it is not-moving (which is opposing Nature) that is hard. The very simile may show it; the rolling ball is the earth. It is as if, to keep ourselves balanced on it, we had to ask: How many miles an hour have *we* to move? What we have to do is not to think about it, to let ourselves move with Nature.

The new spirit does not fill out the dead forms, but moulds them into living ones; it does not fit itself into the crystal, but moulds it into the leaf. It does not enter into and maintain with a new power the rigid things absence of love has imposed, but brings its own forms with it and makes them bud and grow, and never any more be the same. The living thing evidently flows with the flowing nature, is in harmony with it, and expresses it; the inorganic—as we apprehend it—does not. But then is not this simply saying that, in so thinking of it, we are thinking of it falsely? We see in the one response to Nature; in the other, as it were, refusal of her. (And here is a great place evidently for art: to fill up this lack, and put aside the seeming of that refusal.) And so even in studying the physical world should not children be taught first to begin with the organic; as presenting it so more truly, giving the right conception to start with? It shows us Nature operating truly and freely; the yielding all throughout to her, a true image or vision of the whole, everything moving and adjusting itself, responding to all influences, exhibiting the play of all powers: that perpetual mutual influence and response which is her being, the organic presents.

So a true *feeling* would, perhaps, be given, and the false feeling which the inorganic gives avoided, its *appearance* of not yielding would be easily derived from the other by a palpable "minus" or non-perception of ours. For the not yielding there is not true; it only seems. The forces operate though they seem not; their effect is present in hidden forms; we only do not see it; it is present as innumerable *tensions* pervading them. (By the bye, is this one secret of electricity?) By the organic our eyes are opened thus to see the inorganic more truly; the latter is virtually what the former is practically.

There is no failure in not attaining when the object is

falsely aimed at. (The success is learning to aim truly.) So in taking in man's life for our point of view, *failure* is eliminated; but failure and evil are one; success is another name for good.

Not *any* physical relations, or order, and none therefore that have even, or are, or can have been, none of them can have been "evil" or failures. No physical relations can have had any true wrong about them, for none is "right;" none is the object. They are, all alike, *forms* merely and alone for the spiritual powers, and for man's having his needed experience; *all* are equally available for this. And this means that some must accompany our experience of evil and wrong, must furnish the means for the emotions of horror, repentance, consciousness of wrong, others for those of good, of joy, of sacrifice, of right, of life. Some forms—for man's needed experience must gain expression, practical value, and power for him—to the conditions of not-regard; others to those of a true regard. But the forms are not therefore good or bad; the physical relations are but vehicles; cannot be bad. Nay, we see the very same may be the vehicles either for the expression of life or of death.

The object is not these things to be done, a physical order to be secured, but man attaining a flexible right, which must come, surely, by the rigid right being made impossible, failing and becoming intolerable to man in *every* form.

And so do we see how the organic arises; how it comes, as it were, from the inorganic—the crystal, say: namely, by a mere disintegration first; by resistances which had withstood the "claims"—the forces operating around and which *mould* the organic through and through—not withstanding completely any more, but *partly* yielding, partly resisting still. And so all sorts of distorted conditions come (which only analysis can unravel), partly the expression of the old arrangement, partly expressing the claims around, but true to neither. That is chaos; and so life comes from chaos. So is not this the key to our condition? it is a mixture of the old arrangement and the yielding to claims that is to be. First mere disintegration, and then reconstruction answering to the forces—and swaying with the varying forces —around; but the coming in of those forces around— the perfect rule of which makes life—operates first as disintegrating, as bringing disorder—a condition true to nothing.

In respect to a different right many would say: "'Yes, when men are better, but it is not now possible; we must now have another." But grant that a different law is only possible when more has been attained, let the necessity for an inferior condition first be assumed, still see the bearing of the fact upon the way we should regard the failure and loss of these other " temporary " rights. Their failure and breach is not evil as otherwise it would be; that failure has to be judged by another test altogether from that which would apply if it were a perfect and final right. (Something has been left out in our thoughts here, and they have been false accordingly.) The failure must be judged radically by its relation to the coming of the better and truer right. Not thinking of that we cannot see it truly; in so far as it arises in any way from even the most distant approach of that, the slightest shaking of the ground from its ever so remote advance, it is good and not evil; in so far as it prepares the way, and above all gives rise to power to bring it, all failure and breach of the other right is good. How else should the truer right come?

Let it be granted that with a truer right certain outside things that with our present right are wrong, would then not be necessarily wrong, but would be judged by a different standard, and might be counted in themselves not wrong, but only wrong if wrongly done; then how plainly a step towards a truer good it is for people to begin to feel those things not wrong. It is the attainment of one element of the better state, though of course it wants the others also added. But in itself it is a distinct advance towards that better, especially one of the conditions of its coming. The new standard must need the old one to fail.

And altogether in respect to our feelings of wrong, we have to learn that it is not only our deeds, but our *standard* that is under judgment. Our feeling of wrong and our condemnation may truly be a condemnation not of the deeds, but of the standard. And the attainment of a truer right must consist in learning to condemn our former standard. And this is the striking point, that has such power within, and that we so forget: that the change in the standard involves *ceasing* to condemn some things as well as condemning others—is *transferring* the judgment from the thing to the act, and so leaves uncondemned as well as condemns. This new leaving uncondemned—this fulfilling the conditions of not having to do—we so overlook.

So let it be granted that a less perfect right must be first, and even still, and that a truer one is but for the future, still let *that* thought also be applied, and remembered in our judgment of the facts of life; its evil and wrong and failure especially stand in quite a new light before it. And there is one thing that surely must follow, namely, a resolve that the truer right should come as soon as it possibly could, because until it does come there can be no real and succeeding good at all; no laws that we can even hope to find really obeyed. Till the better law does come, law itself *must* be a failure; and the very approach of good must mean evil and distress to us. We cannot be content with its absence, if it is to come at all; our only real good must be in its having come. Its delay is a turning good to evil. The very promise of a better prevents our possession of the less. There is no contentment possible but in having it.

And here would be a good study for us: to test our life in this way, and understand it better, by seeing what elements in it are due to the fact of this approaching better and truer good; to see what effects must result from such approach, and to look at our life and to see what facts there are in it that are its result. So might we not apprehend it more truly, and see that it was a thing less to be discontented with perhaps? And even by such an examination might we not judge how near it was come?

Which is wrong (in any case), the deeds or our standard, is an open question. When we feel a wrong, it is evident there is something wrong, either our standard or the things, but which is it? If our standard is false (and how *can* it not have been?), it will have produced all sorts of twisted results. And if we look, how plainly men's standards have been false. And we see a consciousness of this in men's efforts, everywhere, to remedy it by the belief in a revelation. Here is one of the impulses which have led to the affirmation of a revelation by each nation for itself.

By the bye, it is curious that Christendom has adopted the revelation not only of another nation, but even of another race. Are there in this at once advantages and disadvantages? Might characters of our relation to it, and of its influence on us be traced to this? Is it not richer and more through this union of the bloods—a Semitic affirmation with Aryan interpretations? For the blood surely asserts itself, and though it speaks in another's words, puts on them its own meanings. Might not this be an advantage through a lack? perhaps a poverty of Europe whereby it could not create a revelation for itself has given it the benefit of an adopted one?

But this attempt to escape (or even if the revelation be as direct from God as ever has been affirmed) from the imperfection of our standards has only a limited success; as is evident, even with ourselves, the revelation does become misunderstood. Necessarily and historically men's standards are false: how should we not always consider what part this bears in our judgments? It is the most important side to consider by far; for the falsity of the standard is of more harm and hurt to life, beyond comparing, than are the wrong deeds; it must bring wrong deeds, and prevent their being cured. And so long as self is too much first, the standard must be falsified; that is evident, though we do not consider it. And who does not hold that self is too much first? Then if we feel wrong things which nature—human nature—persistently produces, obstinately, unyieldingly presents, does it not mean that our standard is wrong? (It does not mean, of course, that the feeling is merely wrong; misjudging that a good thing is evil; but that there has come through our wrong standard a confusion and disorder, and that the change is needed *there*.)

What is this feeling that our standard must be the wrong thing in such cases, but doing what science teaches us to do, learning from Nature and being humble, and not holding our assurances against her teaching? Has not morals to learn a true "morality" from science?

And indeed must it not be thus in fact: that the wrong must always be in the standard, that is, in the feeling, in the assumption, that this is always what is "wrong?" So that we have here to make a change, the same as the universally-needed change, of taking into ourselves what we had put outside. And the falsity of the standard is simply the expression of the not-regard; it means that our judgment is at fault, and we cannot get on.

How curiously true it is, practically, that this new thought of morals is "looking to see if the ancients had not a better way." It is exactly so; one finds it constantly. And then the parallel could not be more exact. One finds that they had; distinctly there was at least suggested among them, a law not of things but of the act. (Plato, for example, emphatically. Will Plato be found to have been a sort of Pythagoras in morals? See his permission of lies to governors, and his freedom of womanhood.)

And our "advance" has been in introducing so great a number of definite things, of rules and laws. The parallel to the position of Copernicus is perfect in this. And then again, finding that "other way," that were so much better if it might but be, among the "ancients," we have to look and see what made it impossible for them, and ask whether what has been added since and been handed down to us has not made the very change necessary—fulfilled the very condition that it needed—the subsequent course indeed having been this very thing, though unsuspected.

See how emphatically this is done in respect to the enthronement of the good of woman, and the condition of freedom there. Nothing could be more marked than this. It is the emphatic attainment; and see how plainly it waits for its true meaning to be shown. There is the aim, the feeling, and it cannot fulfil itself; such desire for her good, and woman—how much better off?

That was what was done by Copernicus. This " better way" proposed by one of the ancients was recognised, and the things which had then made it "wrong" and impossible, recognised too, and seen to be the very things that the work done since had put away. It was recognised that some conditions wanted fulfilling, and that man's toils had been their fulfilling. (So how visible a relation would be between Plato and Christ. Christ with the same thought — might it even have been from Plato that it had flowed, not to his soul but to his ears?—putting into operation the powers by which the conditions for that *right of the soul* were fulfilled. That would be a beautiful order indeed. And it would perhaps render more plain why the "Christian" Universities have held so to the reading of Plato's "Republic." There would be an instinct visible in that.) For it must be seen that Copernicus did not merely re-adopt a former " way ; " he recognised that it needed a condition fulfilled, and that it had been fulfilled. (Now is this what is always done in the re-adoption of any former position by genius?)

Christ introduced *love*, the very thing that is necessary —the sympathies; for Plato's right was not the right exactly of love; though it was one which did make human things such as infanticide, which, to us, would be brutally inhuman. He had the thought of a right that was on the soul, and made not evil what otherwise would be intolerably so. So by the very process of putting aside comes the bringing back.

In Plato, the human soul looked towards that "right" —such an aim or object as should make things that were brutal otherwise good and human—and pronounced it good. For no one questions that the old "heathen" morality attained its summit in Plato. The human soul looked at that and pronounced it good, and then it passed away as if it had been a dream, and man went quite another way, as if he had turned his back on it for ever, binding himself with rules and outside laws instead. Is it not like showing man his life in a vision, picturing it before him so as to give his soul an irrevocable tendency, never to be effaced however it might be even forgotten?

Is it not reasonable to propose purity to make things free? It restores Nature to her course, and, above all, love to its freedom. The love between man and woman has this exquisite magic in it: its freedom means purity, because it wants and needs all things free, and cannot be free without being pure. That love is gifted with this power by virtue of its union with the body. (Virtue in an impure person's mouth means opposing Nature.) There is a muddle here, and I propose *purity*, by virtue of its power of making things free, to heal it, to deliver from false bonds (of course counted sacred). This power of purity we have not recognised or used. Many times purity has been urged on us for its own sake and value, as a thing to be prized, attained, and held: and that is well. But there is another reason for it too (and one for which also man was made), another value we have not noticed: it brings in its hand the gift of making things free, of restoring love to its freedom, and Nature to her course.

It is the true "heaven"—the fact of that dream: the perception that earth may be good. "Heaven" is a duty to be glad; feeling that earth may be good is gladness.

We have impulses which we feel are not "bad;"

yet they cannot merely go unchecked, they want some ordering; then we so naturally think they must be *controlled*. But that is not enough; it comes too late. It is not really even what it is called; it is not the impulse, but only the deed, which is so controlled. We need a different thing, *to be able to obey them*. And we see the difference perfectly in food.

One accepted thought—the evolution-thought—represents the whole on the idea of man as the highest, as the most advanced "fringe," as it were, of Nature. Now, if the case is representable so, it is of course certain that it is representable *conversely*; if that one can, the converse relation might be carried through consistently: namely, of man as not the highest, but as the least perfect. Let us try this way.

That Nature differs from man in being *more*; the things that seem wanting are positively, not negatively, denied. This is a new thought, a new key. (Evidently a central new thought, or new method is our want. The old ones divide us.) And is it not certain that if it may be one way it may be the other; that everything that is true or discovered on view of man as a *plus*, *edging* Nature, will work equally on the view of him as a *minus*? It is only changing the sign.

So there is a definite aspiration for man—to be as Nature; and a meaning in the old command: Do not separate yourself from Nature.

How simple and restful all our thoughts are when we have seen that man is *rising* to Nature; that all his self-things and self-attainments, all are his being on the way to the Nature-state; that he needs to value those only from lack of that. What a light and what a rest has descended upon everything.

How striking the direction of the mental activity of this age is. It seems becoming even intensely like that of the Middle Ages again: surely it is hardly an exaggeration to say so. The very same subjects are coming again to the fore, and receive the greatest attention. Science itself turns to them, as if in its merely physical attitude it had been a sort of interlude, to supply something wanting perhaps, but only for return to the very same set of problems. Take merely these three papers coming at the same time: Clifford's "Mind and Body" in *Fortnightly*; mine in *Contemporary* on "Emotions;" and Morley's in *Fortnightly* on Mill's "Nature." How strikingly the tendency of thought is to these old subjects again—surely with new prospects.

Because man cannot succeed in poising himself against Nature, it does not follow that he cannot take her hand and be lifted to her level. But this would be his becoming *unmoral*, as a little child. (Here perhaps is why the precepts of Christ have appeared unpractical or impossible. We have not noticed this basis of them all. He is supposing men to have accepted the becoming as a little child.) We have not recognised this element in being raised to the level of Nature, and have sought it (if at all) combined with our morality. The question is: Is Nature infra-moral or supra-moral?

So there is plainly a new view possible of the moral world, a view which makes the failure to put away evil things right instead of wrong, a success to be turned to account, not a mere failure to be repaired. (Yes, this is it. By this new view man's disasters may be seen as successes, calling for use, for understanding, for following up with joy. This is the delight of recognising a *reductio ad absurdum*.) There may be a call to put away, not the things, but that which makes them evil. We *dread* (as Mrs. Lewes about killing the sick); but we should remember that in this we should be going towards and with Nature, not trying to be above. We have an example before us of success in that. It is certainly possible. (This is what we attach so much value to in Christ—the example proving possibility of success.)

In Nature we see a witness and example that the absence of that which makes things evil is possible; nay, it *is* everywhere except in us. Now, what can we think? Is it really true that the presence of this (the thing that makes things evil) is the one great excellence and eminence of the world? When we know, too, that a change for good in man does have more or less—and might have still more—the effect of making things not evil; when we know that exactly in proportion as a man is more a man and worthier, so are things not evil to him which are evil to those less worthy, and when we know, too, that Christ set a little child as His pattern, to whom things are not evil. Now, since by a progress in good some things are made not evil which otherwise are evil, why should not this be a process which might embrace all things? Why should it not go on without stopping at any particular point? How should it stop? What is there in it to account for its stopping? Is it not the nature of progress in good, without any limit at all, to make things that were evil not evil?

Through not condemning the *act* (of not-regard) we are obliged to put evil in *things;* and then what mischiefs come, and even our own hands are unable to avoid inflicting them. I would carry up the moral judgment again to the act, making it more intense, more inclusive; again reclaiming the soul for its dominion, and so restoring freedom to the things, taking away the omission that has perverted the moral thought to them.

We must insist on the right act absolutely, in order to prevent the perversion of the moral judgment; we obstruct the true channel, and nothing remains but all sorts of perverted ones. We must insist that not-regard is the sin, or else we must make up a whole number of fictitious sins.

And this is so curiously parallel to the intellect and emotions making up for themselves a fictitious sphere, because debarred from their true interpretative action. It is but another form of the very same fact. Give it its true work or it does mischief. So the breaking of the thing-laws is parallel to the denial of the "intelligible" world, and now of our invented "spiritual" world.

The amount of force that is *within* the human soul is to be known by the amount of hard, restraining, effortful things that man has set up, and that have ceased. There the absorbed force is presented to us in obvious forms.

There are two ideals: the self-ideal which excludes the physical, and the true or nature-ideal which includes it. The ideal comes first in the excluding self-form. (I perceive the word "ideal" has come back to me available for use. I have a place for it.) So in this we see one whole function of science; it raises man's ideal from a self-ideal to a nature-ideal. Its entry accomplishes the including of the physical.

The accepted not-regard makes into lusts and mischiefs needing restraint, feelings and tendencies which are not lusts at all, nor evil, but wholly natural, necessary, innocent, indispensable for good; about which no question need be raised if only there were a true regard maintained to the demand for good.

It is said: "There must be that law—or that restraint—till men are fit." But then we do not direct our effort to getting that which makes fit. Does not history bear on this? Has not England above all nations taken the risk, and has it not been wise?

The advance comes through the children. The difficulty of the grown-up men and women is not that they cannot take up the new right, but that they cannot let go the old. But this latter has not to be done by the children at all. The change is in two portions, one hard, one not hard. Now the children have only one of these to do, that which is not hard; the hard one does not come to them.

Might it not be urged that there have been morally grand periods in the lives of nations, times when it seemed natural and rational to aspire, to act as if some humanity might be calculated on in man, and when that acting did not prove chimerical? Such a time there was something of, for example, with us in Elizabeth's age. Now do not these times seem often to have corresponded with great intellectual advance—as, for example, with the dawn of science, with the entrance of the mind on some expansion of its domain? And is not that come again to us? The mind of man is now visibly entering again on a new expansion of its domain, gaining a new sight of

Nature, and drinking therefore more of her spirit (which *is* man's becoming more human). Well, if such a time is approaching again for the thought-life of man, with it, we may feel confident, is coming a time when his soul-life also may spring up and grow, and despondency cease to be rational. So may we not hope, and even try?

And so, again, we should see what we are refusing in refusing the thought of a new advance in the method and aim of thought: we are refusing freedom and power of advance to the moral life. There is this reason for hoping it. Nay more, there is all this added evidence that it is to be expected.

This absence of good-will in man brings these things. Now can we get the good-will? Yes: by the present force; but we must *transfer* it. (This is gained for us by physics; all fresh doing is leaving off doing. It is as men tried in vain to get perpetual motion; but that does not prevent us from getting any we want. So we try in vain to get perpetual motion in morals; but that does not hinder our having any we want.) And it is easier to get a man to seek good than, not seeking, to be "honest." We have put in (or left in) an obstacle that is enormous. That "not seeking" *makes* such a difficulty. Instead of a simple direct task, as is the seeking of good, there is put one with a direct opposition and hindrance to it; we have to obtain a result in presence of an opposing force.

Why do we spend our strength for nought, and our labour for that which is not bread? Are not the milk and wine here, without money and without price? And this is what men do still recognise in this; only it is mixed up with things apart from fact. It *is*: Come and seek the true (not happiness but) *goodness*: good-will instead of restraints.

The thoughts about sin, which made it a serious thing before and nerved men and women up to resist it—those of personal sinfulness, and punishment—are losing their force. Now we want some other apprehensions and feelings which shall restore that power; shall again give seriousness and vigour in respect to them. Whence are they to come? (Is there not here a clear suppression? Now what perfecting is needed to restore it? May it be that there is some law for this, that the lacking thing that makes a suppression necessary is always of a certain order, and that we might know in what direction to look?)

We have failed in working at morals because we have not sought rightly. The moral results are not harder to attain, but it takes longer to find the way. This is the change in our thoughts that I seek to introduce. We think moral success lags because it is harder to get; I would change this view to the thought that it lags because the true method takes longer to find.

It is the same as "The Mystery of Pain." That said: Do not get rid of suffering, but hold that and get rid of that which makes it bad. So now of liberty, of pleasure, of indulgence: Do not get rid of that, but hold that, and get rid of that which makes it bad. And in this parallel we have a guide, for we see it is not the very same things we keep when that which makes indulgence wrong is put away. (We have a pattern in art.) So surely it is not the same things we shall keep when that which makes it evil to us is put away from sacrifice. There is a misapplied thought in each case—of pain and of wrong. This "thing" is evil: get rid of it. No, not so; but let it be different.

The question of a flexible right turns so much on truth and its necessity in the liberalest sense for social confidence. But I see this is not so. As a doctor, I perceive that my holding service as the law of truth does not in the least interfere with my absolute confidence in a doctor. It gives me more trust, for it means that his thought is on me and not on himself, and that is what I want. Not to know he won't deceive me when he finds me morbid and incapable of using my thoughts aright; but absolutely acting, not with his eye on himself, but on me. And this is the trust society wants; not trust in verbal truthfulness, but trust in the soul.

*The Mystery of Pleasure.*—This is the question: Was our discipline through pleasure merely single; to train us to its due restraint and limiting and abstaining merely? Was this single process the end? (Is any process in Nature or in man's life merely single? And see what it means; how little restraining on the part of the capable; how much abstaining inflicted on the weak. That an end? Look at it in its relations, give it life.) Or is there a double process, another besides this; for which it —even in its excesses—is a preparation; a farther step beyond—to have no reason for its putting away or restraining? (So that its putting away or bringing is left to Nature, to fact, to God; nor needs doing by ourselves.) Is this discipline by pleasure only one step; or does it call on us for two?

Obeying impulse and pursuing pleasure are not parallel but *contrasted* terms. But is it true that obeying impulse comes oftenest in the form of doing pleasant things, and looks outside like pursuing pleasure? Is it so in fact? It is doubtful: only when it is not in this form it is not thought of as obeying impulse; the fact of impulse in the opposite direction is overlooked, even as the fact of pleasant things being serviceable; and so there comes a false connection in our thought of obeying impulse with doing pleasant things.

Obeying impulse is adding elements besides those which are in our rational consciousness, so that we can base arguments upon them. Now it may oftenest come in the form of doing pleasant things because—owing to our thoughts, and the way our having self first makes our goodness be in refusing pleasure—our reason mostly tends to refuse it; our conscious thoughts have a bias in that direction, and so the added elements must tend to correct that. For it is inevitable that this should be the case with any being which has let self be an end; he will have set himself falsely against pleasant things.

In truth, when men have come to see truly and to feel naturally, will they not see, in all our feeling of life, an intense perversion of feeling, as of pleasure made less good? This on the one hand, and a not less wonderful succumbing on the other to pleasant things that do disservice. For see, we have no clear guide, no help; nothing to give us either light or strength, for pleasure does (and must) make things less good to us. (That is, to men; and women are muddled and succumb, and don't see; and practically take the same thought, only either less firmly, or with a morbid firmness.) And yet we must have pleasure and take pleasant things all the same; and so how can we look and see if they do disservice? The wrong is not to us in the disservice—for our thought is on our goodness, on "right"—but in the pleasure, and we can't put it away; we have to succumb to it. If pleasure was never suffered to be less good to us—never allowed to make less good—then we should be able, should be obliged, to look at the service or disservice. But, as it is, our thought remains on one thing as making less good, and yet we are obliged to succumb to it, cannot put it away. And how we feel —those that do feel—the confusion, the unreason, and yet can't help it.

People say: "Yes, this ought to come, but the truer life must come first, and then the inferior one will cease. First must come the inner life, and then the outer forms will cease of themselves; but till that comes they are necessary." (This means really that they are bent on keeping the outward forms as well. This is the true secret.) This is the point that has to be made clear; that it is the forms standing in the way that keep the true law from having its power; that it is not for us to bring in this better and truer life, to build this larger edifice around the smaller. God does this; does it even without our knowing; and we must open our eyes to see the true call He gives us; to see what our maintenance of these forms really is.

God gives man as much power as he needs, not more; if he will put away that which is innocent he will succumb (he or another for his evil) to that which is not innocent. (Nature were wasteful else.) So in respect to the innocent endearments women long for: till man has a different power from self-virtue how can he consent to them?

Man with his eye on his pleasure thinks that of course when he has arranged all things rightly round that— settled how much, and on what conditions, he may give, and consented to bind himself by that—he has done everything. He does not see that the centering round his pleasure is the wrong. It wants dreadful calamities, terrible ruin and destruction, hopeless else, to make him feel that the centering round his pleasure at all is the wrong; that there is no *way* that can make that right.

If we suffer no question to be but about motive, it is impossible to be that the motive should not be regarded, and regarded with the intensest force. (If other questions come in—about the *things*—then the force is put aside from that.) But before this can be assented to there must be a different feeling about Nature. For it means really the ceasing of the difference between men and Nature; the giving up and ceasing of all that attitude which makes him feel he is so *above* her. This is wanted as a condition: a different feeling respecting Nature. So that our grasp should be loosened upon those things. So is not this the thing to be first sought; a truer and fuller feeling about Nature, that she may stand to our feeling above us, and the becoming one with her be consciously a rising and a gain?

This is a universal thought: the true channels for man's life are blocked up; we are suffering under the effects of that throughout. And one chief remedy is to open them, according to God and Nature. Then the effects of the stoppage will cease. And the cause is clear; wrong within makes evil what is good; and then that good is put aside; that is, a natural channel of the life is blocked. This is how it has come and must have come. And the evil is everywhere, but most in one part of our life.

It is not so much: Do not regard self, as: Regard self *as means*. It may be regarding self even more and more perfectly, but ever in that way. The question is not of even doing that but of the way; even this one and absolutely evil thing is right with its conditions fulfilled; and not it, but the mode of it, is evil.

And so "the self" may be most intensely thought of. And here again the not-doing is the condition and very fact of the utmost doing. Is it not even as seeing the physical as phenomenal is the most absolute possession of it? For then it is the only world; and there is no spiritual for us but it. Now, is not this a thing women feel very clearly—the regarding self as a means, or for the sake of others? And have we not too much spoken of putting regard to self away instead of having it rightly; that is, instead of fulfilling the conditions of not having to put it away?

So a man who engages in philanthropy but is personally selfish and a tyrant, is like a man trying to work without taking care of his tools: his own self is each man's instrument.

And in connection with this may one see that a person may seem to see something new and important merely by seeing it imperfectly? But then, if so, is it not always the case that the true understanding is limited, and needs extending; that there are some who do not see at all?

Whenever there is anything spiritual there is sure also to be something material. Not that the material is the cause or basis; it is the spiritual fact apprehended in another way. But there will be that other way of apprehending it. One mischief of thinking that the spiritual and physical are different existences, instead of one diversely apprehended by diverse perceiving modes of ours, is that we are apt then to let ourselves take up each by itself, without the other, and so to get each falsely. We never truly apprehend either without both.

It is as one may touch an object truly enough; but if we open our eyes we shall see it also, and if we don't see it there is something amiss. Now, take art for example: we not only see how there is the material fact together with the spiritual, but also how emphatically the material fact *is* the spiritual. The spiritual is but the material read in its true significance. Take the "painting the spirit of an object:" it is truly enough a spiritual fact we are in contact with, but also it is the plain material fact of drawing two things at once, of doing one thing *in* the not doing of another. The material fact *is* the spiritual fact, and only in that is the spiritual fact truly seen or known. It *is* that being in another, that act of sacrifice, that living in the dying. And the senses can perceive it just as well as the soul; why should they not?

There is such an effect in not being able any more to feel that one knows right and wrong, in having our firmest convictions overthrown, and things we thought right proved not right, and what we felt most absolutely wrong proved not wrong. So that one can rely no more upon one's present assurance, but has to feel one does not know. It throws all our thoughts absolutely upon the question of benefit or mischief; nothing else remains, and so all goes to this. Must it not keep the thought alert, and the feeling keen? It is the absolute falling-off of the law of things. This law, this freedom, is upon the soul: there is no right, no duty, which can bar the way to service.

In respect to self-virtue and its aspirations, restraints, and beauty, we must not forget the positive value of the elements thus added; they are not only beautiful and true, but indispensable; things the absence of which made necessary the suppression. As in the intellectual the fiction-region is absolutely necessary to gain the expression of man's demands; so in the moral it is necessary. And these results are to be perfectly maintained, just as in the training of the faculties. All the not-regard rights are a fiction-region by leaving out.

It is plain that there is—and so much in Christians—the distinctly anti-Christian feeling of virtue. Christ put the traceable needs above virtue, and made loving God demand loving man as its precursor and condition. The other feeling is that man's goodness is the thing to be put highest, and traceable good is to be sacrificed for that; that we are to love our (else not lovable) fellow-creatures through first loving God. That is, that the self is *end;* and that we are to turn to our own thoughts, not to facts.

But it is to be noted that this attitude of mind is needed as a preparation; here is the justification of the cleaving to it (though it is so strange to call it Christian). The perception that man's life exhibits the relations which we term those of force, gives the key to the two thoughts; there are needed the two forms of life; one is the storing up of force, the other the *using* it. (It is interesting to see that treating the self as an end answers to the storing up of force.) And these two things go together.

Surely there is a fatal lack in virtue; it will not do *for us,* for it has no power to transfer the regard from self to facts. So that we might say, perhaps, that it is excellent, even best and worthiest, but that it is not suitable for us. We want the right *foundation* laid. It cannot put this wrong right. It is, as it were, food; we want medicine. It is good, perhaps, for beings who have a true regard, but not suitable for those who have to gain it. So here is the necessity for recognising the (essentially *Christian*) thought that man is diseased and wants healing. Christ's problem was not how man shall be good (that is a future one perhaps), but how he shall get *life*, that is, have his regard made true.

Man will wake up and say: "If I am regarding this world—and I must—then it must be for others." And is not this proof indeed that this world is spiritual? It has the virtue to so turn man's regard, and what could be more a spiritual work than that?

Christ, by putting the traceable—this world—first, instead of virtue, made that transfer. And we have partly reaped the fruits, but not wholly. In respect to the relations of men and women we have not learnt His lesson.

It may be that there is an error even in our attempts to transfer our thoughts from ourselves to others. We do not proceed in the true order. The real power is not in trying to think of others, but in thinking of facts, in attending to the traceable. By doing that the transferring of the thought to others is brought. And is this the real means of it and the only means that can truly achieve it? And do we tend to err in trying to gain it apart from this? Is the attempt to think of others directly, instead of through the effect of thinking of the traceable, really a delusion?

Do the words: "These ought ye to have done and *not* to leave the others undone" indicate a period in Christ's thought when He sought to attain both the outward and the inward rights, the true state within, and *also* the external laws? And is not this a period through which the human race, and also every individual who attains a truer right, passes?

Rigidity is always deadness; the law is unchanging and absolute, but that is because its unchangingness is not rigidity, but lies in a perfect flexibility, having that flexibility for its very expression. And this is the demand always: inflexibility *with* flexibility.

And in this there is one of the prerogatives of science, one of the characters that (with all its lacks) make it so satisfying and so strong: it presents perfect unchangingness united with perfect changeableness, the unchanging "force" in the constantly changing forms. Science could not stop till it had attained this, nor can morals; man's thought of his own life must be as his thought of Nature.

And then see what has been done for us, what power has been put into bringing this condition—so simple, and of course since it involves women. See the power that means. And yet what a simple thing! What we tend to do—in our laws of things—is to stop at the body, that it may be fixed. We dread to give our statue a soul; for then it won't be still!

What I want is, that men may not have to put away things because they are pleasant. (This seems a grand, fitting attitude; but we see what comes of it—comes of it, of course, where pleasure chiefly comes.) I stand seeking that pleasure should be absolutely and wholly free, and the means I find for it, the only means and essential condition, is that men's thoughts should not be on pleasure: there must come the limiting and refusing if it is. There is no way for having pleasure made wholly free, but in having the thought first set free from it, and standing in complete response to facts. And so is it not inevitable that in order to attain that true response we should insist and take our stand on this: pleasure must be wholly free?

See now, if we are thinking of ourselves, what are the pleasures we shall put away. Not the wasteful, mere self-enjoying ones, but those in which affection, emotion, the very soul-life—the soul-life of others—are. These are the pleasures which—if we let our right be in limiting our pleasures—we shall limit; not the wasteful ones.

This we must keep our eyes open to; that there be no thought of good in limiting pleasure (which comes of course to every being whose thought is on himself), but that instead of it, absolutely, there be the thought of good in being such as to have no need for that.

And in this relation there comes a practical error it is most necessary to be on our guard against: this thought of a good in limiting pleasure not only takes place as a "good," and therefore as being service, and so having claim in the name of service (as simple self-virtue); but it embodies itself in *institutions*, and these claim emphatically to be upheld for service. So men have not only not-regard virtue, but not-regard institutions, and these demand obedience as if in the name of service.

And their power to delude is increased and prolonged by this: that even when their real reason ceases, then men surround them with projected ones; with reasons, or values, which are not their origins or supports, but which are made up because they exist. There is emphatic need for not being deluded here; it is the mode in which the not-regard of man most deceives him, and so longest struggles with him—this embodiment of his not-regard in institutions, which then make reasons for themselves;

but all turn on accepted not-regard at the bottom, and are really its guardians and protectors.

It is curious to note limiting of pleasure thus coming in the name of service, because, in these days, the seeking and extending of pleasure—the rule and pursuit of self-interest—has come also so emphatically in the name of service. Is it not curious how both these opposing things have come, and indeed come still, in the name of service? (How can the latter, at any rate, be without the former also?) It shows, by the bye, a caution necessary in insisting on service as the law: it must be carried to the bottom that false service-things, made "good" by not-regard, may not come in.

Woman carries this talisman with her: the cure of man from having his goodness in limiting his pleasure. By the very demands of her good she does it. And what a light this casts on the resolute attitude of women to join themselves with men and not be kept apart. Surely it means much more than might appear. Is it not in reality God's spirit—humanity—in her insisting on man's life? Is not this the instinct that is guiding her: man shall no more have his goodness in putting away pleasure, that is, *me?* We cannot see the meaning of that splendid, impulse-led nature of hers, and of these irrepressible instincts, unless we see thus. It is man's life she is carrying and taking charge of, even if she does not know it; and this charge it is that prompts her and will not let her be subdued. Neither violence, nor ridicule—" nor any other creature."

So one sees again how much truer a frequent thought is than has been supposed; namely, that of women having to secure the "purity" of men. They have that task, much more deeply and intensely than has been thought;

and this not by the constraint but by the fulfilment of their own impulses to joy.

Here is the hope: there is an instrument we have not thought of using; a means we have not employed; the thought on self does make pleasure evil; so there *is* this instrument to use; pleasure is a power—we have not made use of it. There is an ideal we have not aimed at, that of having pleasure perfectly free; a motive, an inducement we have not employed: liberty to do all the good that can be. (What a simple, natural thing it is too, when once the thought is drawn to it.) Here is a demand we have not thought of urging, not to make pleasure evil (and so good refused if it be one with pleasure thus made evil); not to turn things against their nature and make them be what they are not.

What could be conceived more adapted to concentrate all of man's energies than that of keeping pleasure free? Then all those energies are concentrated on not having self as end. And the reason this is concentrated in the relation of man and woman, summed up and achieved only there, is that that relation, even after all life has become sacred, may still remain infinitely sacreder than all.

Thinking whether one must not be at liberty to take away from others the burden of one's life, when it becomes a burden to them, this became evident: Is not the idea of a right which has regard to our own duties, which turns on our self in any way, apart from the simple good of others as shown to us in facts, proved impossible? Has it not come to a *reductio ad absurdum;* and proved to end (or tend to end) in a miserable pretence? It has been tried two ways, and both ways betray. It gave men

Egypt, with half the population monks, once; now it has given us Manchester. For Egypt it might be pardoned; but Manchester can never be condoned. Has it not been proved that this thought of goodness betrays? It lands us either in asceticism on the one hand, or in such conventional morality as ours on the other.

That this thought of subordinating our virtue to the needs of others so attracts and delights, and has such a power, might seem at first strange, but it is plain: the reason is that it gives liberty for devotion, liberty for putting others altogether first; it sets that impulse free, justifies it, makes it not ashamed of itself. For it lies there crushed and bound in all of us, and only this can free it. For otherwise it is bound down by our virtues. The whole way and manner of our *right* is contrary to it, and prevents it; implies that it is not.

So it is no matter if a being made for one law cannot, or does not, or will not, obey another; there is no wrong in that; what wants rectifying is his turning from his true law to another. (Now surely in the organic there must be parallels to this.) And again, if it is supposed women are chaste, in the sense of thinking a great deal about their bodily relations, it is a mistake. It is not so at all, but the very contrary; women are made so as not to need to think about their bodily relations. And that other kind of chastity is artificially put upon them, which accounts for the facts we see. It is a complete twisting of their natural chastity; a twisting at once *away* from that which is natural to them, and *to* a thing quite unnatural.

And how this throws light on their intense feeling about some eternal right, some great and unfathomable goodness. Of course, reverencing this twisting forced on them and never suspecting its true meaning, or that it can be anything but an expression of good and right, they must set up before themselves something to account for it, to explain it; something of an absolute authority and majesty for it to be done *for*. Here may there not be a clue to the character of the moral feelings of women: they have to make up some absolute authority that demands of them to be so twisted, and be thinking so much of their bodily relations, never dreaming that that is, above all, "a commandment of *men*," a mere reflex of their not-regard. And so too we see how it betrays and leaves without guide or support other women—women who cannot thus make up reasons. One might say it leaves women at the mercy of their power of making up nonsense-reasons. They can be happy or safe only by being in presence of men who are such as not to need them to be thinking of their bodies.

This is the difference: not to put away a thing which has been made impure, but to put away that which makes it impure. This is all: then Nature's standard comes in, and her law. It is to restore us joy made pure, to open a gate of paradise which impurity has barred. What a double blessing: it gives us not only the things—the things of joy, very many of them simply or chiefly the privilege of *giving* joy to others. (See how it is this to women: how what it makes pure is above all that privilege of giving.) But also this alone is really giving us purity; for putting away the things made impure still leaves the impurity; that is there just as much. The putting away the things is at least as much a sign and fruit of its presence as anything else can be.

Will it not be a freedom and a power when we have learnt to remember (whatever we may choose to do ourselves) that the great thing we have to guard against is making things wrong (that is, letting evil come into our hearts;) or letting them be thought or regarded as wrong; that this is what we must guard against; things being suffered to be regarded as wrong. For that means consenting to the condition in men that makes them wrong; the thought must be: We must not let that condition come which would make things wrong. That is, we must not be forbidding other people to do things, whatever we ourselves may choose to do or not to do. What a freedom and power it will be. What force now wasted will be given us to use.

How soon it may come that men shall look back and say: Our forefathers were bound by all sorts of limitations and restraints, making *things* right and wrong apart from their reasons, so barring themselves even from giving; nay, barring even others from giving; forbidding even delight to be, merely because it was delight, because *they* had made impurity. And we see what does it at once and inevitably. Now we have learnt and see that it is our business to be capable of joy, free for delight; we must take care we do not let ourselves be not so; we must guard our thoughts, our desires; we must be looking within.

And here is a new meaning again: "The kingdom of heaven is within you!" You must keep your eye on that which is within you; there is the secret of its coming. And so for the kingdom of heaven to come, is not one thing only needful? Is it not ready to come at any moment? The conditions of its presence are within.

By making evil what is not evil, and so by needing too much to be put away, making the law too hard (besides so sending the weak to hell), besides this, by making the law too hard there comes the pressure on men, the desire and effort we cannot wonder at, to gain such a "position" that the right may mean to us something not too hard, that is, the struggle for wealth.

It is the very same to say that things are true which oppose physical facts as to say things are right which oppose physical good. These are two forms of the same attitude of mind, the very same struggle as maintaining the Bible against science. And so how curious it is that the very persons who so clearly see the one is a mistake yet most intensely insist on the other. They also set up their Bible against facts, and think it just as sacred a duty, just as necessary.

Is there not a parallel in opinions? It is proposed now that a man shall be at liberty to 'do' anything, but his desires shall be true. There shall be sincerity, in this sense, in his action. Now of old false opinions were the great crime; it was thought fatal, impossible, to allow them; but we allow any opinions to be held—and find it quite possible—and only insist on sincerity in holding them. And we see how much easier it is to succeed in obtaining sincerity in holding them than uniformity in them. The one can be gained, the other could not. The attempt to gain the uniformity indeed was fatal to the sincerity. (So what does our attempt of uniformity of deeds come to? There is the seed; here the fruit.) If we put our aim on the true desire it comes. This very change suggested has come in respect to opinion. And what has come is that we are on the way even to oneness of *desire*.

This is the proposal: to transfer all our feeling (in respect to wrong and right; feelings of repugnance, love and aspiration) from "things" to motives, or acts. (With hope, of course, that so they will *grow* in power; and also even in truthfulness and justice.) But in order to do this—it is an obvious condition—right and wrong must be transferred also from things to act. The thing must be considered as not having any such character in itself, but only as expressing the act. Visibly the effort to hold the thing has falsified our action, has misdirected our effort. Not being able to let go of the things has thwarted us, and leaves us really doing neither one thing nor the other. And it is visible too how the miscarriage has come, namely, through our starting point; because by having the regard on self the only right possible (which is not any at all in reality) is in things; and so we come from a mere thing-right and have to go through the process of this transference altogether. And really we are very far advanced; we may almost be said to have done it (though not completely or with full vision) in all respects but one. The completeness and perfect truth of any must wait for that. That one yet left out (as organic life in science) will give a new perfectness to all; for "if one member suffers the whole body suffers with it;" that unincluded state of one mars all the rest; when it is brought in, then life will be "made *whole*."

Our duty is not to restrain our passions; but to *keep pleasure free*. There is that in man which makes things evil (every one allows that "evil" is only in the soul, not in physical things), and he tends accordingly to put away the things, the *made*-evil things instead of the *making*-evil things. (So he has to fight many things instead of one.) Here has been his error, in the direction of his effort. But all the while he has had before his eyes a model in Nature.

And it is evident what in man is the making-evil thing. Here we see his condition. It is a clear wrongness. Is not here a harmony of all questions about depravity? Would not seeing this, and accepting it, be essentially a religious revolution? In truth has not every religious revolution been essentially one of morals and not of theology? Are our attempts so vain because they seek to be of theology instead of life? Is not the revolution of *life* the only real and true religious revolution?

There are two ways of gaining a result: one to introduce new forces, another to use forces already existing. Now if the latter is done there must be this result also: *something will cease to be done.* The ceasing of something is an inevitable result of the use of existing forces for something new. Then also the use of forces that are already present is easier than the introducing new ones; easier by all the difficulty of gaining the new force. (The difficulty indeed is rather in the ceasing than in the new doing.) Every correction of a premiss is a using of already present forces for new results; this gives it its character. It is like pouring water from one cup into another. Now the present proposal is not to introduce new force, but to use force already present. And it has the ceasing of certain effects of force for its condition.

And may we not say this also: there are certain things for which we intensely want force now in our life. Then should we not look around and see where there is any force which may be used for these purposes? Should we not look and see if there are any things, and what and how many, among us in which force is employed and which might cease?

And as for our need, our special need, of force to do some fresh things for us: may it not be that this need becomes more urgent as society advances, and that we distinctly now have need of conditions requiring force to produce them to a degree which did not exist in former times? Is it not pretty to see if this be Nature's plan? Because force will be needed for some great results in the future, she stores it up in human life, in the form of men doing a number of force-needing, but quite needless things. Then there the force is ready. And so this is the way we should look at our life; what a number of quite needless things there are which we do, but then they bring force to us available for use. But is not this storing up of force even the great mass of our present civilised life? Nay, will this present stage of civilisation be seen as the storing up of force in "things," for use in the heart? Here too is a key to this relation of morals: the place respectively of the heart and of external things. Read from this dynamical relation do not the phenomena of morals appear necessary? Unless we see the special forms of our life thus as reservoirs, as it were, of force, we cannot comprehend it rightly.

Also it is interesting to note how these reservoirs of force *must* come; how the very need of them within compels the things in which they are embodied.

But is not the need of a truer *foundation* for life—of a true regard, in a word—more urgent as society advances? And so the order is visibly yet more perfect. These stores of force are made while the need for them is not visible; not felt at all.

And so do they come to be more felt as being merely for themselves; more felt as ends instead of means; and so grasped as things to be held instead of used? But is not this also part of the power? Would they otherwise really contain the power? For is not the giving up of that feeling at the claim of need the very change within?

But now the need for a change in the *basis* of our life becomes more and more plain, more urgently felt; the old idea also of referring to an isolated God becomes more and more untenable; and at the same time is not the hold upon the thing-rights visibly loosened? Do not the very gains, the very improvements, tend more and more to make felt this need of a truer basis? The very points in which our life is better convict it of hollowness.

The great tragedy of the world has been the fight about right. What we must insist on, for the sake of peace, is not that the rules shall not cease, but that the condition of their ceasing shall come. It is a question of putting away made-evil or making-evil, of the ceasing of rules, the coming of being led by the Spirit. Have we not a test then for changes of a true kind, a guide to the true course? And one source of strife—surely the great one—is visibly put to rest. There is a clear principle to which to refer. In a word the advance is from things, or rules, to principles; from fixity to fluency. We start with fixity and go to unfixity; that is to something deeper, and more; which reveals the former fixed things as forms and rightly fluent. This is so marked in science: it is seeing deeper that makes fluent.

The ceasing or avoiding of strife then will ever be the consenting to an internal. Might we not have the end clear, at least discuss and explore it in general terms, not in deeds that could make anger, and have the question only of time and preparedness?

Now the next change, or one of the next and chief, must be about the relations of men and women. Would it not be sad that this also should be by great strife and clashing? Were it not blessed indeed if it could come without, by an understanding of the real nature of the true changes for the better and the conditions they must fulfil? And that if strife came it should not be of rights, but of good against evil, not with itself? Were it not a boon indeed to avoid strife there? For where else could it be so bitter or so sad? Is it for this—that it may be without that sadness—it has been reserved till last?

Is not this the principle we see, alike in reason and in fact, that with a change of the details (always a ceasing from restrictions which are rigid and not fluent) there comes *a general change as well?* A different attitude, feeling, mode of action; in a word, a fulfilling of the conditions of the change. The change is not of form, but of relation of correlated changes. The commandments are "of men," that is, expressing man's state, and these are known by being rigid. Nature's are fluent—nay *to be fluent* is in one sense all. That the whole attitude must alter with the particular thing; this is the essential. And so we come evidently on marks of reason and relation in things; the special "things" or details are as means of effect upon this general condition, the channels through which it is operated on; the particular agencies through which operations are effected upon it. And so when every particular relation has thus had its part and passed from rigid to fluent, with corresponding general change, will not that general change be complete?

---

PRINTED BY BALLANTYNE, HANSON AND CO.
EDINBURGH AND LONDON.

www.ingramcontent.com/pod-product-compliance
Lightning Source LLC
Chambersburg PA
CBHW031853220426
43663CB00006B/607